THE KNAPP COMMISSION

REPORT ON

POLICE CORRUPTION

THE KNAPP COMMISSION

REPORT ON

POLICE CORRUPTION

George Braziller   *New York*

For information address the publisher:
George Braziller, Inc.
One Park Avenue, New York, N.Y. 10016

Standard Book Number:
0-8076-0688-X, Cloth
0-8076-0689-8, Paper

Library of Congress Catalog Number:
73-76969
Printed in the United States of America

FOREWORD

This report was submitted to Mayor John V. Lindsay on December 26, 1972, bringing to a close the Knapp Commission's two and one half year investigation into corruption in the New York Police Department.

Informally named for its chairman, Whitman Knapp, the Commission was made up of five private citizens appointed by the Mayor. It was established after serious charges of police corruption had been made in the press. A committee of law enforcement officials, named by the Mayor to examine these charges, had recommended that the job of looking into corruption in the Department could best be done by an independent citizens commission with a full-time staff of its own. Both the Commission and the staff it assembled were composed of people whose preconceptions, if any, were sympathetic to the police. Three of the five commissioners and six of the eight staff attorneys were former prosecutors. The twelve investigators all had extensive backgrounds in law enforcement.

The Commission investigated the extent and patterns of corruption in the Department, held public hearings and, finally, issued the recommendations and findings contained in the report which follows. The report is divided into two main sections. The first, originally issued on August 3, 1972, is a summary of the Commission's investigative findings and a presentation of its principal recommendations. The second is the main report, containing a history of the Commission's activities, a topic-by-topic analysis of corruption in the Department and analyses of the anti-corruption efforts of the Department and related agencies. A short interim report, issued on July 1, 1971 is included in the appendix.

A word about a few things that are not in this report. Police officers, wounded by criticism which they feel was generated by the Commission's disclosures rather than by the conditions which were disclosed, have objected that too little attention was paid to the good work they do and to corruption elsewhere in a society from which they feel singled out. Both subjects are, in fact, dealt with in the Commission's report. Neither is dwelt upon at length because, quite simply, it was not the Commission's job to do so. The Commission was charged with investigating a single problem, corruption, in a single city agency, the Police Department. Having found police graft to be a serious problem, it was obliged to focus in its report upon the reasons for its finding and the steps that are being and might be taken by way of remedy. The heroism and distinction with which countless police officers, whether or not they accept graft, perform their difficult and dangerous jobs is relevant to a study of graft only in shedding light upon police attitudes having a bearing upon the problem of corruption. Similarly, the obvious fact that corruption is not found only among policemen must be recognized in order to put police corruption in something of a proper perspective. However, the Commission had neither the legal authority nor the resources to investigate other governmental agencies, much less society as a whole. However great the need may be for further investigations, that need affords no excuse for discounting or ignoring the results of this one.

Another thing the report is not is a blanket indictment of all police officers. This charge has been made by some who misinterpret in order more easily to attack—even at the cost of perpetuating in the public mind the very impression to which they object. When the president of the Patrolmen's Benevolent Association complains that the Commission report condemns the entire police force many people accept his characterization—and tend to believe it. Anyone seriously interested in evaluating the Commission's efforts must begin—as the PBA president did not before making his public observations—by reading the report.

The report describes in specific detail patterns of corruption which no knowledgeable police officer or law enforcement official has challenged, which the Department's new leadership acknowledges, and which recent indictments confirm. In helping to bring these patterns out into the open, the Commission has made its contribution to the vigorous efforts now being made to deal with a problem that for too long could not adequately be met because those in a position to do something about it could not—or would not—recognize it for what it was.

MICHAEL F. ARMSTRONG

Commission to Investigate Allegations of Police Corruption and the City's Anti-Corruption Procedures

COMMISSION REPORT

(With Summary and Principal Recommendations, Issued August 3, 1972)

WHITMAN KNAPP
Chairman

JOSEPH MONSERRAT
JOHN E. SPRIZZO
FRANKLIN A. THOMAS
CYRUS R. VANCE

MICHAEL F. ARMSTRONG
Chief Counsel

DECEMBER 26, 1972

WHITMAN KNAPP, CHAIRMAN
JOHN E. SPRIZZO
JOSEPH MONSERRAT
FRANKLIN A. THOMAS
CYRUS R. VANCE
MICHAEL F. ARMSTRONG, CHIEF COUNSEL

December 26, 1972

Honorable John V. Lindsay
Mayor
City Hall
New York, New York

Dear Mr. Mayor:

In submitting this our final report, I should
like to express the appreciation of the Commission for
the support received from you and your Administration.
It would be unrealistic to assume - and I don't suppose
anyone does assume - that there were never differences
of opinion between the Commission and the Mayor's office.
However, you made it clear that it was our function to
exercise our own judgment, and you supported us in the
exercise of that judgment whether or not it agreed with
yours.

Any enterprise as complex as this one requires
the cooperation of many areas of city government. Such
cooperation was forthcoming, notably from the Corporation
Counsel, the Mayor's Criminal Justice Coordinating Council, the Bureau of the Budget, the Department of Personnel,
and the Police Department itself. In addition, as outlined more fully in the report, significant assistance was
provided - often at your urging - from a variety of independently elected public officials and from officers and
agencies of the federal and state governments.

Speaking for myself rather than for the Commission, I should like to call attention to the outstanding
services rendered by my fellow Commissioners. I don't
suppose there is any way they can get the public recognition that is their due. Pursuant to our joint decision,
all the noise was made by me. However, responsibility was

always shared in common and all significant actions - not infrequently agreed upon over my initial dissent - were jointly authorized. It was truly a partnership enterprise.

In closing, may I express the hope that the ultimate benefits to the Department will justify your unprecedented step, as Mayor of a city, of creating an independent commission to investigate a police department responsible to you.

Respectfully,

Whitman Knapp

THE CITY OF NEW YORK
OFFICE OF THE MAYOR
NEW YORK, N.Y. 10007

December 27, 1972

Honorable Whitman Knapp
United States District Court
United States Courthouse
Foley Square
New York, New York   10007

Dear Judge Knapp:

We have come a long way since the Serpico case in
1967 raised allegations of corruption which began the
process which culminated in my appointment of your
Commission. That was more than five years ago, and for the
last 2 1/2 years, the Commission has worked diligently
to create greater public understanding and a climate for
action. As you have pointed out, this is the first time
in the history of New York that a Mayor has created an
independent commission to investigate corruption of the
City's police. Although one would think that this
project would win wide support, you and I will remember
the strong opposition to the creation of the Commission
and the renewal of your subpoena powers. Those were
important political battles that required the most
intensive efforts of my Administration to sustain the
authority of the Commission.

With full independence, you conducted your own
inquiry and reached your own conclusions. Your procedures,
hearings and findings have, at times, been controversial,
and even painful, and no single observer will agree with
all of your conclusions. There may well be conclusions
which I cannot agree with. But you have performed a vital
task for our City and its police, focusing full public
scrutiny and debate on one of government's more sensitive
areas.

At the same time, Police Commissioner Patrick V.
Murphy has been waging a tough, persistent campaign against
corruption in the Police Department. With my full support,
Commissioner Murphy has been taking dramatic steps to
reform the practice, procedures and codes of conduct of

the Department. That has been the hardest fight of all
-- to improve supervision and the daily actions of
30,000 police officers. No Police Commissioner in our
City's history has set such high standards of integrity
and accountability -- and few have taken on such for-
midable obstacles.

        These combined efforts have resulted in
enormous progress. There is good reason to believe
that the problems faced by Patrolman Serpico six years
ago would not recur today. But it is just as obvious
that the problem of police corruption is not yet fully
solved. Last week's startling revelations that hundreds
of pounds of narcotics were stolen from the Police
Department, going back over a ten year period, shows how
deep this problem is and how much work remains to be done.

        But we have made a substantial start. I be-
lieve that never before in our City -- not in the 80
years since serious investigations into police corruption
have been conducted -- has there been a more forthright,
rigorous, and sustained attack on this problem. No goal
has had higher priority in my Administration than protecting the integrity of the administration of criminal justice.
Against considerable political opposition, we have insisted
that the Police Department be accountable to the elected
civilian leadership of the City and to the public. This
has not been easy. But in seven years of fighting for
improved police productivity and professionalism, I believe
that we have proved that it is essential for the Mayor to
demand accountability for the policies and performance of
the City's police. I consider this seven year effort, and
particularly the focus on corruption of the past 2 1/2
years, aided by the work of your Commission, to be one of
the most important accomplishments of my Administration.

        I am determined that this work continue in the
years to come. That will require the continuing courageous
leadership of police commissioners like Pat Murphy, and the
strong support of the Mayor in what will not always be a
popular or easy effort.

And it will mean some real legislative creativity in Albany if the promise of your report is to be fulfilled and the historical cycle of corruption that has persisted for almost a century is to be truly broken for the first time. As your report shows in detail, the State government, through its outmoded and unrealistic criminal laws, must bear its share of the responsibility for the continued opportunities for corruption. It is therefore essential that we intensify our efforts to win reforms in next year's State Legislature to remove these unfair burdens from our police.

For your personal role in leading this historic Commission, and for the diligent work of your fellow Commissioners and your able staff, you have my warm thanks and those of all New Yorkers.

Sincerely,

John V. Lindsay
Mayor

ACKNOWLEDGMENTS

The people responsible for the day-to-day work of the Commission were, of course, the members of its full-time staff, headed by our chief counsel, Michael F. Armstrong. Mr. Armstrong was the architect of the investigation, the public hearings, and this report.

The rest of the Commission's staff personnel changed as we moved from one phase to another and consisted of a maximum of thirty people during the investigation, about half that number during the hearings, and no more than six for the writing of this report.

Commission attorneys, whose various functions included supervising the investigations and preparing the hearings were Associate Counsel Nicholas Figueroa, Julius S. Impellizzeri, Otto G. Obermaier, Paul K. Rooney, Nicholas Scoppetta, Milton L. Williams and Assistant Counsel Lisa L. Barrett. In addition, the Commission was ably assisted by two volunteer attorneys, Warren H. Colodner and Paul Ford; by two attorneys on loan from the U.S. Department of Justice, John W. Sweeney, Jr., and Stephen Stein, who was replaced by David Ritchie; and by law students Patricia Farren and Susan Lissitzyn.

The investigators, whose efforts provided the witnesses for the hearings and the basis for our findings, were Adolph J. Alessi, Brian M. Bruh, George J. Carros, Ralph A. Cipriani, James P. Donovan, Mark K. Hanson, Seymour Newman, Frank J. Nemic, Jr., Ralph A. Parente, James Rogers, Patrick J. Stokes and Gordon E. White.

While the preparation and editing of this report was a group effort of the Commission and its staff, a large part of the writing was done by Margo Barrett, assisted by researcher and editorial assistant Anne C. Beane.

Members of the administrative and clerical staff, who supported the Commission in all phases of its activities, were Josephine Amalbert, Carol Ash, Anita Kennedy, Natalie D. Marra, Nathania Miles, Denise Morrissey, Arney Rosenblat, William C. Spitzner, Veri Sweete and Nettleton G. Wells.

The Commission is also indebted to Professor Herman Goldstein of the University of Wisconsin, who acted as a consultant to the Commission and gave us valuable help in charting our course.

The Commission received help in its investigation from many people in law enforcement agencies, in particular, Assistant U.S. Attorney General Will Wilson, U.S. Attorney for the Southern District of New York Whitney North Seymour, Jr., Bronx District Attorney Burton B. Roberts, New York District Attorney Frank S. Hogan, and many members of the New York Police Department, including Commissioner Patrick V. Murphy, First Deputy Commissioner William H. T. Smith, Assistant Chief Inspector Sydney Cooper, Inspectors Harold Hesse and John Clark, and Captains Daniel McGowan and Patrick Murphy.

Martin Danziger and Joseph A. Nardoza of the Justice Department's Law Enforcement Assistance Administration, were instrumental in helping the Commission obtain federal funds which enabled it to continue its work.

Many City officials gave assistance and guidance to the Commission, in particular, Norman Redlich, Corporation Counsel; Henry S. Ruth, Jr., Director of the Mayor's Criminal Justice Coordinating Council; Thomas J. Cuite, Vice Chairman and Majority Leader of the City Council; and Arthur G. Fox and Denis J. Conroy of the Division of Administrative Services, Law Department.

Others to whom the Commission is indebted for advice and assistance are James Ahearn, Joseph Armstrong, William Browne, Bernard Cohen, Mary Forcellon, Lawrence S. Goldman, Irving Hest, Kenneth Kemper, David McCall, Warren Pfaff and Robert Rice.

Six of the Commission's twelve investigators were lent to us by federal agencies. The Commission is indebted to the Federal Bureau of Narcotics and Dangerous Drugs, the United States Postal Service and, particularly, the Internal Revenue Service, which supplied four of its best agents and, during a period when the Commission was in financial need, declined to accept the usual salary reimbursements.

The Commission worked in cooperation with and received valuable assistance from the State Commission of Investigation and its Chairman Paul J. Curran, and the New York State Joint Legislative Committee on Crime, chaired by the late Senator John H. Hughes.

Particular thanks is due the following private foundations which made funds available to the Commission: Edna McConnell Clark Foundation, Field Foundation, Fund for the City of New York, Howard Z. Leffel Fund in Community Funds, Inc., The J. M. Kaplan Fund Inc., Joint Foundation Support, Inc., on behalf of the Bernhardt Foundation and the Joyce and John Gutfreund Foundation, New York Community Trust, The New York Foundation, New World Foundation, The Rosenblat Charitable Trust and The Stern Fund.

Table of Contents

SUMMARY AND PRINCIPAL RECOMMENDATIONS

COMMISSION REPORT
Section One: Commission Activities

Section Two: Patterns of Police Corruption

Section Three: Anti-Corruption Efforts

APPENDIX

SUMMARY AND PRINCIPAL
RECOMMENDATIONS
(Issued August 3, 1972)

PREFACE

The Commission's Mandate

The Commission was established in May, 1970 by Executive Order of Mayor John V. Lindsay. The Mayor acted upon the recommendation of an interdepartmental committee he had appointed in response to an article appearing in *The New York Times* on April 25 which charged widespread police corruption and official laxity in dealing with such corruption.

We were given the basic tasks of determining the extent and nature of police corruption in the City, examining existing procedures for dealing with corruption, and recommending changes and improvements in those procedures.

Commissioner Leary resigned in August, 1970 and was replaced in October by Commissioner Patrick V. Murphy. Almost immediately, Commissioner Murphy announced—and began to carry into effect—an intention to make sweeping changes in departmental procedures for dealing with corruption. This development had an important effect on the nature of our task. The extent and nature of corruption still had to be determined, but suggesting changes in procedures for dealing with corruption was reduced in importance. It became more important to make our findings on patterns of corruption clear to the public, so that the public would encourage the new Commissioner in his announced intentions of reform, and would support him in putting them into effect.

The ability to carry out our mandate was enhanced by the nature of our appointment. Our authority was derived from the Mayor who, as the City's chief executive officer, is ultimately responsible for the conduct of the Department we were called upon to investigate. This was the first time—in this or perhaps any other city—that the official ultimately responsible for a police department's conduct had authorized public investigation of allegations of police corruption.

The fact that the Mayor appointed us encouraged cooperation between the Department and us. This did not mean that serious differences did not arise between our Commission and the Department but, as the investigation progressed, cooperation became increasingly real and fruitful. While it is too early to say to what extent our investigation will help to bring about permanent changes in the Department, it may well turn out that any such change will result in part from the cooperation that has existed between us.

SUMMARY

The Extent of Police Corruption

We found corruption to be widespread. It took various forms depending upon the activity involved, appearing at its most sophisticated among plainclothesmen assigned to enforcing gambling laws. In the five plainclothes divisions where our investigations were concentrated we found a strikingly standardized pattern of corruption. Plainclothesmen, participating in what is known in police parlance as a "pad," collected regular bi-weekly or monthly payments amounting to as much as $3,500 from each of the gambling establishments in the area under their jurisdiction, and divided the take in equal shares. The monthly share per man (called the "nut") ranged from $300 and $400 in midtown Manhattan to $1,500 in Harlem. When supervisors were involved they received a share and a half. A newly assigned plainclothesman was not entitled to his share for about two months, while he was checked out for reliability, but the earnings lost by the delay were made up to him in the form of two months' severance pay when he left the division.

Evidence before us led us to the conclusion that the same pattern existed in the remaining divisions which we did not investigate in depth. This conclusion was confirmed by events occurring before and after the period of our investigation. Prior to the Commission's existence, exposures by former plainclothesman Frank Serpico had led to indictments or departmental charges against nineteen plainclothesmen in a Bronx division for involvement in a pad where the nut was $800. After our public hearings had been completed, an investigation conducted by the Kings County District Attorney and the Department's Internal Affairs Division—which investigation neither the Commission nor its staff had even known about—resulted in indictments and charges against thirty-seven Brooklyn plainclothesmen who had participated in a pad with a nut of $1,200. The manner of operation of the pad involved in each of these situations was in every detail identical to that described at the Commission hearings, and in each almost every plainclothesman in the division, including supervisory lieutenants, was implicated.

Corruption in narcotics enforcement lacked the organization of the gambling pads, but individual payments—known as "scores"—were commonly received and could be staggering in amount. Our investigation, a concurrent probe by the State Investigation Commission and prosecutions by Federal and local authorities all revealed a pattern whereby corrupt officers customarily collected scores in substantial amounts from narcotics violators. These scores were either kept by the individual officer or shared with a partner and, perhaps, a superior officer. They ranged from minor shakedowns to payments of many thousands of dollars, the largest narcotics payoff uncovered in our investigation having been $80,000. According to information developed by the S.I.C. and in recent Federal investigations, the size of this score was by no means unique.

Corruption among detectives assigned to general investigative duties also took the form of shakedowns of individual targets of opportunity. Although these scores were not in the huge amounts found in narcotics, they not infrequently came to several thousand dollars.

Uniformed patrolmen assigned to street duties were not found to receive money on nearly so grand or organized a scale, but the large number of small payments they received present an equally serious if less dramatic problem. Uniformed patrolmen, particularly those assigned to radio patrol cars, participated in gambling pads more modest in size than those received by plainclothes units and received regular payments from construction sites, bars, grocery stores and other business establishments. These payments were usually made on a regular basis to sector car patrolmen and on a haphazard basis to others. While individual payments to uniformed men were small, mostly under $20, they were often so numerous as to add substantially to a patrolman's income. Other less regular payments to uniformed patrolmen included those made by after-hours bars, bottle clubs, tow trucks, motorists, cab drivers, parking lots, prostitutes and defendants wanting to fix their cases in court. Another practice found to be widespread was the payment of gratuities by policemen to other policemen to expedite normal police procedures or to gain favorable assignments.

Sergeants and lieutenants who were so inclined participated in the same kind of corruption as the men they supervised. In addition, some sergeants had their own pads from which patrolmen were excluded.

Although the Commission was unable to develop hard evidence establishing that officers above the rank of lieutenant received payoffs, considerable circumstantial evidence and some testimony so indicated. Most often when a superior officer is corrupt, he uses a patrolman as his "bagman" who collects for him and keeps a percentage of the take. Because the bagman may keep the money for himself, although he claims to be collecting for his superior, it is extremely difficult to determine with any accuracy when the superior actually is involved.

Of course, not all policemen are corrupt. If we are to exclude such petty infractions as free meals, an appreciable number do not engage in any corrupt activities. Yet, with extremely rare exceptions, even those who themselves engage in no corrupt activities are involved in corruption in the sense that they take no steps to prevent what they know or suspect to be going on about them.

It must be made clear that—in a little over a year with a staff having as few as two and never more than twelve field investigators— we did not examine every precinct in the Department. Our conclusion that corruption is widespread throughout the Department is based on the fact that information supplied to us by hundreds of sources within and without the Department was consistently borne out by specific observations made in areas we were able to investigate in detail.

The Nature and Significance of Police Corruption

Corruption, although widespread, is by no means uniform in degree. Corrupt policemen have been described as falling into two basic categories: "meat-eaters" and "grass-eaters." As the names might suggest, the meat-eaters are those policemen who, like Patrolman William Phillips who testified at our hearings, aggressively misuse their police powers for personal gain. The grass-eaters simply accept the payoffs that the happenstances of police work throw their way. Although the meat-eaters get the huge payoffs that make the headlines, they represent a small percentage of all corrupt policemen. The truth is, the vast majority of policemen on the take don't deal in huge amounts of graft.

And yet, grass-eaters are the heart of the problem. Their great numbers tend to make corruption "respectable." They also tend to encourage the code of silence that brands anyone who exposes corruption a traitor. At the time our investigation began, any policeman violating the code did so at his peril. The result was described in our interim report: "The rookie who comes into the Department is faced with the situation where it is easier for him to become corrupt than to remain honest."

More importantly, although meat-eaters can and have been individually induced to make their peace with society, the grass-eaters may be more easily reformed. We believe that, given proper leadership and support, many police who have slipped into corruption would exchange their illicit income for the satisfaction of belonging to a corruption-free Department in which they could take genuine pride.

The problem of corruption is neither new, nor confined to the police. Reports of prior investigations into police corruption, testimony taken by the Commission, and opinions of informed persons both within and without the Department make it abundantly clear that police corruption has been a problem for many years. Investigations have occurred on the average of once in twenty years since before the turn of the century, and yet conditions exposed by one investigation seem substantially unchanged when the next one makes its report. This doesn't mean that the police have a monopoly on corruption. On the contrary, in every area where police corruption exists it is paralleled by corruption in other agencies of government, in industry and labor, and in the professions.

Our own mandate was limited solely to the police. There are sound reasons for such a special concern with police corruption. The police have a unique place in our society. The policeman is expected to "uphold the law" and "keep the peace." He is charged with everything from traffic control to riot control. He is expected to protect our lives and our property. As a result, society gives him special powers and prerogatives, which include the right and obligation to bear arms, along with the authority to take away our liberty by arresting us.

Symbolically, his role is even greater. For most people, the policeman is the law. To them, the law is administered by the patrolman on the beat and the captain in the station house. Little wonder that the public becomes aroused and alarmed when the police are charged with corruption or are shown to be corrupt.

Departmental Attitudes Towards Police Corruption

Although this special concern is justified, public preoccupation with police corruption as opposed to corruption in other agencies of government inevitably seems unfair to the policeman. He believes that he is unjustly blamed for the results of corruption in other parts of the criminal justice system. This sense of unfairness intensifies the sense of isolation and hostility to which the nature of police work inevitably gives rise.

Feelings of isolation and hostility are experienced by policemen not just in New York, but everywhere. To understand these feelings one must appreciate an important characteristic of any metropolitan police department, namely an extremely intense group loyalty. When properly understood, this group loyalty can be used in the fight against corruption. If misunderstood or ignored, it can undermine anti-corruption activities.

Pressures that give rise to this group loyalty include the danger to which policemen are constantly exposed and the hostility they encounter from society at large. Everyone agrees that a policeman's life is a dangerous one, and that his safety, not to mention his life, can depend on his ability to rely on a fellow officer in a moment of crisis. It is less generally realized that the policeman works in a sea of hostility. This is true, not only in high crime areas, but throughout the City. Nobody, whether a burglar or a Sunday motorist, likes to have his activities interfered with. As a result, most citizens, at one time or another, regard the police with varying degrees of hostility. The policeman feels, and naturally often returns, this hostility.

Two principal characteristics emerge from this group loyalty: suspicion and hostility directed at any outside interference with the Department, and an intense desire to be proud of the Department. This mixture of hostility and pride has created what the Commission has found to be the most serious roadblock to a rational attack upon police corruption: a stubborn refusal at all levels of the Department to acknowledge that a serious problem exists.

The interaction of stubbornness, hostility and pride has given rise to the so-called "rotten-apple" theory. According to this theory, which bordered on official Department doctrine, any policeman found to be corrupt must promply be denounced as a rotten apple in an otherwise clean barrel. It must never be admitted that his individual corruption may be symptomatic of underlying disease.

This doctrine was bottomed on two basic premises: First, the morale of the Department requires that there be no official recognition of corruption, even though practically all members of the Department know it is in truth extensive; second, the Department's public image and effectiveness require official denial of this truth.

The rotten-apple doctrine has in many ways been a basic obstacle to meaningful reform. To begin with, it reinforced and gave respectability to the code of silence. The official view that the Department's image and morale forbade public disclosure of the extent of corruption inhibited any officer who wished to disclose corruption and justified any who preferred to remain silent. The doctrine also made difficult, if not impossible, any meaningful attempt at managerial reform. A high command unwilling to acknowledge that the problem of corruption is extensive cannot very well argue that drastic changes are necessary to deal with that problem. Thus neither the Mayor's Office nor the Police Department took adequate steps to see that such changes were made when the need for them was indicated by the charges made by Officers Frank Serpico and David Durk in 1968. This was demonstrated in the Commission's second set of public hearings in December 1971.

Finally, the doctrine made impossible the use of one of the most effective techniques for dealing with any entrenched criminal activity, namely persuading a participant to help provide evidence against his partners in crime. If a corrupt policeman is merely an isolated rotten apple, no reason can be given for not exposing him the minute he is discovered. If, on the other hand, it is acknowledged that a corrupt officer is only one part of an apparatus of corruption, common sense dictates that every effort should be made to enlist the offender's aid in providing the evidence to destroy the apparatus.

The Commission's Actions

The Commission examined and rejected the premises upon which the rotten-apple doctrine rested. We concluded that there was no justification for fearing that public acknowledgment of the extent of corruption would damage the image and effectiveness of the Department. We are convinced that instead of damaging its image a realistic attitude toward corruption could only enhance the Department's credibility. The conditions described in the Commission's public hearings came as no surprise to the large numbers of City residents who had experienced them for years. If, then, the Department makes it a point to acknowledge corrupt conditions the public already knows to exist, it can hardly damage its image. On the contrary, it can only promote confidence in the Department's good-faith desire to deal with those conditions.

The Commission looked at the question of morale in much the same way. We did not—and do not—believe that the morale of the average policeman is enhanced by a commanding officer who insists on denying facts that the policeman knows to be true. We believed —and continue to believe—that such false denials can only undercut the policeman's confidence in his commander. If a policeman listens to his commander solemnly deny the existence of an obvious corrupt situation, the policeman can draw only one of two conclusions: Either the commander is hopelessly naive or he is content to let the corruption continue.

Once we had rejected the premises of the rotten-apple doctrine, the Commission determined to employ one of the techniques that adherence to the doctrine had made impossible, namely to persuade formerly corrupt police officers to work with us in providing evidence of continuing corruption.

The mere decision to use the technique did not automatically produce a body of officers able and eager to assist us in this manner. Indeed, knowledgeable persons assured us that the code of silence was so strong that we would never find a corrupt officer who could be persuaded to assist in exposing corruption. We ultimately did persuade four officers, including Detective Robert L. Leuci and Patrolmen William Phillips, Edward Droge and Alfonso Jannotta to undertake undercover work. Of these, all but Detective Leuci did so under the compulsion of having been caught by Commission investigators. Patrolmen Phillips and Droge testified at public hearings held in October 1971. Patrolman Jannotta was unavailable due to illness at the time of the hearings. The information disclosed by Detective Leuci was so vital that we did not, since our time was limited, feel justified in keeping it to ourselves. Leuci and the Commission staff members who had debriefed him and worked with him on his initial undercover operations were turned over to the Federal Government for the long-term investigation which was required. Leuci's work as a Federal undercover agent is now resulting in the series of important narcotics-related indictments being obtained by United States Attorney Whitney North Seymour, Jr.

Success in persuading these officers to assist in the investigation was a first step in demonstrating that the rotten-apple doctrine was invalid. Patrolman Phillips' three days of testimony about systematic corruption in various parts of the Department, corroborated by tape-recorded conversations with many police officers and others, was in itself enough to make the doctrine seem untenable. Patrolman Droge described how departmental pressures gradually converted an idealistic rookie into an increasingly bold finder of bribes and payoffs. Former Patrolman Waverly Logan, who volunteered to testify about corruption in which he had been involved, corroborated Droge's testimony and went on to tell about policemen in Harlem who received monthly as much as $3,000 each in narcotics graft. Patrolman Logan also introduced the Commission to two addicts who were willing to work with us in obtaining evidence to corroborate these assertions. The Commission's work with these addicts produced movies and recorded conversations of policemen selling narcotics. Some of the narcotics were paid for with merchandise the policemen believed to be stolen. Captain Daniel McGowan, a police officer of unquestioned integrity and experienced in anti-corruption work, testified that the picture of corruption presented by Patrolmen Phillips, Droge and Logan was an accurate one. In addition, there was testimony from, among others, a Harlem gambler,

Commission agents describing their investigations, and witnesses in the business community revealing corrupt police dealings with the hotel and construction industries. Recorded conversations and movies documented instances of police corruption, including gambling and narcotics payoffs, fixing court cases and shaking down a tow-truck operator. The cumulative effect of these two weeks of testimony made it not only unrealistic but absurd for anyone thereafter to adhere to the rotten-apple doctrine, either publicly or privately.

The doctrine did not die easily. Institutional pressures within the Department seemed to force the high command to continue giving lip service to the doctrine even when speaking out against corruption. Commissioner Murphy in his early statements about corruption regularly included a pointed statement indicating that the corruption in the Department was limited to a few officers. On one occasion he went so far as to imply that there were no more than about 300 corrupt police officers in the entire Department. After Patrolman Phillips had completed two of his three days of testimony at our public hearings, Commissioner Murphy found it necessary to discount his testimony of widespread corruption, referring to him as a "rogue cop."

However, one week later, after Phillips had completed his testimony and had been followed by Patrolmen Logan and Droge and others, the Department, speaking through First Deputy Commissioner William H. T. Smith, forthrightly rejected the rotten-apple doctrine by name. Smith defined it as standing for the proposition that "police departments are essentially free of corruption except for the presence of a few corrupt officers who have managed to slip into police service and also into key assignments such as gambling investigations, despite rigorously applied screening procedures designed to keep them out." He said that traditional police strategy had been to react defensively whenever a scandal arose by "promising to crack down on graft, to go after the 'rogue cops,' to get rid of 'rotten apples.'" Smith said the Department now rejected this approach "not just on principle,

but because as a way of controlling corruption it had utterly failed."
He acknowledged that the result of adherence to the theory had been
a breakdown in public confidence: ". . . they [the public] are sick of
'bobbing for rotten apples' in the police barrel. They want an entirely new barrel that will never again become contaminated."

Changing Departmental Attitudes

The public hearings, in addition to helping bring about official
abandonment of the rotten-apple doctrine, have had dramatic effect
on the way members of the Department discuss corruption. This change
was graphically described shortly after our hearings by former Assistant Chief Inspector Sidney C. Cooper in colorful language: "Not very
long ago we talked about corruption with all the enthusiasm of a group
of little old ladies talking about venereal disease. Now there is a little
more open discussion about combatting graft as if it were a public
health problem." In short, the first barrier to a realistic look at corruption has been overcome: The problem has been officially, and
unofficially, acknowledged.

Some time after the public hearings were over, it was revealed
that Detective Leuci had been doing undercover work for the Federal
Government for over a year and a half, and that he had been doing it
with both the knowledge and protection of the Department's high command. News also began to spread throughout the Department that
other formerly corrupt policemen were doing undercover work for the
Department's Internal Affairs Division and for at least one District
Attorney's office. These revelations had considerable impact, both
direct and indirect, upon attitudes toward corruption within the
Department.

To put the direct impact in proper perspective, it should be
pointed out that any criminal activity, within a police department or
elsewhere, cannot thrive unless all of its participants are able to maintain confidence in each other. Patrolman Phillips' testimony made

this very clear. In testifying about his own corrupt activities, he described how he could, by making a few telephone calls within five or ten minutes, "check out" the reliability of any other officer whose assistance he might require in a corrupt enterprise. By way of illustration, he described instances where he had been similarly checked out while doing undercover work for the Commission. This ability to check out, and rely upon, an officer with whom one has had no previous contact rested on the assumption—unchallenged before the advent of our Commission—that no police officer who had once become involved in corruption could ever be persuaded to disclose the corruption of others. The actions of Detective Leuci and Patrolmen Phillips and Droge and of others as yet unnamed who are presently working undercover have undermined this assumption.

Even more important was the indirect effect produced by general knowledge that the undercover activities of these formerly corrupt policemen had been known to—and protected by—the Department's high command. Traditionally, the rank and file have shown a deep cynicism, well justified by history, concerning pronouncements of new police commissioners. They carefully examine the new commissioner's every word and action, searching for "messages": Does he mean business? Can he stand up against institutional pressures?

The initial lack of clarity in Commissioner Murphy's statements on the rotten-apple theory and his "rogue cop" reaction to the first widely publicized defiance of the code of silence were interpreted by some as suggesting a lack of commitment to total war on corruption. However, the Department's final repudiation of the doctrine, and the general knowledge that the Department was using and protecting policemen who had agreed to do undercover work, gave reassurance to the doubters.

In short, we believe that the Department's recent reactions to the Commission's activities have promoted realistic self-criticism within the Department. This spirit of self-criticism is an encouraging sign. For one thing, it is becoming less unusual for police officers to report evidence of police corruption. If this tendency continues, the day may be approaching when the rookie coming into the Department will not be pressured toward corruption, but can count on finding support for his desire to remain honest.

The present situation is quite like that existing at the close of previous investigations. A considerable momentum for reform has been generated, but not enough time has elapsed to reverse attitudes that have been solidifying for many years in the minds of both the public and the police.

After previous investigations, the momentum was allowed to evaporate.

The question now is: Will history repeat itself? Or does society finally realize that police corruption is a problem that must be dealt with and not just talked about once every twenty years?

Both immediate and long-term actions are mandatory. The reforms already initiated within the Department must be completed and expanded; there must be changes, both legislative and administrative, to curb pressures toward police corruption and to facilitate its control; and the momentum generated by the events before and during the life of this Commission must be maintained.

A PLAN FOR IMMEDIATE ACTION

We are convinced that there is an immediate need for a supplement to the agencies currently charged with combatting police corruption.

A basic weakness in the present approaches to the problem of police corruption is that all agencies regularly involved with the problem rely primarily on policemen to do their investigative work. The

Department relies exclusively on its own members. The District Attorneys in the five counties and the Department of Investigation, although they have a few non-police investigators, depend primarily upon policemen to conduct investigations. In the case of the District Attorneys, there is the additional problem that they work so closely with policemen that the public tends to look upon them—and indeed they seem to look upon themselves—as allies of the Department.

At the present time a citizen wishing to complain about a policeman knows that his complaint will ultimately be investigated by other policemen. This discourages complaints, because many New Yorkers just don't trust policemen to investigate each other.

We saw much evidence of this distrust. Many people—sometimes represented by experienced lawyers—brought the Commission evidence of serious corruption which they said they would not have disclosed to the police or to a District Attorney or to the City's Department of Investigation. Even today, complainants who call the Commission and are told that the investigation has ended often refuse to take down the phone numbers of these agencies. It makes no difference whether or not this distrust is justified. The harsh reality is that it exists.

This distrust is not confined to members of the public. Many policemen came to us with valuable information which they consented to give us only upon our assurance that we would not disclose their identities to the Department or to any District Attorney.

Any proposal for dealing with corruption must therefore provide a place where policemen as well as the public can come with confidence and without fear of retaliation. Any office designed to achieve this must be staffed by persons wholly unconnected with the Police Department or any other agency that routinely deals with it. Our experience is illustrative. Our investigative staff was wholly drawn from non-police sources. Four investigators were lent to us by the Bureau of Internal Revenue, one by the Bureau of Narcotics and

Dangerous Drugs, and one by the Post Office Department. We also obtained the services of ex-members of the FBI, of Army Intelligence and of the Immigration Service. A new office could be similarly staffed.

Further, any proposed office must have jurisdiction going beyond the Police Department. In recent months there have been numerous accusations of corruption among prosecutors, lawyers, and judges. There is need for a public demonstration that society is genuinely committed to a war on corruption and is not simply indulging in a foray against the police. An office is therefore needed where everyone —including the policeman—can go with a corruption complaint against anyone involved in the criminal process. A City agency is inadequate to this task since prosecutors and judges are not all subject to City jurisdiction.

Any new office must also have authority to prosecute corruption cases in order to insure its independence of the agencies which may come under its scrutiny. This does not mean that it may not cooperate with local or Federal authorities as the Commission did with good results. There should, however, be independent access to grand juries and the right to issue subpoenas and grant immunity. In addition, there must be City-wide jurisdiction. Corruption patterns do not stop at county lines, and jurisdictional niceties have often severely hampered corruption investigations. Moreover, District Attorneys' offices are reluctant to encroach upon each other's jurisdictions, much less investigate each other's personnel.

Finally, there is a need for an office that can be established immediately, without the delays that would be inevitable should implementing legislation be required.

To meet these needs, we recommend that the Governor, acting with the Attorney General pursuant to §63 of the Executive Law, appoint a Special Deputy Attorney General with jurisdiction in the five counties of the City and authority to investigate and prosecute all crimes involving corruption in the criminal process.

The powers of such Deputy Attorney Generals are traditional and well established. They include the power to use the grand jury and employ all investigative techniques incident to grand jury proceedings. They also include the power to suggest grand jury presentments and make other public reports.

The proposed Special Deputy Attorney General should use these powers to the widest extent. While he should provide a well-publicized channel for the reception of complaints, his activities should not be complaint oriented. He should concentrate on the identification and elimination of patterns of corruption, and should keep the public advised of conditions requiring administrative or legislative change.

We recommend that the Governor specify that this Special Deputy Attorney General be limited to a term of five years. It should be possible at the end of five years to make an informed judgment of whether this special Deputy Attorney General should continue to supplement regular anti-corruption efforts in the criminal justice process.

A PLAN FOR ANTI-CORRUPTION ACTION IN THE POLICE DEPARTMENT

Although the Commission believes that an anti-corruption agency outside the Police Department is required at this time, the Department's own anti-corruption effort must also be strengthened. Two actions are necessary for improvement. First, departmental doctrine that every commander is responsible for rooting out corruption in his command must be strictly adhered to in practice by requiring command accountability, as emphasized in many reforms ordered by Commissioner Murphy. Second, the Commission recommends that the Inspectional Services Bureau, which includes the anti-corruption agencies in the Department, be reorganized along the lines of the Inspections Office of the Internal Revenue Service. The Inspections Office is responsible to the Commissioner of Internal Revenue, but it plays no part in the collection of revenues. Its sole responsibility is to seek out evidence of corruption and to assist in the prosecution of Bureau agents and civilians who become involved in corruption. Its agents expect to spend their careers in the Inspections Office. Therefore, no inspections officer need ever contemplate the possibility of serving in a unit with or commanded by someone he has investigated. An Inspectional Services Bureau similarly organized would place full responsibility upon the Commissioner and at the same time provide him with an anti-corruption arm which is unhindered by the various handicaps we have discussed.

OTHER RECOMMENDATIONS

A significant reduction in police corruption can be achieved if the momentum for reform is maintained and if the following objectives are vigorously pursued:

First, corrupt activity must be curtailed by eliminating as many situations as possible which expose policemen to corruption, and by controlling exposure where corruption hazards are unavoidable.

Second, temptations to engage in corrupt activity on the part of the police and the public must be reduced by subjecting both to significant risks of detection, apprehension, conviction and penalties.

Third, incentives for meritorious police performance must be increased.

Fourth, police attitudes toward corruption must continue to change.

Fifth, a climate of reform must be supported by the public.

Commissioner Murphy has instituted a host of managerial changes aimed at achieving all the above objectives. In the recommendations which follow, we single out some that need particular support and others that have not yet been implemented. But we concentrate mainly on reforms which require action by others than the Commissioner.

Reducing the Opportunities for Corrupt Activity

Changing Laws

The laws against gambling, prostitution, and the conduct of certain business activities on the Sabbath all contribute to the prevalance of police corruption in obviously different degrees of seriousness. However, they have one characteristic in common—they are laws which are difficult to enforce because the "victims" of these crimes are usually willing participants and seldom complain to the police. Consequently, if a police officer for whatever motive decides to condone a violation, he need only fail to report it. Such a situation is an invitation to corruption. To curtail the opportunities for corruption fostered by these laws, the Commission makes the following recommendations:

Gambling. The criminal laws against gambling should be repealed. To the extent that the legislature deems that some control over gambling is appropriate, such regulation should be by civil rather than criminal process. The police should in any event be relieved from any responsibility for the enforcement of gambling laws or regulations.

Sabbath laws. The present Sabbath laws should be repealed as they have been in a number of states. To the extent they are retained, enforcement should not be a police function.

Prostitution. Although our evidence with respect to police corruption resulting from prostitution was not as strong as in other areas, the Commission believes that prostitution is a corruption hazard. It has been suggested that one way to eliminate the hazard would be to legalize prostitution, but this has usually included some regulatory control and other countries which have taken this approach do not seem to have eliminated the related police corruption. To the extent that prohibition or regulation of prostitution is deemed necessary or desirable, the Commission can suggest no alternative agency for enforcement.

Narcotics

The Commission believes that the police must continue to assume responsibility for enforcement of laws forbidding narcotics sale and possession as long as society deems it necessary to invoke criminal sanctions in this area. However, increased study and attention should be given to ways other than criminal sanctions for dealing with the addict.

The laws against marijuana are particularly controversial because of their growing unenforceability and the conviction of many that they are undesirable. However, the Commission has not found evidence that the marijuana laws are a distinct factor in police corruption.

Regulated Industries

Any industry subject to regulations whose enforcement is entrusted to the police presents a serious corruption hazard. Our investigations focused in particular upon the construction industry, and bars and other premises having liquor licenses which are subject to detailed and intricate regulations which are highly conducive to corruption. We believe that many opportunities for corruption can be eliminated by making such laws more reasonable.

The Commission recommends that in any area where a regulatory agency has jurisdiction, police officers should, insofar as possible, be relieved of the responsibility of enforcement unless (1) the agency requests police assistance or (2) a threat to order exists and must be dealt with on an emergency basis. Moreover, there must be publicly recognized means for waiving regulations where necessary, for example in construction, but we recommend that the police have no responsibility in this connection. We recognize that this approach will not in itself eliminate corruption but may simply transfer its hazards from the police to some other agency. But we believe that corruption in other agencies—undesirable as it is—has far less impact upon the body politic than corruption among the police.

The progression found again and again in the course of our investigation, from the acceptance by a police officer of petty graft to more serious corruption, makes it desirable to remove as many sources of such petty graft as possible. By eliminating the opportunity for petty graft, the Department can change the current attitude that such graft is an accepted part of the police job. This attitude makes it easier for a police officer to accept or solicit graft of a more serious nature when the opportunity presents itself. Moreover, policemen are more likely to pursue vigorously a corrupt public official who is not one of their own.

Finally, as a simple matter of efficiency there is no justification for using the police—with all their powers and prerogatives—in the enforcement of many miscellaneous reglations. It is ridiculous to have an armed police officer wasting his time (and that of his partner and supervising sergeant) checking restaurant washrooms to find out whether they are properly supplied with soap. We believe that the police should be taken out of bars and restaurants and away from building sites and returned to their principal job of protecting lives and property.

Reducing the Temptations and Increasing the Risks

Penalizing Bribe Givers

The Commission was struck by the apparent immunity from arrest enjoyed by givers as opposed to the takers of bribes. If the Police Department procedures in the past have been inadequate to apprehend members of the force who accept bribes, efforts to bring to justice those who give them have been almost non-existent.

Recently, a campaign was initiated to publicize the fact that the Police Department would hereafter arrest anyone offering a bribe. The Department has in fact increased its activity in this area. Bribery arrests in 1971 were up 440% over 1968 but the absolute numbers are still small. Further, the message conveyed by bribery arrests will be much stronger if the arrested bribers include individuals of some standing in the community like lawyers, hotel managers, restaurant or nightclub managers, and construction superintendents. The publicizing of such bribe arrests will deter offers of bribes and afford a legitimate excuse for refusing to pay them.

An effective way to supplement a campaign against bribers is to let it be known that specially assigned policemen will be used to apprehend bribers. In several instances, Commission investigators received offers of bribes from gamblers, bar owners, and prostitutes who mistook them for policemen. In one case, two investigators entered a bar for the purpose of checking records. Before they could make their request, the bartender informed them that the precinct captain had already been paid and asked them what they wanted. Experiences such as this indicate that this approach can be effective.

Procedures to Facilitate Corruption Investigations

Personnel Records. This Commission was hampered in its investigations by the lack of an efficiently organized system of personnel records. There is no centrally located personnel file for each police officer. For example, his applicant record, his Academy record, his service record, his disciplinary record and his award record, his medical record, his marksmanship record, his continuing education and training record, and his examination scores and promotion records are all maintained in different places. In order to check the record of an individual officer we found it necessary to go to as many as twelve different locations and search fourteen different files, since there was not even a central index to the various personnel files. It was not uncommon in these searches to discover all or part of a record missing or misfiled. Some records, maintained only at the precinct or unit headquarters level, are virtually inaccessible to investigators without alerting the subject of the investigation.

The Department has had a stated intent for several years of creating a central personnel file for each member of the Department. A centralized index summarizing the dispersed records is in the initial stages of construction. Both steps are necessary. The system of personnel records centralization should provide for two sets of records. One set of confidential records should contain all facts and allegations concerning a police employee's career. It should be maintained by the Internal Affairs Division and located in their headquarters. Access to this confidential set of records should be rigidly controlled to maintain the integrity of the files, and the files should be so structured as to make the unauthorized removal of a record difficult and obvious. Their principal use would be in investigations. A second set of accessible personnel records duplicating the first should be located at Police Headquarters, but this set should omit unsubstantiated allegations. This second set could be maintained by the Chief Clerk's staff or the Personnel Bureau or any other unit which could provide response to legitimate inquiries.

Both the quality and accessibility of photographs of police officers on active duty increase the difficulties faced by investigators of possible corrupt activities. Our investigators found that the pictures maintained in the files frequently appeared to be many years old and were taken in a rigid pose not conducive to ready identification. Moreover, investigators, including the Department's own, must go to a central photographic file in order to obtain photographs of suspected police officers and often must engage in elaborate subterfuges to conceal their interest in a particular individual.

The Commission recommends that two photographic files of police employees be maintained, one at the Internal Affairs Division and the other with the accessible central personnel file. The rule that photographs be taken every five years should be enforced, and the photographs should include several poses.

Complaints of Corruption. A complaint from a citizen or a police officer is one starting point for detecting corruption and apprehending corrupt officers. Such complaints must be encouraged by informing the public specifically how and where to make complaints and what details are necessary for action. More effective procedures must be established, with strong controls for insuring that complaints get immediately recorded wherever in the Department they may be received. These actions are necessary to mesh with the new departmental procedures for ensuring adequate complaint follow-up.

Line-ups. Commission investigators had one experience where they were called upon to identify allegedly corrupt officers in a line-up. The line-up was conducted in such a way that our investigators were exposed to full view before a number of police officers not connected with the case and, indeed, the suspects themselves. While such conditions did not deter our professional investigators, it was apparent to them that they would have intimidated civilian witnesses. Line-up procedures should insure that a complaining witness can identify an officer in a manner that protects the witness' anonymity.

Treatment of Cooperative Police Witnesses. If the Department is to use formerly corrupt policemen as undercover agents, it must be prepared to keep them on duty at full pay during the time that they are serving as agents and witnesses. When their services are no longer required, the Police Commissioner should allow them to resign in good standing as he did Patrolman Droge.

Enforcement Responsibility

Departmental Action Against Infractions Indicative of Corruption. Anti-corruption investigators often know the identities of corrupt police officers and from observing their behavior can be certain of the fact that they are engaged in corrupt activities. Proving a criminal case, however, is a different matter, since corrupt activities are inherently covert and involve mutually trusting parties. Although a more vigorous and effective effort to make criminal cases is certainly desirable and possible, one solution to the corruption problem may lie elsewhere.

There are a number of regulations and procedures in the Department that call for disciplinary punishment for a variety of infractions related to corrupt behavior, such as the regulation against associating with gamblers, criminals, or persons engaged in unlawful activities except in the discharge of official duty or with the permission of the Police Commissioner. The rules require that the fact and purpose of such a meeting in the course of duty be recorded. Whenever this kind of meeting is observed and has not been recorded, the excuse commonly given by the officer is that he was attempting to get information from an informant and had merely forgotten to report the matter. Invariably, no charges are brought for such infractions if the commander is satisfied with the excuse given in the particular case. Such rules as this one are designed to deter corruption. Yet their uneven enforcement undermines the achievement of this goal.

The Commission recommends that the required reporting procedures be strictly enforced and that Departmental charges be brought against violators in all instances. The validity of the excuse for such meetings should bear only upon the penalties imposed. However, since it would be unfair to change the enforcement policy abruptly, the Department should publicize its intention to punish with maximum severity any infraction of these rules. The threat of severe penalties may have a deterrent effect on an officer who knows how difficult it is to prove a corrupt conversation between him and a gambler or other criminal but who also knows how easy it is to prove the simple fact of the meeting.

Expanded Penalties in Department Hearings. Perhaps the most troublesome issue in the disciplining of policemen found guilty in Departmental hearings is the inappropriateness of the available penalties. The Administrative Code provides no gradations of penalty between outright dismissal from the force and a fine of 30 days pay or vacation followed by a year's probation. The Commission recommends that the disciplinary alternatives available to the Police Commissioner be broadened. Penalties under the Administrative Code should be changed so that there are penalties available between dismissal and a thirty-day fine.

The Police Commissioner can now reduce any officer above the rank of captain to captain. The Commission further recommends that provision be made for a penalty of reduction of one civil service rank after conviction on serious charges. This would mean that captains, and officers above captain, could be reduced to lieutenants and removed from command posts, lieutenants could be reduced to sergeants, and sergeants could be reduced to patrolmen.

This latter recommendation of rank reductions is necessary to provide meaningful penalties for failures to exercise supervisory and command responsibilities. At present, the usual penalty for such failure is transfer to a new assignment. Such a light penalty does little to motivate superior officers to move vigorously to eradicate corruption and laziness.

Hearing Officers. The Commission urges that the City Council approve the pending bill providing for additional Hearing Officers in departmental trials. The present requirement that only Deputy Commissioners can conduct such trials has created an unnecessary backlog.

Pensions. Another serious defect in the Department's disciplinary options is the present law requiring that any officer dismissed from the Department automatically forfeit his pension regardless of the nature of the offense bringing about his discharge, or how many years he may have worked to earn his pension, or how exemplary his prior record may have been. Although a Police Commissioner should be able to dismiss any policeman found to be corrupt, it by no means follows that a single act of corruption justifies what may amount to a fine of several hundred thousand dollars, the commuted value of many officers' vested pension rights. No civilian would be subjected to a comparable penalty.

The result of the present forfeiture rule has been that the courts on appeal have directed the reinstatement of patently unfit officers because they could not tolerate the injustice involved in the forfeiture of vested pension rights.

The solution recommended by the Commission is to separate considerations of pension from departmental disciplinary proceedings. Disciplinary proceedings within the Department should be concerned solely with the question of whether the offense has been established and whether the offender should be removed from the force or suffer some lesser departmental punishment. In the event of dismissal, and upon recommendation of the Police Commissioner, there should be a wholly separate proceeding conducted by the Corporation Counsel to determine whether the offender should be deprived of his accumulated pension rights.

Under present procedures, officers suspected of misconduct are permitted to put in their retirement papers and retire thirty days later, at which time they become immune to departmental disciplinary proceedings and become eligible to receive their pensions. This results in a thirty-day race, with a suspected officer seeking to retire before charges can be brought against him. The statute of limitations for beginning a pension proceeding should commence to run the day the officer is separated from the Department—either by disciplinary action or by resignation—and there should be no arbitrary period of time for the completion of such a proceeding. The normal rules for civil actions where issues of comparable importance are customarily decided should apply to such a proceeding.

Until these new procedures are adopted, the thirty-day limitation should immediately be extended to ninety days by passage of the bill to that effect now pending before the City Council.

Effect of Disciplinary Records upon Promotions. Officers with lengthy records of disciplinary infractions have, in the past, been promoted to supervisory and command ranks—even repromoted after demotion. The system of departmental recognition provides for the Department of Personnel to add extra points to the scores of officers taking a promotion examination. But a disciplinary record is never counted by imposing specified negative points for convictions of various rule infractions. The Commission recommends that revisions be made in the formal system of promotion points to include both positive points for good performance and negative points for convictions of rule infractions.

Changing Procedures Which Encourage Corruption

Policemen sometimes engage in corrupt practices because alternative means of solving problems are not available or are too bothersome. For example, expense money is inadequate or too slow in being paid and procedures for handling contraband are too complex and too time-consuming. These situations, and others like them, can be readily corrected. Many such improvements have already been ordered by Police Commissioner Murphy.

Reimbursement of Expenses. Although plainclothesmen have traditionally been faced with the greatest temptation for corruption because of the nature of their work, the Depatment has made their job even more difficult by not giving them sufficient funds to do it properly. A plainclothesman incurs various expenses in the course of doing his job, but the Department has in the past allowed him only $100 per month. To facilitate the work of plainclothes officers, an expense advance should be provided, the amounts allowed should be flexible, and reimbursement for expenses should be prompt.

Arrest Quotas. The existence of informal arrest quotas is an inducement to a particular kind of corruption, the arrest of individuals not actually apprehended in the commission of the charged crime. Testimony before the State Investigation Commission in its investigation of narcotics described a pattern of requiring a quota of four felony arrests per month and concluded that this requirement led to "flaking" of individuals—the planting of narcotics upon a suspected individual. Our investigation confirmed the existence of such an informal quota as well as similar flaking in policy arrests. The Commission also found that plainclothesmen assigned to prostitution details were faced with the necessity of producing a stipulated number of arrests a night and, in order to do so, often arrested persons they considered to be "obvious" prostitutes, without obtaining sufficient legal evidence.

The emphasis on quality arrests which the Department has now established should be pressed vigorously, and steps should be taken to insure that individual commanders do not replace formal quotas with informal quotas.

Informants. Abuses with respect to the use of informants have, in the past, been facilitated by the loose control exercised over them. According to Departmental Rules and Regulations, informants must be registered to an individual police officer. But in fact the Commission has found that this rule is not enforced and informants deal with a number of police officers. This leads to corruption because officers will not usually engage in illegal activities, such as selling narcotics, with informants registered to them. The Commission recommends that rules requiring the registration of informants be enforced. We further recommend that officers be required to report all contacts with informants.

Paid Informants. At the present time, it is the policy of the Department that informants are not paid. This leads to corruption because of the temptation to reward informants with narcotics or other contraband. The Commission recommends that realistic appraisal be made of the funds necessary to maintain the Department's registered informants and that adequate funds be made available to the Department for this purpose. Procedures for accounting for the expenditure of these funds should be simplified to the maximum extent possible and should be no more complicated than a regular expense report.

Gratuities. Although the acceptance of "any valuable gift" is against Departmental regulations, the rule has not been enforced with any regularity. Maintaining that a free cup of coffee is the acceptance of graft while finding no wrongdoing when a Chief of Detectives accepts a meal for himself and guests worth $84 promotes an attitude of cynicism in the Department leading to corruption. The Commission recommends that the Department bring practice and policy into accord, and enforce diligently whatever policy is finally adopted. If the Department decides to permit policemen to accept free meals and goods, the Commission urges that all such gratuities be reported in memorandum books or on Daily Field Activity Reports, which should be reviewed daily by supervisory officers. Supervisory personnel should then be held responsible for insuring that such privileges are not abused.

Sleeping Accommodations. Since there are many occasions, such as a morning court appearance after a night of duty, when it is difficult for an officer to return home to sleep, the Department should acknowledge this fact and arrange for sleeping accommodations. The City should make appropriate arrangements to reimburse hotels to permit officers to occupy hotel rooms on a space-available basis.

Management Procedures

The Department will always have to cope with opportunities and temptations for corruption. In part, the Murphy administration's strategy for doing so is to reduce exposure to corruption hazards and to fix responsibility and insure individual accountability. Many steps have been taken in these directions, and others are required.

Field Activity Reporting. To make the concept of accountability work it is important to have an officer's account of what he did while on duty—to be compared with what he was supposed to do. The necessity for having on record an account of a policeman's daily doings that can be verified or proved false was made clear to this Commission when it subpoenaed several dozen memorandum books of policemen about whom questions had been raised. At that time the only record of a police officer's activities was his memorndum book, and he kept the only copy in his possession. We discovered that these books were uniformly useless, not just because they contained falsifications but because they were full of blanks. Under the memorandum book system, many patrolmen customarily leave large blanks and/or perhaps spend an hour or two a week reconstructing (or inventing) their activities. Since memo books are retained by the officers, it is easy to go back and add entries to provide an account of an officer's daily activities when an investigation of his activities creates a need to do so. To provide an improved record, the Department is now experimenting in twelve precincts with Daily Field Activity Reports for all patrolmen and is requiring them from plainclothes officers assigned to the Organized Crime Control Bureau (OCCB). These reports are filled out in triplicate, turned in every day, and signed by a superior officer. Whether or not the experimental Daily Field Activity Report form is satisfactory, there is a clear need for all field officers including detectives to prepare during their tour a reporting form or book specifying where the officers were and what they were doing at specific times. At least two copies of this daily report should be submitted at the end of each tour for supervisory scrutiny and signature. One copy should be retained by the Department and one by the officer. Other copies should be prepared as required for administrative review, as is now done in the OCCB.

Arrest Procedures. Corruption in connection with the arrest of an offender is facilitated by the reporting form used by the Department to record arrests. The Commission found that, particularly in gambling arrests, the description of the alleged offense is often written by the police officer in such ambiguous terms that he can later testify in a manner exculpating the defendant. This fact enables a police officer to make himself available for a change of testimony in exchange for financial consideration. A forced-choice arrest form which removes the possibility of a change of testimony in key areas involving search and seizure and the legality of an arrest is necessary and should be adopted after field experimentation.

Name Tags. We have already referred to the fact of police isolation from the community. To many citizens, the police officer on the street is the nameless embodiment of authority. The present badge numbers cannot be easily read. The Commission recommends that the uniformed officers in the department be required to wear name tags on the outside of their uniforms. This is standard practice for identifying individuals who deal with the public like doctors on hospital staffs, bank tellers, and airline personnel. Men and women in the armed services of the United States have worn name tags for years.

Reducing the Susceptibility to Corruption

There are two general approaches to reducing the susceptibility to corruption among police officers. The first is to improve screening and selection methods and standards. The second aproach requires no less than a change in police attitudes.

Background Investigations. To prevent the few situations that have arisen in which unsuitable candidates were admitted to the force and sent out to the field before their full background investigations had been completed, there should be established in practice, as well as by rule, an absolute ban against the swearing in of police officers until their background investigations have been finished and reviewed.

Lateral Entry to Supervisory Ranks. A controversial reform in police practice involves the infusion of new blood at supervisory levels. Currently, all supervisory and commanding officers must rise through the ranks, and the officer-enlisted man relationship which contributes to a sense of discipline in the military is often entirely lacking. The quality of superior officers is necessarily limited by the refusal of the Department to accept supervisory personnel from outside its own ranks. If, as it appears to the Commission, the Department is imbued with an attitude of tolerance towards corruption, officers rising through the ranks cannot help but be conditioned by this prevailing attitude. Moreover, many superior officers are, rightly or wrongly, the subject of rumors as to their own past corrupt activities. The Commission recommends that provision for lateral entry to the Department be established by amendments to the present Civil Service regulations to permit individuals of outstanding qualifications from other law enforcement agencies to assume supervisory ranks.

Police College. A long-range reform which could facilitate lateral entry into all police departments would be the establishment of a National Police Academy at a college level. Suggestions for a National Academy have usually revolved around the idea of retraining officers already on the job. A national, Federally-funded academy patterned after the military service academies would provide a free college education for highly qualified young men and women who wish to make a profession out of police service. Application to the college should be open to any high school graduate. Entrance to the college, however, should be delayed until after the appointee has served one year, after completion of training, in any police department. Following a regular four-year education leading to a bachelor's degree and including on-the-job training in several police departments, a graduate should return to the city where he originally served and assume the rank of sergeant. He would have a four-year obligation in that Department. As in the military service, provision would also be made for education in the same college of officers rising from the uniformed force through an officers' candidate school along the lines of the British Police College. An academy of this sort would add to the professionalism of police service.

Partners for New Officers. Under Commissioner Murphy, the Department is providing, for the first time, thorough training for all ranks in dealing with the hazards of corruption and the proper response to them. To supplement this, the Commission recommends that the Department develop a new approach for the first field assignment of new recruits. After their first assignment to a model precinct, officers should be assigned a senior "training" patrolman as their partner. Specially selected and carefully screened patrolmen with considerable experience, both in the Department and in the particular precinct or unit, should be used for this purpose. A precinct training syllabus should be provided to cover all phases of police work within the precinct.

Master Patrolmen. For men of patrolman rank, the Commission recommends a system of promotion to create a new classification of Master Patrolman. These Master Patrolmen would be promoted from the ranks of veteran patrolmen and would be given responsibilities for training new recruits.

Enlisting Public Support

Progress Reporting. If concerned citizens are to be encouraged in bringing reports of corruption to the attention of the Police Department, they must be promptly informed of the final disposition of their complaints. This will give the aggrieved citizen who feels that the action taken was inadequate an opportunity to seek a remedy from other agencies.

Publication of Statistics. Besides providing specific information to complainants, general information concerning corruption should be provided to the public. Raw data concerning disciplinary actions is difficult to collect because it exists only in individual records. Furthermore, statistics relating disciplinary dispositions to charges are not even compiled. A monthly report should be prepared and made available to all communications media showing the changes and dispositions of all departmental actions against corrupt officers by rank and command. Such a report would be complementary to the Department's publication of bribery arests. Similar reports are published in other cities, and in some the names of the accused officers are included.

* * *

The remaining sections of the Commission's report, which are to be issued shortly, set forth in detail the substantive findings upon which these recommendations are based.

August 3, 1972

COMMISSION REPORT

Section One: Commission Activities

Chapter One

HISTORY OF COMMISSION

Origin of Commission

On April 25, 1970, *The New York Times* printed a story presenting lengthy and detailed accusations of widespread corruption in the Police Department. The story charged that police officers received systematic payoffs from gamblers, narcotics peddlers, and other law violators, and that the police hierarchy as well as officials of the City administration had been informed of specific charges of serious corruption and failed to take any action.

Mayor John V. Lindsay responded to the allegations by appointing a committee to investigate them.* The committee met several times and reported by letter** to the Mayor that a full-time citizens' commission was needed to investigate the problem. The committee said that it had received 375 complaints in response to a public plea by the Mayor for information and that the regular duties of the committee members prevented their devoting sufficient time to an independent investigation. Moreover, the committee noted the reaction among some segments of the public that an investigation of allegations of police corruption should not be conducted by those who conceivably might be responsible for the conditions they were supposed to examine.

In response to the Rankin Committee's recommendation, the Mayor, on May 21, 1970, issued an executive order† appointing this

---

* The committee was headed by Corporation Counsel J. Lee Rankin and its members were Frank S. Hogan and Burton B. Roberts, District Attorneys of New York and Bronx Counties, respectively; Commissioner of Investigation Robert K. Ruskin and Police Commissioner Howard R. Leary.

** Appendix, Exhibit 1.

† Appendix, Exhibit 2.

Commission* and charging it with the tasks of determining the extent and nature of police corruption in the City, examining existing procedures for dealing with corruption, recommending changes and improvements in these procedures, and holding whatever hearings were deemed appropriate.

The City Council passed a bill** giving the Commission power to issue subpoenas and authorized $325,000 in funds to last through December 31, 1970. On July 25, the Board of Estimate ratified the authorization of funds. On the same date a legal challenge to the Commission's legitimacy was rejected by the courts.

Purposes and Goals

The Commission's efforts were directed first at conducting investigations to identify the patterns of corruption, if any, which existed within the Police Department. Although using traditional law enforcement investigative techniques, Commission investigators did not set out to seek evidence for criminal charges against individuals but instead concentrated on the broader problem of identifying the nature and extent of corruption in the Department. Information which afforded a basis for criminal prosecution was turned over to the appropriate district attorney.

Once the Commission had determined the existence and extent of patterns of corruption, it could evaluate whether proper supervisory action had been taken by those in authority, including the police hierarchy, and devise recommendations to meet the problems found in the investigation.

---

* The formal title of the Commission is: Commission to Investigate Allegations of Police Corruption and the City's Anti-corruption Procedures. Whitman Knapp was named as its chairman and Arnold Bauman, Joseph Monserrat, Franklin A. Thomas and Cyrus R. Vance were named as commissioners. In February, 1971, Mr. Bauman resigned to devote full time to his private law practice. He was replaced by John E. Sprizzo.

** Appendix, Exhibit 3.

Just as the Commission's investigation was getting under way in September, 1970, Commissioner Leary resigned and was replaced in October by Patrick V. Murphy.

This change necessitated a shift in the Commission's emphasis. Commissioner Murphy announced in no uncertain terms that it was his intention to institute major reforms in an all-out attack upon a corruption problem which he acknowledged to be of top priority. He quickly began to replace personnel in supervisory positions and institute changes in the Department which seemed to address some of the major problems the Commission's investigation was beginning to uncover. For the Commission, fixing responsibility at the command level and focusing upon managerial and organizational reforms assumed less importance while the Department was in the midst of this necessarily lengthy reform effort.

The job of investigating and exposing patterns of corruption remained. Its importance was emphasized by the fact that even the new Police Commissioner seemed to adopt an ambivalent public position on the actual extent of the conditions he pledged himself to eradicate. He often spoke in terms implying that corruption was limited to a few aberrant members of the Department, and this view was echoed by others engaged in the anti-corruption effort.

Assembling a Staff

Plans called for a chief counsel, six associate and assistant counsel, approximately a dozen field investigators, and a small stenographic and clerical staff. Recruiting and organization proceeded through August and most of September, 1970. Although limited investigations were begun in August, it was not until the first week in October that a full investigative staff was assembled.

Whether the Commission's efforts were to succeed clearly depended upon the competence and experience of its investigators, all but one of whom had formerly been investigators for various federal agencies.* Of the investigators, only two (a former uniformed patrolman and a federal agent who had been a detective on the New York County District Attorney's squad) had any prior experience with the New York Police Department. The former patrolman left the Commission in October, 1970, leaving the staff with virtually no investigators experienced in actual police work.

Although the investigative personnel lacked police experience, the Commission counted on the fact that skilled investigators could familiarize themselves quickly with the workings of the Department. From the outset, individuals of long experience with the Department had pointed out that the intense group loyalty that existed among police officers would make it extremely difficult to find policemen or former policemen who could bring enthusiasm to the job of investigating corruption among men who were or had been their comrades.

The decision to use investigators from outside the Police Department proved to be a sound one. In the course of its investigation, the Commission confirmed the impression that, with some outstanding exceptions, policemen operating in the climate of opinion that prevailed in the Department did not make the most effective investigators of other policemen.

Investigative Activities

As the end of 1970 approached, the Commission's investigation was just getting under way but subpoena power and funds had been provided only through December 31. The City was in dire fiscal trouble and it seemed clear to the Commission that members of the City Council and Board of Estimate, who had been considerably less than unanimous in their enthusiasm over the creation of the Commission, would

---

* The Commission's investigative staff consisted of three former FBI agents, two former Immigration Service agents, one former U.S. Army counterintelligence agent, one former New York City policeman, and, on loan from their respective agencies for the duration of the Commission's work, two Internal Revenue Service Intelligence agents, two Internal Revenue Service Inspection agents, one Federal Narcotics agent and one Postal Inspection agent.

be reluctant to authorize any expenditure of City funds to extend the Commission's life. The Commission therefore approached the U.S. Justice Department's Law Enforcement Assistance Administration (LEAA) and received the promise of a grant which would enable the Commission to continue for another six months. With the cooperation of the Mayor and Commissioner Murphy, the grant was approved and a bill was passed by the City Council extending the Commission's subpoena power for the same period.

On July 1, 1971, upon the expiration of the six-month period for which funds and subpoena power had been provided, the Commission cut its staff from approximately thirty to approximately six, including two attorneys and two investigators.* Several of the most important investigations were not completed but further governmental funds were unavailable in substantial amounts, help could not be sought from private sources without revealing confidential investigations and most staff members had commitments elsewhere. No attempt was made to gain further subpoena power and the Commission continued operations out of unspent monies and a small additional grant from LEAA.

An interim report was issued on July 1, 1971, setting forth in general terms the factual findings of the Commission's investigation to that date.**

During the summer of 1971, despite its limited staff, the Commission carried forward some of its most productive investigations, aided

---

* In May, 1971, Assistant Attorney General Will Wilson, who headed the Justice Department's criminal division and had greatly assisted the Commission in recruiting federal agents and obtaining federal funds, assigned two additional lawyers from the Organized Crime Strike Force and the Racketeering Section to act as liaison with the Commission and to assist in its work. These assignments, which lasted through August and October, 1971, were made in recognition of the fact that in March, 1971, the Commission detailed one of its supervisory attorneys and two investigators to work exclusively with federal authorities on a criminal investigation arising out of the Commission's work. This investigation is discussed on pp. 48-50.

** Appendix, Exhibit 4.

somewhat by the impression on the part of the general public and the rank and file of the Police Department that the investigation was over.

The Commission worked increasingly with various law enforcement agencies to insure that the results of its investigation could be translated, insofar as possible, into criminal and departmental cases. Since much of the investigative effort was concentrated in Manhattan, particularly close liaison was maintained from the outset with the United States Attorney's Office for the Southern District of New York and later with the District Attorney's Office of New York County. The Police Department Internal Affairs Division, which came under the command of Assistant Chief Inspector Sydney Cooper on July 31, 1971, was also brought in on a number of matters and provided effective assistance.

In all, the Commission's investigation lasted for nine months using approximately ten to twelve investigators and continued for another three months using two and sometimes only one investigator.

Public Hearings

The Commission recognized the dangers inherent in public hearings, which would inevitably lead to public attention being focused on the most sensational aspects of the testimony. Nevertheless, the persistent tendency of public officials in and out of the Department to characterize police corruption in terms of a few "rotten apples" and the apparent ignorance of large segments of the public of the dimensions of the problem of police corruption led to the decision that public hearings were essential. The Commission felt that the public was entitled to hear and evaluate witnesses rather than being asked to accept determinations based upon testimony taken behind closed doors.

In October, 1971, the Commission held nine days of public hearings during which it heard testimony from fifteen witnesses.* Three police officers detailed their own corrupt activities. Three Commission

---

* Commission Chairman Whitman Knapp's opening statement at the First Public Hearings appears as Exhibit 5 in the Appendix.

agents testified to the results of various investigations. A police officer experienced in anti-corruption work and the chairman of the New York State Commission of Investigation testified about their work in the corruption field. A gambler, a tow truck driver, and five members of the business community described police corruption which they had encountered. Tape recordings and films made in undercover operations were presented during the testimony of various witnesses.

In December, 1971, a second set of hearings was held lasting five days.* The purpose of these hearings was to provide a public airing of the circumstances surrounding the handling of charges of corruption made in 1967 and 1968 by Officers Frank Serpico and David Durk, the two men whose experiences had provided the basis for much of *The New York Times* article which had prompted the creation of the Commission. During these hearings, testimony was heard from the two police officers who had made the charges, the former Police Commissioner, the former Commissioner of Investigation, various high ranking police officers, the District Attorney of Bronx County and a mayoral aide.

Insofar as possible, names of individuals allegedly involved in corrupt actions but not yet tried for them were not used in either set of hearings. Opportunity was provided for rebuttal testimony and two police officers took advantage of this opportunity, one to deny implications of his own involvement in corrupt activities and the other to disagree generally with the Commission's efforts.

After the conclusion of the hearings in December, the Commission devoted its time to the preparation of its report and to cooperative efforts with the Police Department and various federal and state prosecutors. Additional funds were obtained from federal, state and private grants which made it possible for the Commission to continue during its hearings and in the preparation of the report. Expenditures for the Commission's activities totaled $749,120.**

---

* Chairman Knapp's opening statement at these hearings appears as Exhibit 6 in the Appendix.

** A list of the sources of grants is set forth in the Appendix as Exhibit 7.

Chapter Two

METHODS OF INVESTIGATION
and
SOURCES OF INFORMATION

Initial Steps

In assessing the degree and patterns of corruption in the Police Department the Commission staff relied upon a wide variety of methods and sources. At the outset, information was gathered from examining complaints and conducting interviews. In all, the Commission received more than 1,700 written or telephoned complaints, 375 of which had been forwarded by the Rankin Committee. Most complaints coming from the public were not appropriate for investigation by the Commission's limited staff, and many of them were either crank complaints or too vague to be of any use. Many, however, presented inbelievable fashion facts which were repeated often enough to give some indication of patterns of police behavior.

Various facets of police corruption were discussed with members of the business community, current and former members of the Police Department, individuals engaged in illegal activities, citizens in high crime areas, and others with relevant knowledge or experience. Commission staff members conducted hundreds of interviews of this sort and soon learned that a vast majority of ordinary citizens—in and out of the Department—shared a somewhat fatalistic belief that the Police Department was permeated with corruption.

Almost any conversation held on a confidential or informal basis with a member of the public, particularly a ghetto resident, elicited a strong opinion that police corruption was widely prevalent and, almost invariably, an illustrative story based on personal experience. Practically no one, however, was willing to allow his information to be used —much less to testify himself. In particular, members and former members of the Department were unwilling even to allow their words to be repeated on an anonymous basis for fear of being recognized as a source of information.

Nevertheless, information received on a confidential basis from many sources gave the Commission staff, at a fairly early stage of its investigation, a pretty clear picture of the patterns of corruption in the Department: organized and systematized payoffs from gamblers to plainclothesmen, payments of large amounts of money by narcotics violators, regular payments by companies engaged in various industries having contacts with the police, payments by tow truck operators, grocery store owners, prostitutes, and many others were detailed enough times and with enough repetitive similarity to indicate that such patterns not only were widely believed to exist but actually did.

Field Investigations

The Commission had, of course, a larger obligation than simply to compile allegations obtained in complaints and confidential interviews. Commission personnel conducted field investigations for the purpose of producing hard evidence of the extent of corruption in the Department. In doing so, they focused upon a number of areas where the opportunity for corruption seemed to present itself. Investigators were assigned to look into illegal activities such as narcotics, gambling, loansharking, prostitution, Sabbath law violations, alcohol violations, and homosexuality. Businesses susceptible to corruption such as the construction industry, drinking places, parking lots, food stores, hotels, taxicabs, tow trucks, trucking companies, and street vendors were also examined.

In their field work Commission agents employed standard investigative techniques. They conducted surveillances to observe areas of open violation of the law ranging from narcotics to illegal parking. They gathered information from paid informants, sometimes from the underworld. They conducted undercover interviews which were surreptitiously recorded with the aid of electronic recording equipment. They reviewed cases of police corruption in the hope that individuals involved in them might be willing to give information. They posed as customers and law violators and capitalized oh instances where they were mistaken for police officers. They persuaded some individuals who provided information to obtain further evidence by participating in electronically recorded conversations under the supervision and surveillance of Commission agents.

Commission investigators were limited in their ability to make use of electronic investigative aids. The law permits such an investigator to use electronic equipment which will enable him to overhear and record a conversation only when one of the participants to the conversation consents to its being overheard. One of the most valuable anti-corruption investigative tools, using an electronic device to overhear or record a telephone or face-to-face conversation involving people who are unaware that the conversation is being monitored, can only be used by regular law enforcement officers after obtaining a warrant.

The Commission also lacked another weapon which is probably the most useful one in investigations of this sort—the power to compel testimony by granting immunity from prosecution.

Indeed, for much of its life, the Commission lacked even the power to subpoena a police officer who chose not to testify. Lawsuits challenging the Commission's authority to issue subpoenas were instituted by some police officers in the fall of 1970. Although these suits were ultimately decided in the Commission's favor, the Commission was restricted in its use of subpoenas until the appeal process was completed in late April, 1971.

In addition, the temporary nature of the Commission operated to frustrate its efforts because potential witnesses were well aware that the police officers against whom they were being asked to testify would probably still be on the job long after the Commission had ceased to exist.

Commission investigators, however, possessed certain advantages over traditional law enforcement officers. Since they were not primarily engaged in making criminal cases, they were not obliged to spend their time developing evidence against specific individuals. Some witnesses felt freer to talk to Commission personnel because, where necessary, assurance could be given that the information would not be used in a criminal prosecution. The investigators' backgrounds as federal officers aided them in that many witnesses who would refuse to talk to a policeman were willing to talk to an investigator with no apparent ties to the Department. This attitude, which reflected a deep-seated mistrust of the Department's ability to police itself, was repeatedly encountered during the investigation.

Commission investigators ran up against a virtual stone wall when they attempted to obtain information from legitimate businesses obviously involved in payments to the police. Businessmen refused to cooperate or to give information. Some small grocery store owners were willing to relate their experiences and even cooperate in attempts at undercover surveillances, but bar owners, construction supervisors, hotel managers, and other similarly situated businessmen refused to cooperate until the Commission subpoenaed records which reflected illegal payments. At this point representatives of certain hotels and of the construction industry agreed to cooperate more fully.

The surveillances conducted by the investigators focused not only upon specific meetings where bribes or conversations relating to them were discussed but also upon conditions indicating the extent of corruption. For example, investigators observed and photographed gambling spots, construction sites, and bars catering to prostitutes and homosexuals. The openness of illegal activities at such establishments, coupled with the occasional appearance of police officers who took no action, indicated either corruption or extremely lax police effort.

Occasionally a general surveillance of this type produced more direct evidence, like the instance in January, 1971, when Commission agents observed police officers in four patrol cars removing packages of meat from a meat packing plant at 3:00 A.M. one Sunday morning in Greenwich Village.

Document Analysis

In addition to the street investigations conducted by the investigators, the Commission served 296 subpoenas *duces tecum* to obtain records from various businesses. Financial questionnaires were obtained from ranking police officers. Police records concerning known gamblers, arrests, and other data were examined. Surveys were sent to members of the construction industry and associations representing Spanish-speaking grocery store owners. Literature relating to problems of corruption and police management was collected and analyzed.

Interviews of Supervisors

In late 1970 and early 1971 supervisory police officers assigned to anti-corruption work and other sensitive posts were interviewed in an attempt to examine the Department's anti-corruption procedures. The continuing reorganization undertaken by Commissioner Murphy made it necessary for the Commission to conduct a second round of interviews in the summer of 1972. By that time all of the personnel and most of the procedures were found to have been changed.

Investigations by Others

The Commission also drew upon the findings of other commissions and law enforcement agencies. When the Commission was appointed, the State Commission of Investigation was already well into a year-long investigation of the narcotics trade in New York, including problems of police corruption. Their public hearings and resultant findings, based chiefly on cases investigated by the New York Police Department, indicated patterns of corruption in narcotics which paralleled the conclusions drawn by Commission investigators. Similarly, the New

York State Joint Legislative Committee on Crime, headed by Senator John Hughes, produced studies with respect to gambling and the courts which provided valuable information. Cases handled by the Police Department, federal law enforcement agencies and the various District Attorneys also provided insights into patterns of corruption.

Executive Hearings

The Commission conducted private hearings in executive session throughout the investigation and heard testimony from 183 witnesses, ranging from high City and police officials to underworld figures. One hundred thirteen police officers were subpoenaed; seventy-nine of them testified and an additional twenty-two testified without subpoena. Sixty-eight civilians were subpoenaed, and all but one testified; fifteen civilians also testified voluntarily. Additionally, 116 subpoenaed witnesses (104 civilians and twelve policemen) testified informally before Commission staff members.

Police Witnesses

Throughout its investigation the Commission staff sought to find police officers actually engaged in corrupt activities who could be induced to describe openly and for the record their activities and their knowledge of the patterns of corruption observed during their careers. We were informed by people experienced in police work that no police officer had ever given such information and that none ever would, even if he himself were caught in a corrupt act and were offered immunity in exchange for his testimony. The tradition of the policeman's code of silence was so strong, we were advised, that it was futile to expect such testimony from any police officer. The most that could be expected was anonymous information or, if we were extremely lucky, testimony given under oath on an anonymous basis. All of the experienced people with whom we spoke agreed that if even one police officer could be induced to give inside information based upon personal experience, the testimony would be of inestimably greater value than any other evidence the Commission might uncover.

The search for a corrupt officer who would speak frankly and openly uncovered not one but five. However, the first and potentially most productive of these proved to be too valuable to keep to ourselves. Robert Leuci was a detective who had spent eleven years on the force and who had been assigned to the elite Special Investigation Unit (SIU) of the Narcotics Division. He had met police officers Durk and Serpico in 1970 and led them to believe that he would back up their charges that SIU had not adequately pursued certain narcotics cases. In the fall of 1970 Durk arranged for meetings between Leuci and various assistant district attorneys, the State Commission of Investigation, and the staff of this Commission. In these meetings Leuci's statements were inconclusive and not susceptible to investigation. He subsequently indicated that his purpose in submitting to questioning had been to discover how much information the Commission and other agencies possessed.

In February, 1971, Leuci was again interviewed by the Commission staff, and this time he was convinced to tell all he knew about corruption in SIU and to help the Commission expose it.

Leuci told of a Narcotics Division infested with corruption. Drawing on personal experiences as well as those he observed and discussed with fellow officers, he described enormous payoffs by narcotics violators, illegal wiretaps used to facilitate shakedowns, involvement of supervisory personnel in narcotics graft, and arrangements between police officers and organized crime members which gave the latter protection from arrest and advance knowledge of legitimate investigations involving them.

Leuci worked with Commission agents for about one month and obtained a number of incriminating tape-recorded conversations with police officers. It quickly became apparent that he had incalculable value as an undercover agent. His work, if allowed to continue for as long as it was productive, could result in criminal prosecutions which might well expose a network of narcotics related corruption involving many police officers and stretching outside the Department.

However, an investigation calculated to accomplish this end would, if successful, last for many months, even years, and would require concentrating on obtaining evidence in specific cases rather than on gathering information for the purpose of identifying patterns of corruption. Because the Commission's investigation was due to end in a few months, we decided that Leuci should be turned over to law enforcement authorities with the time and manpower necessary for such an investigation.

In March, 1971, Assistant United States Attorney General Wilson and Whitney North Seymour, Jr., United States Attorney for the Southern District of New York, were apprised of Leuci's activities to date and advised that the Commission was willing to forego any use of Leuci or the information he had provided in favor of an investigation directed at criminal prosecutions. The Commission also offered to refrain from revealing or further pursuing certain investigations into narcotics and related corruption which might draw attention to Leuci, and to allow the attorney and the two agents who had been working with Leuci to devote their full time to the proposed investigation. The Commission's offer was accepted.

The following month Commissioner Murphy and First Deputy Commissioner William H. T. Smith were informed of the investigation and arrangements were made to transfer Leuci back into SIU where he could work most effectively. The Commissioner agreed to keep his knowledge of the investigation entirely confidential and to give his full assistance whenever requested to do so.

The investigation was pursued with great success by the original investigative team aided by personnel from Mr. Seymour's office and, as the scope of the investigation broadened, by agents of the Federal Bureau of Narcotics and Dangerous Drugs, and a few carefully selected police officers. By the spring of 1972 federal authorities were confident that the investigation would result in far-ranging indictments involving organized crime members, police officers, and others in the criminal justice system including even judges.

However, Detective Leuci's participation in the investigation came to an end in June, 1972, when a story printed in *The New York Times* precipitated a general disclosure of his activities. Six indictments have so far been returned alleging corruption on the part of four police officers, an assistant district attorney, three lawyers, a bail bondsman and a private investigator. Other indictments are anticipated, but some of the most important cases have undoubtedly been aborted by the premature disclosure of the investigation.

The Commission could not, of course, call Leuci as a witness in its public hearings since at that time he was still working as a federal undercover agent. Moreover, findings in other Commissions investigations were withheld during the hearings so as to avoid areas where the focusing of attention might threaten his undercover activities.* With his exposure some of the information disclosed by Leuci and certain of the results of his undercover work can now be discussed and have been included, where relevant, in this report.

A second police officer who agreed, under significantly different circumstances, to cooperate with the Commission was Patrolman William Phillips. Phillips was a decorated police officer with fourteen years' service who had made arrests in every precinct in Manhattan. He had served as a foot patrolman and in a radio patrol car in the Nineteenth Precinct in mid-Manhattan, as a plainclothesman in the Sixth Division in Central Harlem, as a member of the Youth Squad assigned to southern Manhattan, as a detective in the Seventeenth Precinct squad in midtown and, finally, as a patrolman in the Twenty-fifth Precinct in East Harlem, which was the headquarters for organized crime figures running illegal gambling operations throughout Harlem. According to his own admission, he had been thoroughly corrupt throughout his career.

---

* Paul Curran, chairman of the State Commission of Investigation, also agreed to limit certain of his investigations into narcotics corruption when informed of Leuci's work by the Commission and Mr. Seymour.

Despite the fact that he had had only one brush with disciplinary authority—resulting in his demotion from detective—Phillips' entire career had been one of virtually unrelieved corruption. He had, in his own words, been a "super thief." He told of having participated in comparatively petty graft involving construction sites, bars, restaurants, garages, bowling alleys, and other establishments making regular payments to officers on patrol. He had participated in organized shakedowns of gamblers which in one six-month period had netted him $6,000 to $8,000. He had dealt with organized crime figures who ran widespread gambling operations and paid for the ability to do so unmolested. He had engineered innumerable "scores" of gamblers, pimps, loan sharks, illegal liquor dealers, and other violators who had paid him as much as several thousand dollars for their freedom following arrest. He had arranged for the alteration of testimony in criminal trials. He had also collected all the traditional emoluments considered by policemen to be their due, from free hotel rooms—or, in Phillips' case, suites—to the traditional free meals—which again in his case had often consisted of dinner at Le Pavillon rather than a free hot dog. He knew all the illegal operations within his area of responsibility and was intimately familiar with the technical regulatory rules which could be used to shake down businesses subject to such rules.

Phillips' knowledge of corruption in the Department was not limited to his own experience. In fourteen years on the force, he had made innumerable friends who had, in the course of their own careers, scattered throughout the Department. He maintained contacts with many such officers and, through them, was quite well aware of conditions in other commands and areas. His use of the Department grapevine was revealing. He demonstrated on several occasions his ability to check on the reliability of any police officer. Invariably, he could find out if an officer could safely be approached with a corrupt proposal simply by placing a phone call to an acquaintance in the officer's command.

Phillips asserted that he drew a firm line reflecting the traditional notion in the Department of "clean" and "dirty" money, and the Commission found no evidence to contradict him. He said that he had never taken money in connection with narcotics or illegal guns because he found narcotics traffic abhorrent and an illegal gun could someday be used against him or another police officer. In addition, on grounds of self-protection rather than morality, he claimed to have followed a general rule of avoiding prostitutes because of their notorious unreliability. He proved the wisdom of this rule when he finally was caught because he ignored it.

Phillips was induced to testify not through appeals to his better nature but rather as a direct result of his being caught by Commission agents in the course of his involvement in the payment of some $11,000 in bribes by a midtown madam. Under this pressure, Phillips agreed to tell what he knew about corruption in the Police Department and to work as an undercover agent for the Commission.

From the outset, it was made absolutely clear to him that his chances of ultimately obtaining immunity from prosecutors with authority to grant it depended upon his veracity. He knew that he would be called upon to testify both before the Commission and in criminal trials resulting from his work, and that defense counsel in those criminal trials would cross-examine him in detail. He was, therefore, made acutely aware of the fact that if he strayed from the truth in an attempt to cover up his activities or to curry favor with the Commission it was virtually inevitable that any such misstatement would be uncovered.

The Commission staff selected certain situations from those described by Phillips which it felt were appropriate for investigation, and he began five months of undercover work. Having agreed to cooperate, Phillips displayed the same ingenuity—and courage—in exposing corruption that he previously had shown in practicing it.

In the two days following his first interview with Commission personnel, Phillips, wearing a transmitter and under surveillance by Commission investigators, contacted seven gamblers operating in East Harlem who were central figures in the Harlem bookmaking and numbers rackets. For several months he collected payments from these and other similar individuals on a regular basis. Several of these individuals, seven of whom have now been indicted by the federal government, were important members of organized crime who had for years been sought by federal law enforcement agencies. Recorded conversations with them demonstrated that payoffs to police were a regular part of their business.

After this start, Phillips continued his undercover work in a variety of situations.

He participated in meetings where an East Harlem organized crime figure, in order to protect a high stakes dice game, paid a lieutenant and, through Phillips, the patrolmen manning patrol cars in the mobster's area. That lieutenant, eight patrolmen and two civilians are now under federal indictment.

After spreading a rumor that he knew an underworld figure anxious to set up a large dice game in midtown Manhattan, Phillips was contacted by members of two plainclothes divisions who set up with him a monthly protection scheme and discussed, in lengthy tape-recorded conversations, the workings of organized graft among plainclothesmen. The operation was terminated after a few preliminary payments, since the Commission was not in a position to go into the gambling business. As a result of this investigation, four police officers and one civilian middleman have been indicted by a New York County Grand Jury.

A police officer had previously told Phillips about accepting $2,000 to cover up two mobsters' connections with a murder. Phillips engaged the officer in a conversation in which the story was recorded by Commission agents. The recording was turned over to the New York County District Attorney and gave rise to an investigation which resulted in five indictments and the reopening of the murder case. Those indicted included three police officers, two retired detectives, and the two men who had paid the bribe—one of whom was also charged with the murder.

Phillips also exploited his acquaintances in organized crime. He was arranging, in cooperation with federal narcotics agents, to participate in illegal shipments of quinine into the country for purposes of cutting narcotics when the operation was aborted because Phillips' underworld contact became the victim of a gangland-style slaying.

A plainclothesman in Queens who was purported to be the bagman for his division took money from Phillips, ostensibly on behalf of fellow officers, to allow a card game to be established in his area. In one tape-recorded conversation during these negotiations, the plainclothesman also told Phillips how he had taken part in an $80,000 payoff in a narcotics case. The case is under investigation by the United States Attorney for the Eastern District of New York.

Phillips accepted money, under Commission surveillance, from two notorious underworld loansharks and cooperated with federal authorities in an investigation of their activities.

Phillips engaged a number of police officers, including a captain, a lieutenant, a PBA delegate, a former narcotics detective, and the chauffeur of an assistant chief inspector, in conversations which further corroborated his descriptions of corrupt activities within the Department.

When Phillips had exploited most of the investigative opportunities available to him as a patrolman, the Commission decided to enlist the aid of Commissioner Murphy in transferring him to a plainclothes division. He attended plainclothes classes at the Police Academy with thirty-four other experienced officers who were part of a program intended to place in plainclothes divisions men of long service who presumably would have a stabilizing and anti-corruptive effect. Phillips reported that the attitudes of these thirty-four officers reflected, in about equal parts, a determination to ''hide'' so as to avoid being implicated in corruption and eager anticipation of the profits to be derived from it.

Phillips was assigned to the First Division in southern Manhattan and continued his work for the Commission. However, shortly after his transfer, and shortly before the Commission's public hearings, his role was discovered and his undercover activities came to an end.

Phillips' work provided the Commission with invaluable information on the patterns of corruption in the Department. He participated in a total of sixty-nine operations in which tape-recorded conversations involving corruption were obtained. In these recorded conversations it was clear that the participants assumed that police officers were almost uniformly tolerant of, if not involved in, the kinds of corrupt practices in which they themselves were involved. They talked openly not only about their own activities but about conditions in various commands and provided solid corroboration of descriptions by Phillips and other police officers who had talked to investigators on an anonymous basis about the widesepread nature of corruption in the Department and the forms it takes.

Phillips' career gave the Commission insights into matters beyond facts indicating the nature and extent of police corruption. It demonstrated, for example, that a corrupt police officer does not necessarily have to be an ineffective one. Phillips possessed qualities of aggressiveness, courage, imagination, intelligence, and a highly developed knowledge of street conditions and the law. These qualities served him well in all his activities in the Police Department—both legitimate and corrupt. Among his fellow officers Phillips stood to gain approval, or at least grudging admiration, both for tough, aggressive police action and for skillful extracurricular money making. He was adept at both.

Phillips himself asserted that few of his comrades embraced corruption with his enthusiasm—and it is clear that the shock expressed by many police officers at the disclosures made in Phillips' public testimony was quite genuine. However, he reported that it was common for fellow patrolmen to pay the officer in charge of assignments for the privilege of being assigned temporarily as his partner. According to Phillips, those whose scruples, timidity or lack of expertise prevented them from attempting to match him in his corrupt endeavors were often quite willing to share the benefits of those endeavors on an occasional basis. One thing is certain—no fellow police officer with whom Phillips served ever turned him in.

Although Phillips' work for the Commission was not directed at making criminal cases, his efforts have, nevertheless, resulted to date in indictments of thirty-one individuals. Six federal and six New York County indictments have named a total of seventeen police officers; and fourteen other persons, most of whom are organized crime members, have also been indicted as a result of his undercover work for the Commission. More indictments flowing from his investigations are anticipated.*

A third cooperative police witness was Waverly Logan. Logan was a police officer of two-and-a-half years' experience who had served for eleven months on the Preventive Enforcement Patrol (PEP) Squad,

---

* The first criminal trial resulting from Phillips' work ended in the conviction of an underworld figure in the United States District Court for the Southern District of New York. Then, on March 20, 1972, Phillips was himself indicted for murder by a New York County grand jury. The crime of which he was accused was the double murder of a pimp and a prostitute which had remained unsolved since its commission in 1968. Phillips had attracted attention to himself in this regard by his public testimony before the Commission and subsequent detailed statements to police investigators to the effect that he had shaken down the pimp in 1965. The charge against Phillips was brought to trial in New York County Supreme Court in August of 1972 and resulted in a hung jury, with ten jurors voting for acquittal. A second trial is presently scheduled to begin in early January, 1973.

an elite group of twenty officers set up to deal with ghetto problems, particularly in narcotics. In June, 1971, he had been dismissed from the Department for corruption. Logan had consented to take part in an interview on WNEW-TV in which he described in general terms his experiences on the PEP Squad involving corruption in narcotics. Afterwards, Commission staff members interviewed Logan and persuaded him to testify in specific terms about corruption he had participated in and witnessed.

Logan described patterns of corruption he experienced in his early days as a patrolman which echoed those already familiar to Commission personnel—payoffs from gamblers and businessmen, thefts by policemen from burglarized premises, acceptance of gratuities, and the like.

Logan's testimony about the PEP Squad described a deepening involvement in corruption which culminated in the acceptance of narcotics payoffs by the whole squad in amounts of as much as $3,000 per month per man. Logan had been dismissed from the police force and, after his television appearance, was obviously in no position to work in an undercover capacity against police officers. However, he worked in several situations to obtain tape recordings and films of open narcotics and illegal liquor transactions and introduced the Commission's staff to two narcotics addicts who had worked with him as police informants. These informants worked for the Commission and obtained tape recordings of transactions with police officers who sold them narcotics in exchange for what the policemen obviously assumed to be stolen merchandise. Ten such meetings with ten police officers took place over a three-week period. An attempt was made at this point to broaden the activities of the informants by having them work with agents of the Federal Bureau of Narcotics and Dangerous Drugs but the informants' undercover roles became known and subsequent operations proved largely fruitless. Two of the police officers who engaged in transactions with the two informants were indicted in federal court in the Southern District of New York. Three others have been suspended and charged with departmental violations. Departmental charges are pending against two officers, and two others have resigned, one without permission, before charges could be filed against them.

Patrolman Edward Droge was the fourth police officer who agreed to testify. Droge was a young police officer assigned to patrol duty in Brooklyn when he became involved in accepting a $300 bribe from a narcotics defendant in a minor case. The defendant's lawyer contacted the Commission, and investigators conducted a tape-recorded surveillance implicating Droge. Not knowing that his illegal action had been discovered, Droge took a leave of absence from the Department and enrolled in a California university where he was contacted, informed of his predicament, and persuaded to cooperate.

Droge agreed to testify regarding his experiences with corruption during his four years in the Department. Again, the patterns were the same as those described by other police officers, involving illegal payments from gamblers, narcotics dealers, businessmen, and others, as well as instances of police theft and acceptance of various gratuities. Droge was neither as experienced nor as aggressive as Phillips, but his testimony was more typical of the involvement of the average police officer. He agreed to operate in an undercover capacity insofar as he was able. Droge's use as an undercover agent was limited because he was now a newly assigned and consequently untested member of a plainclothes unit and the Commission's public hearings were only a few weeks off. On one occasion Droge attempted to engage two police officers with quite notorious reputations in a transaction involving protection payments for an imaginary gambler. The officers apparently became suspicious and reported the matter to their superiors. The result was a meeting observed and recorded by agents both of the Commission and the Department, with each group unaware of the other's involvement until they met and recognized each other.

A fifth police officer, Patrolman Alfonso Jannotta, gave information and worked undercover but was unable to testify because of ill health. Jannotta, who had been in the Department for five years, was assigned to a radio patrol car in the Nineteenth Precinct in mid-Manhattan. He and his partner took a $30 payoff from a tow truck operator who was working as a Commission operative. The transaction was tape-recorded by Commission agents and filmed by a local television station which had made its equipment and personnel available to the Commission. Jannotta and his partner noticed the cameras, became suspicious, and Jannotta telephoned the tow truck operator to arrange a concocted story to be used in the event of an investigation. The telephone conversation was recorded by Commission agents. Jannotta was confronted with the evidence against him and agreed to tell what he knew about corrruption. He told of sporadic participation in low level corruption involving construction sites, bars, tow trucks, and the like. He said that his yearly illegal take was less than $1,000. Jannotta, working with Commission agents, obtained a tape-recorded conversation with the police officer who had been involved with him in the payoff from the tow truck operator. Jannotta proved unwilling or unable to provide further cooperation with the police or the district attorney's office in making criminal cases and both he and his partner were indicted by a New York County Grand Jury.

Other police officers, including plainclothesmen and detectives, who had themselves been involved in corrupt activities, spoke to the Commission staff on a strictly confidential basis. They described patterns of corruption which lent added credibility to the testimony of police witnesses who spoke openly. One of these officers testified anonymously in public hearings held by the State Commission of Investigation and described patterns of corruption in narcotics enforcement which were similar to those described by Detective Leuci, Patrolman Logan and other Commission sources.

Honest police officers also provided the Commission with information about patterns of corruption in the Department. Captain Daniel McGowan has been a member of the Department for twenty-five years and had spent most of his distinguished career assigned to various anti-corruption units. Early in 1971 he provided information to the Commission regarding the handling—or mishandling—of corruption investigations particularly those involving allegations of corruption on the part of police officers which had been referred by federal law enforcement agencies. Although Captain McGowan testified at the Commission's public hearings, some of his most important information could not be presented because it would have focused attention upon conditions in SIU and jeopardized the federal investigation then under way involving the undercover work of Detective Leuci. Captain McGowan testified about his knowledge of conditions in the Department and confirmed the accuracy of the testimony of Officers Phillips, Logan and Droge. Other police officers, experienced in anti-corruption work privately confirmed the patterns testified to at the public hearings.

Another police officer who testified about his own experiences with corruption was Frank Serpico, whose charges of police mishandling of corruption had been presented in *The New York Times* story in April, 1970, which ultimately led to the creation of this Commission. Officer Serpico had refused to participate in corrupt activities but testified to patterns of corruption, particularly among plainclothesmen, which he had observed and which exactly paralleled the patterns described by the other Commission informants and witnesses.

Section Two: Patterns of Police Corruption

Chapter Three

INTRODUCTION

At the time of the Commission's investigation, police corruption was found to be an extensive, Department-wide phenomenon, indulged in to some degree by a sizable majority of those on the force and protected by a code of silence on the part of those who remained honest.*

Police Corruption: A Historical View

The Commission's findings were hardly new. As long ago as 1844, when the state legislature created the New York police force as the first municipal police department in the country, historians record an immediate problem with extortion and other corrupt activities engaged in by police officers.

Since that time, the New York Police Department has been the subject of numerous corruption scandals followed by investigations. In each case, the investigators turned up substantial evidence of corruption, which was greeted by public expressions of shock and outrage. While some reforms usually followed each of these periodic scandals, the basic pattern of corrupt behavior was never substantially affected and after the heat was off, it was largely back to business as usual.

In March, 1894, in response to allegations of police corruption made by commercial and reform organizations, a New York State Senate committee, financed by private organizations because of the state's refusal to provide funding, conducted an investigation of the New York Police Department. The committee, known as the Lexow Committee, found systematic police extortion of "disorderly houses," systematic

---

* The Commission's investigation ended on October 18, 1971, the day the first public hearings began. In discussions of the existence and extent of corruption, this report speaks as of that date—unless otherwise clearly indicated.

payoffs by gambling operations to policemen throughout the City, and payoffs by organized confidence games. The committee also found that small grocery stores, builders, and "all classes of persons whose business is subject to the observation of the police, or who may be reported as violating ordinances, or who may require the aid of the police, all have to contribute in substantial sums to the vast amounts which flow into the station-houses . . ."

Seventeen years later, following the Times Square murder of a gambler who had reported police corruption to the newspapers, the Board of Aldermen (predecessor of the City Council) appointed a committee, headed by Henry Curran, to investigate the police. The committee found that corruption and inefficiency in the Department were in large part due to administrative methods which made intelligent direction and accountability impossible. The committee found systematic monthly police extortion of gambling and brothel operations, made possible by weak discipline and a failure of supervision within the Department. It found that the Department was hostile to civilian complaints, and that the police commissioner was not aware of the most important complaints. The aldermanic committee recommended, among other things, the establishment of an internal security squad, composed of men other than policemen, to secure evidence of police corruption.

A citizens' committee working at the same time reported that "corruption is so ingrained that the man of ordinary decent character entering the force and not possessed of extraordinary moral fiber may easily succumb." That committee recommended, among other things, separation of vice control from the constabulary forces of the police.

Some twenty years later, on January 25, 1932, Samuel Seabury, counsel to a committee appointed pursuant to a joint resolution adopted by the state legislature, reported the same condition of police corruption to committee chairman Samuel H. Hofstadter. The committee was granted special powers to grant immunity to witnesses and found that the Police Department was deeply involved in extorting large sums from speakeasies, bootleggers, and gamblers.

On September 15, 1950, Harry Gross, the head of a mammoth New York City gambling syndicate, was arrested and subsequently agreed to cooperate with the district attorney. Having indicated his willingness to tell the district attorney and the grand jury about the police officers who protected his bookmaking operation, he was brought in for questioning. After giving his early background, he told of his first arrangements with members of the Police Department in the early 1940's.

He had been operating in the area of Flatbush and Church Avenues. Two plainclothesmen apprehended him while he was making book. They told him he was operating like a small-timer by cheating (making book without police protection). From this point, his payoff system snowballed. As Gross opened new spots he met and paid more police officers. He quickly reached the point where payments to each division's plainclothes squad were insufficient. He needed protection from squads having boroughwide and citywide jurisdiction over gambling. At the height of his operation, the payoff system was substantially as follows:

On the first and fifteenth of each month Gross paid the plainclothes squad in every division in which he had a gambling spot. In addition, he paid a set fee for each telephone he used in a given division. There were extra payments to precinct plainclothesmen and precinct commanders. The borough plainclothes squads were paid for each location in their jurisdiction. The chief inspector's squad and the police commissioner's squad, having citywide jurisdiction, were paid off for all locations. Inspectors in charge of divisions received regular payments as did lieutenants in charge of plainclothes squads.

The intricate workings of the system need not be detailed. Payoffs were made to each squad which had responsibility for the suppression of gambling. In addition, hundreds of personal gifts of television sets, suits, furs, jewelry, theater tickets, and cars were given to members of the Department. The payoff system was most notable for its sheer magnitude: One million dollars was paid annually to the police for protection, in addition to numerous personal gifts.

Gross told the story of this operation to a grand jury. He named the men he paid, where he met them, and how he made his contacts.

In May, 1951, the grand jury filed an indictment charging twenty-one police officers with conspiring to protect the Gross syndicate. Fifty-seven other police officers were named in the indictment as co-conspirators but not as defendants because there was insufficient corroborative evidence against them to meet the requirements for a criminal prosecution.

Gross took the witness stand in Kings County Court, identified all the defendants as men he knew, and testified to the point where he implicated the defendants in the conspiracy. Then he refused to continue. In an extremely dramatic courtroom incident, he was held in contempt for refusing to obey directives to answer questions. The district attorney was left with no alternative but to ask the court to dismiss the indictment. The trial had begun and, under the constitutional ban against placing a defendant in double jeopardy, the defendants could not be retried and were free. On September 27, 1951, in the Court of Special Sessions, Gross received twelve one-year sentences on his plea of guilty to sixty-five counts of bookmaking.

Studies of police corruption in other cities have likewise uncovered systematic police extortion of bookmakers, mutuel racehorse policy operators, brothels and prostitutes, and legitimate businesses.

It seems that the pressures upon policemen, the nature of the job, and the inevitable temptations are similar enough in any large municipal police department at any time to give rise to the kinds of problems found by this Commission and its predecessors.

Grass-Eaters and Meat-Eaters

Corrupt policemen have been informally described as being either "grass-eaters" or "meat-eaters." The overwhelming majority of those who do take payoffs are grass-eaters, who accept gratuities and solicit five- and ten- and twenty-dollar payments from contractors, tow-truck operators, gamblers, and the like, but do not aggressively pursue corruption payments. "Meat-eaters," probably only a small percentage of the force, spend a good deal of their working hours aggressively seeking out situations they can exploit for financial gain, including gambling, narcotics, and other serious offenses which can yield payments of thousands of dollars. Patrolman William Phillips was certainly an example of this latter category.

One strong impetus encouraging grass-eaters to continue to accept relatively petty graft is, ironically, their feeling of loyalty to their fellow officers. Accepting payoff money is one way for an officer to prove that he is one of the boys and that he can be trusted. In the climate which existed in the Department during the Commission's investigation, at least at the precinct level, these numerous but relatively small payoffs were a fact of life, and those officers who made a point of refusing them were not accepted closely into the fellowship of policemen. Corruption among grass-eaters obviously cannot be met by attempting to arrest them all and will probably diminish only if Commissioner Murphy is successful in his efforts to change the rank and file attitude toward corruption.

No change in attitude, however, is likely to affect a meat-eater, whose yearly income in graft amounts to many thousands of dollars and who may take payoffs of $5,000 or even $50,000 in one fell swoop (former Assistant Chief Inspector Sydney Cooper, who had been active in anti-corruption work for years, recently stated that the largest score of which he had heard—although he was unable to verify it—was a narcotics payoff involving $250,000). Such men are willing to take considerable risks as long as the potential profit remains so large. Probably the only way to deal with them will be to ferret them out individually and get them off the force, and, hopefully, into prisons.

Pads, Scores and Gratuities

Corruption payments made to the police may be divided into "pad" payments and "scores," two police slang terms which make an important distinction.

The "pad" refers to regular weekly, biweekly, or monthly payments, usually picked up by a police bagman and divided among fellow officers. Those who make such payments as well as policemen who receive them are referred to as being "on the pad."

A "score" is a one-time payment that an officer might solicit from, for example, a motorist or a narcotics violator. The term is also used as a verb, as in "I scored him for $1,500."

A third category of payments to the police is that of gratuities, which the Commission feels cannot in the strictest sense be considered a matter of police corruption, but which has been included here because it is a related—and ethically borderline—practice, which is prohibited by Department regulations, and which often leads to corruption.

Operations on the pad are generally those which operate illegally in a fixed location day in and day out. Illegal gambling is probably the single largest source of pad payments. The most important legitimate enterprises on the pad at the time of the investigation were those like construction, licensed premises, and businesses employing large numbers of vehicles, all of which operate from fixed locations and are subject to summonses from the police for myriad violations.

Scores, on the other hand, are made whenever the opportunity arises—most often when an officer happens to spot someone engaging in an illegal activity like pushing narcotics, which doesn't involve a fixed location. Those whose activities are generally legal but who break the law occasionally, like motorists or tow-truck operators, are also subject to scores. By far the most lucrative source of scores is the City's multimillion-dollar narcotics business.

Factors Influencing Corruption

There are at least five major factors which influence how much or how little graft an officer receives, and also what his major sources are. The most important of these is, of course, the character of the officer in question, which will determine whether he bucks the system and refuses all corruption money; goes along with the system and accepts what comes his way; or outdoes the system, and aggressively seeks corruption-prone situations and exploits them to the extent that it seriously cuts into the time available for doing his job. His character will also determine what kind of graft he accepts. Some officers, who don't think twice about accepting money from gamblers, refuse to have anything at all to do with narcotics pushers. They make a distinction between what they call "clean money" and "dirty money."

The second factor is the branch of the Department to which an officer is assigned. A plainclothesman, for example, has more—and different—opportunities than a uniformed patrolman.

The third factor is the area to which an officer is assigned. At the time of the investigation certain precincts in Harlem, for instance, comprised what police officers called "the Gold Coast" because they contained so many payoff-prone activities, numbers and narcotics being the biggest. In contrast, the Twenty-Second Precinct, which is Central Park, has clearly limited payoff opportunities. As Patrolman Phillips remarked, "What can you do, shake down the squirrels?" The area also determines the major sources of corruption payments. For instance, in midtown Manhattan precincts businessmen and motorists were major sources; on the Upper East Side, bars and construction; in the ghetto precincts, narcotics, and numbers.

The fourth factor is the officer's assignment. For uniformed men, a seat in a sector car was considered fairly lucrative in most precincts, while assignment to stand guard duty outside City Hall obviously was not, and assignment to one sector of a precinct could mean lots of payoffs from construction sites while in another sector bar owners were the big givers.

The fifth factor is rank. For those who do receive payoffs, the amount generally ascends with the rank. A bar may give $5 to patrolmen, $10 to sergeants, and considerably more to a captain's bagman. Moreover, corrupt supervisors have the opportunity to cut into much of the graft normally collected by those under them.

Sources of Payoffs

Organized crime is the single biggest source of police corruption, through its control of the City's gambling, narcotics, loansharking, and illegal sex-related enterprises like homosexual afterhours bars and pornography, all of which the Department considers mob-run. These endeavors are so highly lucrative that large payments to the police are considered a good investment if they protect the business from undue police interference.

The next largest source is legitimate business seeking to ease its way through the maze of City ordinances and regulations. Major offenders are construction contractors and subcontractors, liquor licensees, and managers of businesses like trucking firms and parking lots, which are likely to park large numbers of vehicles illegally. If the police were completely honest, it is likely that members of these groups would seek to corrupt them, since most seem to feel that paying off the police is easier and cheaper than obeying the laws or paying fines and answering summonses when they do violate the laws. However, to the extent police resist corruption, business interests will be compelled to use their political muscle to bring about revision of the regulations to make them workable.

Two smaller sources of payments to the police are private citizens, like motorists caught breaking the law, and small-time criminals like gypsy fortune tellers, purse-snatchers, and pickpockets who may attempt to buy their freedom from an arresting officer.

Organization of the Department

To understand police corruption in New York and have some idea of how such corruption involves supervisors and commanders as well as the rank and file, one must first know a little about how the Department is organized. The following brief account is by no means complete, but it should suffice to provide some understanding of the Department's organization.*

Patrol Force: Of the thirty thousand men and women in the New York Police Department, approximately two-thirds are assigned to the Patrol Services Bureau, which is headed by the Chief of Patrol. The patrol force is divided into seven borough commands: Manhattan North, Manhattan South, Brooklyn North, Brooklyn South, Queens, Bronx, and Staten Island. Each borough command supervises several divisions,** which are, in turn, subdivided into seventy-four precincts. Most uniformed patrolmen are assigned to the precincts, where they are supervised by sergeants. The sergeants in turn report to lieutenants, and the lieutenants to precinct commanders, who are generally captains although they may be of higher rank.

Plainclothes: The Department's 450 plainclothesmen are patrolmen, sergeants, lieutenants, and captains who wear civilian clothes and work primarily in the areas of gambling, narcotics, and such vices as prostitution and pornography. At the time the Commission's investi-

---

* Exhibit 8 of the Appendix is a map showing the geographical organization of the Department as of January, 1972.

** Except in Staten Island, where there is no division. Staten Island Borough Command directly supervises the island's three precincts.

gation began, plainclothesmen, like the patrol force, were assigned to precinct, division, and borough commands. However, plainclothes has since been reorganized several times with control now centralized in a special Organized Crime Control Bureau under a deputy commissioner.

Detectives: The 3,000-man Detective Bureau is headed by the Chief of Detectives who, like the Chief of Patrol, reports to the Chief Inspector who reports to the Police Commissioner. At the time of the Commission's investigation, detective squads were assigned to precinct, division, and borough commands. But the Detective Bureau has since been reorganized, and detectives are now assigned to specialized squads within detective districts, which are coterminous with patrol divisions.

The Commissioner's Office: At the top of this vast pyramid is the Police Commissioner, who is assisted by seven deputy commissioners. The Commissioner is appointed by the Mayor to a five-year term designed to overlap the four-year term of the Mayor. Of the twelve Commissioners appointed during the last forty years, only two have served the full term to which they were appointed. One of these served for eleven years. The other eleven served an average of twenty-three months each.

Patterns

In its investigation into police corruption, the Commission found that each area under investigation had its own distinctive patterns. Each is therefore discussed in a separate chapter which describes what the Commission investigation found, the reasons for the payoffs, the methods of paying, and, where appropriate, setting forth the Commission's comments.

Chapter Four

GAMBLING

"You can't work numbers in Harlem unless you pay. If you don't pay, you go to jail . . . You go to jail on a frame if you don't pay."

—Numbers Operator, Executive Session, January 15, 1971

Policemen, especially those in plainclothes units, were found to shake down gambling operations throughout the City on a regular, highly systematic basis. The collection of tribute by police from gamblers has traditionally been extremely well organized and has persisted in virtually unchanged form for years despite periodic scandals, departmental reorganizations, massive transfers in and out of the units involved, and the folding of some gambling operations and the establishment of new ones.

The Commission received numerous complaints of illegal gambling operations, most allegedly located in ghetto neighborhoods. In those areas where Commission investigators went to check out these allegations, they found the situation to be just as described, with some neighborhoods having a numbers spot every block or two. Investigators also found numerous bookmaking operations and some high-stakes, organized card and dice games. The operators of these games apparently had little fear of police intervention in their enterprises, and their confidence was well-founded. Payments to police insured that their operations would be protected from police action, except for token arrests made to give an appearance of activity.

Reasons for Gambling Payoffs

In New York State it is perfectly legal to buy a ticket in the state-run lottery or to place a bet on a horse either at the racetrack or at a state-run betting parlor, and other forms of legalized gambling have been proposed. Although gambling was considered morally objectionable at the turn of the century when most laws against it were passed, that attitude has largely evaporated, with most citizens, public officials, and policemen feeling that there is nothing wrong with it. There is, therefore, no public pressure to crack down.

The courts, too, take a lenient view of gambling offenses, dismissing a high percentage of cases and imposing light fines in most others.

A State Commission of Investigation study of eighty-eight gambling arrests made during one year at a Bronx social club revealed that forty-seven of the arrests—slightly over one-half—resulted in conviction, and of these, one resulted in a jail sentence—and then only because the convicted gambler chose to go to jail for five days rather than pay a $50 fine. In the remaining forty-five convictions, the offenders were either given conditional discharges or ordered to pay fines ranging from $25 to $250.

A similar study by the Policy Sciences Center, Inc., came up with comparable figures. This study analyzed 356 numbers bank arrests made in Bedford-Stuyvesant over the past ten years. Such arrests can be assumed to have greater impact on the gambling power structure, because an arrest in a policy bank involves a greater number of slips and larger money volume, yet the courts did not show significantly greater punishments for such offenses. Of the 356 arrests, 198 resulted in dismissals, sixty-three in acquittals, and ninety-five in convictions. Of the ninety-five convictions, twelve resulted in suspended sentences, seventy-seven in a fine/time option, and six in jail sentences. Of the six jail sentences, one was for one year and the other five averaged seventeen days.

Our study of 108 gambling arrests made by the plainclothes squad in one division over a five-month period showed that, of fifty convictions, not one resulted in a jail sentence: two resulted in conditional discharge; forty-seven in fines of under $300; and one in a $500 fine. (Five were pending.)

Police officers, sharing the general attitude that gambling does no harm, themselves regard gambling money as "clean" graft. But, despite the changed attitudes toward gambling, most forms of gambling remain illegal, and corrupt policemen at the time of the investigation considered gamblers fair game.

As for gamblers, they were found to regard payments to the police as a necessary business expense. They often pointed out that a numbers operation couldn't exist unless it was under police auspices. As one gambler told the Commission, the police "are the insurance company, and unless you pay your monthly rent, you can't operate."

Plainclothesmen and Gambling

At the time of the Commission's investigation, plainclothesmen bore primary responsibility for enforcing anti-gambling laws, and it was among plainclothesmen that the Commission found the most pervasive and systematic police corruption, particularly in relation to gambling. The Commission received its information about plainclothes payoffs from gamblers, former and current plainclothesmen, police supervisors and anti-corruption officers; law enforcement officers outside the Department, and, most significantly, from tape-recorded conversations with plainclothesmen actually going about the business of setting up or receiving payments.

At the start of the Commission's investigation, plainclothes units were assigned to precinct, division and borough commands. By February, 1971, borough and precinct units had been eliminated. Finally, in November, 1971, division plainclothes units were merged with the central Public Morals Division and placed under the new Organized Crime Control Bureau, headed by a deputy commissioner.* Reorgan-

---

* The Thirteenth Division in Brooklyn, which was at that time the subject of a major anti-corruption investigation, was left intact in order not to jeopardize the investigation. The public explanation for leaving this one division out of the reorganization was that it was to be a "control" against which the performance of the new OCCB could be measured.

izations have not in the past made any noticeable dent in plainclothes corruption, and it remains to be seen whether the latest attempt will be successful.

The Pad

The heart of the gambling payoff system was found to be the plainclothes "pad." In a highly systemized pattern, described to the Commission by numerous sources and verified during our investigation, plainclothesmen collected regular biweekly or monthly payoffs from gamblers on the first and fifteenth of each month, often at a meeting place some distance from the gambling spot and outside the immediate police precinct or division. The pad money was picked up at designated locations by one or more bagmen who were most often police officers but who occasionally were ex-policemen or civilians. The proceeds were then pooled and divided up among all or virtually all of the division's plainclothesmen, with each plainclothes patrolman receiving an equal share. Supervisory lieutenants who were on the pad customarily received a share and a half and, although the Commission was unable to document particular instances, any commanding officer who participated reportedly received two full shares. In addition, the bagman received a larger cut, often an extra share, to compensate him for the risk involved in making his collections. Some bagmen made extra profits by telling gamblers there were more plainclothesmen in the division than there actually were, collecting shares for these non-existent men and pocketing the proceeds. Division plainclothesmen generally met once a month to divide up the money and to discuss matters concerning the pad—*i.e.*, inviting plainclothesmen newly assigned to the division to join, raising or lowering the amounts paid by various gamblers, and so forth. A man newly assigned to plainclothes duty in a division would be put on the pad after he had been with the division for a specified period, usually two months, during which time the other members would check him out and make sure he was reliable. This loss of revenue was customarily made up to him when he was transferred out of the division at which time he would receive severance pay in the form of two months' payments after his transfer. Plainclothesmen who put a new gambling operation on the pad were entitled to keep the entire first month's payment as a finder's fee.

This pattern of collection and distribution appeared to Commission investigators to be quite standardized. It was evident in the four Manhattan divisions and the one Queens division which were the focus of the Commission's investigation. Evidence of the same patterns was also turned up in the other Manhattan division and in one division each in Brooklyn and the Bronx, for a total of eight divisions out of the sixteen divisions and Staten Island.* In addition, the Commission received allegations of similar pads in most of the other divisions in the City.

William Phillips, then recently assigned as a plainclothesman in the division covering lower Manhattan, testified on the basis of his own experiences and conversations with fellow plainclothesmen that the average monthly share per man ranged from $400 to $500 in midtown Manhattan divisions, to $800 on the Upper West Side, $1,100 in lower Manhattan, and $1,500 in Harlem. He stated that the reported "nut" (share per man) in two Queens divisions was $600, that in the three Bronx divisions it was $600, $800, and $900, and that in one Brooklyn division it was $800. These figures corroborated quite precisely those received by the Commission from the many sources willing to talk privately but who did not want to take the risk of public testimony, and further corroboration has come from similar sources since the Commission's hearings.

The pad was a way of life in plainclothes. According to Patrolman Phillips, the pad was openly and endlessly discussed whenever plainclothesmen got together. The Commission found no reason to doubt Phillips' opinion, echoing that held by other knowledgeable police officers and informants: "In every division in every area of plain-

---

* There is no division in Staten Island. The three precincts in that borough report directly to borough command.

clothes in the City, the same condition exists. There is a pad in every plainclothes precinct and division in the City of New York.''

Revelations made before and after the Commission's investigation bore out the consistent nature of plainclothes gambling pads. Prior to the Commission's existence, Patrolman Frank Serpico told about his experience in a Bronx plainclothes division in 1967 and 1968 and described an almost identical pattern of payoffs. In May, 1972, after the Commission's hearings, Kings County District Attorney Eugene Gold announced the indictment of virtually an entire division plainclothes squad in Brooklyn, which collected payments from gamblers without interruption during the Commission's public hearings in precisely the same fashion being described by Commission witnesses. The indictments and related departmental charges involved a total of thirty-six current and former plainclothesmen, twenty-four of whom were indicted. According to Mr. Gold, at one time twenty-four of twenty-five plainclothesmen in the division were on the pad. It is highly significant that this investigation was carried out without the Commission's knowledge, and yet, like the information given by Frank Serpico, it revealed a pattern of share payments, severance pay, and bagmen that matched in detail the patterns described by Patrolman Phillips and other Commission witnesses and informants.

The corrupting influence of gambling operations is not limited to plainclothes. Gambling pads of various sorts were also found to exist in the uniformed patrol force.

Generally, where such pads existed among uniformed men, the sector car had its own pad, the sergeant theirs, and the desk lieutenant and precinct commander had their own personal pads if they were so disposed. (Precinct commanders who received graft almost always designated a patrolman, ''the captain's man,'' to make their pickups, and in some instances, when a corrupt captain was transferred out and an honest one took over, the captain's man continued to collect payments ''for the captain'' and kept the money.)

At the time of the investigation, certain precincts in areas with widespread gambling had special gambling cars (patrol cars with the words "gambling car" painted on them) to which two uniformed patrolmen were assigned with the ostensible mission of harassing gamblers. According to Phillips, these patrolmen were notorious for the extensiveness of their pads.

Different Kinds of Gambling and Different-Sized Payoffs

There are three major forms of illegal gambling in New York: numbers, bookmaking, and card and dice games. The size of a payoff was found to vary considerably according to the nature of the gambling operation, with the most lucrative and conspicuous operations paying the highest monthly tariff. Conspicuousness plays an important role in determining the amount of the payoff because the more overt a gambling operation is, the easier it is for police to make arrests and generally harass employees and players. Also, highly conspicuous operations are more likely to generate citizen complaints, which can put the police in a compromising position. Numbers is by far the most conspicuous of the three, depending as it does on numerous permanent locations, large numbers of players coming and going, and crowds gathering outside to hear results. Bookmakers who operate on street corners or from telephone booths are also fairly conspicuous, although bookies who operate from apartments using telephone answering services or elaborate electronic equipment designed to prevent detection often escape police notice and thus the pad. High stakes card and dice games, which involve many players, were generally found to pay if they stayed in one location, but "floating" games are less conspicuous and often didn't pay.

For intelligence purposes, the Police Department maintains two special sets of files relating to gambling. One of these is a file on "known gamblers," individuals who generally have a long history of gambling arrests. The files contain their pictures, arrest records, and any other pertinent data the Department may have collected. The

Department also maintains files on known gambling combines, which contain whatever information the Department may have on given gambling operations, including the location and the names and functions of employees. These files, which are intended to aid in gambling enforcement, often influenced the size of the payment a given gambler made to the police, the payment rising accordingly to the number of known gamblers employed by the combine.

Numbers

In many New York neighborhoods, there are spots every block or two, in candy stores, tobacco stores, unadorned storefronts, and first-floor apartments, where one can place a 25¢, 50¢, or $1 bet on a number. Various kinds of bets may be placed on one to three digits. The winning number each day is determined by a complicated formula based on the amounts of money wagered and paid out at various racetracks. In essence, the numbers game is a lottery, with odds ranging from 10-1 to 1000-1, depending on whether one bets on one, two, or three digits. The payoff ranges from 6-1 to 600-1, with the game's sponsors keeping forty per cent of the amount bet to cover their operating expenses and profits.

Bets are taken by numbers runners, who either collect bets door-to-door, or accept them at a fixed location which may be anything from a street corner to a store to a first-floor apartment. For his services, the runner receives a percentage of the amount bet with him. Before the first race is run at whatever track is being used to determine the winning number, all betting slips and the money bet are collected from the various runners and taken either directly to the "bank" or to a "drop" from which they will later be taken to the bank. At the bank, clerks with adding machines tally the day's take and figure the money owed to winners, which is sent by messenger back to the runners, who then take ten percent of the winnings as a tip and pass on the remainder to the winners.

The banker in a numbers operation is the central figure in the setup. Until recently, almost all bankers were organized crime figures from outside the ghetto.* But there has been a growing trend toward numbers operators from within the ghetto becoming bankers themselves. A banker usually has working for him several "controllers," each of whom in turn controls a number of runners.

The Commission's gambling investigation in Harlem was initiated by a citizen complaint, referred to the Commission by the Department of Investigation, alleging that an unidentified gambler, driving an auto with a specific license plate number had given money to a police officer in a sector patrol car. Commission investigators then followed the auto in question and established a pattern of regular stops at various gambling spots which always ended at a specific spot located in a rear apartment in a residential building on a main thoroughfare in the division. The investigators then made observations at that location and filmed the coming and goings of apparent customers and members of the gambling combine. They observed that certain men would stand in front of the spot acting as lookouts, that there was an unusually heavy flow of people in and out of the hallway, and that there was a heavier flow of people in the early afternoons when it was alleged that single action play was being accepted.

From police records and the later testimony of division personnel in Commission executive hearings, it became clear that the police were aware of the spot's existence and business. Police records indicated a significant number of arrests in the vicinity of the spot including the frequent arrest of the presumed operator of the spot. Yet the business went on seemingly unhampered by police arrests. A very graphic example of this lack of effectiveness was displayed at the Commission's public hearings in the form of a film showing a police raid on the premises. A large number of people were seen constantly

---

* As a result of the Commission's investigation, the FBI, in October, 1971, raided several policy operations in East Harlem resulting in federal indictments of eight individuals associated with organized crime. The FBI raid uncovered one bank and five numbers spots, one of which also made book on sporting events.

going in and out of the hallway; police officers were seen arriving in front of the building, entering the hall, and leaving with one man. Then a single man was seen to leave the hall, look up and down the street, and wave a handkerchief. Apparently this was a prearranged signal because a number of people then left the hall and dispersed on the street. The normal pattern of comings and goings then resumed.

The man designated in police combine records as the operator of the spot was first arrested in 1948 and since then has been arrested fifty-one times. These cases led to twenty-six dismissals, six acquittals and seventeen convictions (three were pending). Of the seventeen convictions only two resulted in a mandatory jail term: In two cases the operator received probation, in three cases a suspended sentence and in eleven cases a sentence of fine or time; in one case he received a fifteen-day sentence and in a second he received a choice of $250 fine or thirty days in jail and a mandatory thirty days in jail. These two sentences did not seem to reflect a growing judicial impatience with his recidivism because his last four convictions in 1969 resulted in fine or time sentences despite the fact that he had at that time a record of forty-five arrests and thirteen convictions. It was learned from an informant in this operation that this alleged operator was only the overseer of the operation and that the actual boss of the spot was a man with a very scanty arrest record. The informant also stated that the boss would oversee the operation when the operator was arrested and that at such times the police would never raid the spot.

When someone decides to start a numbers operation, the first thing he does is to get in touch with the other gamblers in the area, to clear his operation with them and make sure he's not encroaching on their territory. Next, he will get in touch with the police, either directly or through other gamblers working in the same neighborhood. Or he may simply start taking bets and wait for the police to come to him.

One ex-gambler, working as an informant for the Commission, made inquiries about setting up a numbers operation in Harlem. While wearing a transmitter monitored by Commission investigators, he spoke to several other gamblers with operations in the division who told him that they were on the pad and that they could get him on with the help of another gambler who acted as contact man for the division.

Gamblers were found to pay policemen amounts which varied according to the nature of their operations. One ambulatory runner, who moved from place to place in Harlem collecting bets in hairdressers' shops, candy stores, and apartment house hallways, paid $200 a month to division plainclothesmen while an operator of a permanent spot paid $600 a month. Another gambler, who ran a fixed spot, told the Commission he paid $750 a month to division plainclothes and $300 to borough, as well as $196 to the detective squad, $180 to the precinct sergeants, $60 to the precinct desk officers, $60 to the precinct gambling car when there was one, and $120 a week to the local patrol car, for a total of $1,600 a month. At another Harlem spot, several police cars stopped by every morning except Sunday* at around 7:00 a.m., and the lookout gave money to the patrolmen in the car.

When borough plainclothes squads were eliminated in February, 1971, Queens division plainclothesmen reportedly demanded, in addition to their own monthly share, the entire monthly share that had been going to borough plainclothes. Queens numbers operators held a meeting to discuss the demand and present a unified front. It was agreed that they would increase the monthly payment by an average of $200 to $300. According to one source, this meeting of numbers operators to resolve a common problem was most unusual in Queens, which the source stated was the only borough where policy operators did not have some sort of unity.

---

* There are no horse races on Sunday, and thus no number.

Uniformed men also scored gamblers on a catch-as-catch-can basis. Patrolman Droge testified about some well-known gamblers in one precinct he worked in, who used to drive around the precinct in a car. Police officers were constantly on the lookout for them, because it was their custom to throw $8 into a police car whenever they came across one.

In Queens, one gambler operating from a fixed spot told the Commission that he paid $2,100 a month, while the operator of a smaller game without a fixed location said that he paid $1,200, split evenly between division and borough. Another Queens gambler, whose spot was said to have been found for him by the police, reportedly paid $1,750 a month for as long as he operated the spot. He later gave up the spot and changed his operation to an ambulatory one, whereupon the police lowered the price to $1,200 a month. Gamblers who operated without a spot often escaped making pad payments at the precinct level, although they were always subject to scores by men from the precinct.

In return for these payments, gamblers were protected from all police action at precinct, division, and borough levels, with the exception of occasional token arrests. These payments did not protect them from action by the Public Morals Administrative Division (PMAD) of the First Deputy Commissioner's office, a unit which Phillips said was generally feared by corrupt police officers. If PMAD made an arrest at a gambling spot, to protect themselves division and borough plain-clothesmen would then make follow-up arrests at the same spot.

But there are indications that a partial pad may also have existed in PMAD involving some members of the unit. Patrolman Phillips, while working undercover for the Commission, was told by a plain-clothes patrolman that arrangements could be made with PMAD to protect a gambling operation at least partially. In addition, a former controller in a Harlem combine stated that he had been approached by a PMAD plainclothesman who sought to put him on what he said was a PMAD pad. The gambler refused even to discuss the pad with the plainclothesman until he had had him checked out by other plainclothesmen he knew, because he wanted to make sure that the PMAD plainclothesman was not setting him up for a possible bribery case. The check indicated that the plainclothesman was corrupt and he put the gambler on what he claimed was a PMAD pad for $185 a month with $25 extra for himself.

Most often, when plainclothesmen needed a token arrest to meet arrest quotas or to give the appearance of activity, they would tell the operator of a spot and arrange a time and place for the arrest. The operator would then select someone to take the arrest, who was usually either one of his employees who had a relatively clean arrest record or an addict who was paid for his trouble. Whoever took the arrest would put a handful of bogus policy slips in his pocket and meet the plainclothesman at the designated time and place, where, often as not, he would get into their car without even waiting to be asked.

Alternatively, when police needed a gambling arrest, they would pick up someone known to them as a gambler and plant phony numbers slips on him (a practice known as "flaking"), then arrest him. They were rather casual about this, sometimes flaking bookmakers with numbers slips or numbers runners with bookmaking records, a practice which infuriated the gamblers more than being arrested. When police decided to score gamblers, they would most often flake people with gambling slips, then demand $25 or $50 for not arresting them. Other times, they would simply threaten a flake and demand money. As mentioned above, they also scored people after arrest by offering to change their testimony at trial. When this happened, the take was higher, usually several hundred dollars.

Another method plainclothesman used to score gamblers was to arrest a gambler, then take money from him for writing up the arrest affidavit in such a way that he would be acquitted. If, for instance, the arresting officer stated he found numbers slips *near* the suspect, perhaps on a radiator or a counter, rather than on his person, defense counsel could make a motion for dismissal and the judge would have no choice but to throw out the case. At other times, officers would make their complaints sufficiently vague so that acquittal or conviction depended on their testimony at trial. One such affidavit reads, "Deponent states that the Defendant had in his possession *on a counter* [emphasis added] in the said premises a total of 118 slips of paper bearing a total of 842 plays MRHP [mutuel racehorse policy] with amounts wagered and identities." When officers had filed ambiguous affidavits like the one above, they would often score the suspect for whatever they could get, then change their testimony so that he was acquitted.

Another common method of scoring numbers operators consisted of policemen confiscating the gambler's numbers slips, which are known as "work." The police officer would then offer to sell the work back to the gambler. Such scores generally involved sizable amounts of money, because it is vitally important to the operator to have his work, so that he can know who the winners are in the day's play and pay them—and only them. If a police officer kept the work, many players would claim that they had the winning number, and the numbers operator would have to pay them all off at 600-1, or not pay any of them, which would ruin his future business since he would get a reputation for welshing on bets.

In his testimony at the public hearings, ex-Patrolman Waverly Logan described an incident in which two uniformed officers walked up to a policy bank and simply rang the bell, whereupon the operator opened the door. The two officers then arrested the banker and took him to the precinct house, where he was booked. Logan testified that plainclothes officers at the precinct said they had known all along where the bank was and were just waiting to raid it.

Bookmaking

Payoffs to police by bookmakers were found to follow roughly the same pattern as those made by numbers operators with certain modifications resulting from the distinctive nature of bookmaking. Bookies in New York City have two quite different methods of operation. There are "street bookies," who work in specific—usually poor —neighborhoods, collecting their bets either at fixed locations or by making rounds of stores, bars, apartment houses, and certain designated street corners. The amounts wagered with a street bookie are generally small. Because he works the same neighborhood every day and visits the same locations, his operations are fairly obvious to the police and, at the time of the investigation, he had to be on the pad to stay in business. How much a street bookie paid was found to depend on whether or not he worked out of a fixed spot, on how large his operation was, and on whether he had others working for him.

The telephone bookie operates a more sophisticated service, generally involving larger wagers. The simplest kind of telephone bookmaking operation involves the bookie stationing himself in a pay telephone booth where he receives his bets. Generally, bookies who operate this way change phones frequently. Since most bettors who deal with these bookies place bets regularly, it is a simple matter for the bookie to tell his customers when they call to place a bet that he is changing locations and to give them the new phone number. Since this kind of telephone bookie can work out of a phone booth in Brooklyn one day and out of one in the Bronx the next, he is never put on any division's pad, although at the time of the investigation such bookies were often scored by any policeman who caught them at work.

One telephone bookie who worked out of various pay phones told the Commission that he had been arrested three times in the last three years. Following the first arrest, the bookie paid $750 to the arresting plainclothesman, who told him he split the money with his partner and with his supervising lieutenant. The case against the bookie was dismissed in court. In the second case, the bookie paid the arresting officers $500 at the time of the arrest and $50 a month for four months, after which the court case was dismissed and he stopped paying. The third and most serious case involved a felony arrest for book-making made by a special plainclothes detail from the borough command set up to go after policy banks. The bookie said that he paid $2,500 to borough plainclothes and ultimately received a $300 fine upon conviction.

Phillips testified about another telephone bookie who regularly worked out of two pay telephones in Harlem. "He has two telephones on the corner and it's his private office," Phillips said. "He's there all day long, him and his associate, answering phones, making call-backs." Because his operation was on the street and stationary, this bookie of course paid off the police.

The more sophisticated telephone bookie uses more elaborate systems. He can employ a telephone answering service to take down bettors' phone numbers, then call them back. Or he can use a variety of complicated electronic devices, some of which are almost impossible to trace. Because the risk of police detection is nil for bookmakers using sophisticated telephone devices, they are not targets of police pads and are rarely scored.

At the time of the Commission's investigation, bookies interviewed in Queens and Manhattan North said they paid amounts ranging from $750 to $800 a month to division plainclothesmen and an equal amount to plainclothesmen assigned to borough, with all payments doubled at Christmas.

Bookies either made their pad payments directly to the police bag-man, or one bookmaker collected from the others and turned the entire amount over to the police, after taking a cut for his trouble. Street bookies, who made pad payments to the police, were less likely to be scored than telephone bookies.

Card and Dice Games

Operators of card and dice games also paid the police in a similar pattern of pads and scores. High stakes organized games generally made pad payments to various units of policemen, from the precinct level on up as high as they could reach. These were expensive games, where thousands of dollars were bet and where players could win or lose $15,000 in an evening.

Patrolman Phillips testified about one such dice game, operated by a gambler named Joe Tough Guy in the Twenty-Fifth Precinct in East Harlem, who made pad payments to division plainclothesmen and to uniformed sergeants and sector car patrolmen. Shortly after the sector car pad of $50 per car per month was established, a lieutenant in the precinct heard about it and approached Phillips to discuss enlarging the pad to include the precinct's lieutenants. While wearing a transmitter monitored by Commission investigators, Phillips attended a meeting between the lieutenant and a representative of the gambler, during which they negotiated a pad of $100 a month for the lieutenants. There was some discussion about also including two captains assigned to the precinct, but no definite arrangements were made.

As a result of these tape recordings, which were turned over to the United States Attorney's Office, federal indictments have been returned against the lieutenant, two gamblers, and eight sector car patrolmen.

Patrolman Droge testified at the public hearings about another card game, held regularly four nights a week in one precinct where he was assigned. On nights when the game was played, sector cars on two shifts would park across the street from the game and wait for the gamblers to send someone across the street with $10. Droge also testified that if the messenger was slow in coming out with the money, the cops would honk the horn "to speed things up."

The Commission was also told of a dice game in Harlem, whose operator paid $200 a month to the sector car bagman, although the police did not know the location of the game and he wouldn't tell them.

Eventually, the Commission decided to set up a bogus dice game. Phillips spread a rumor that he knew a gambler who wanted to set up a floating game. He was introduced through an intermediary to plainclothes patrolmen from the Third and Fourth Divisions in mid-Manhattan. The negotiations that followed were monitored by means of a transmitter worn by Phillips. The plainclothesmen first asked for $2,000 for each division, then later they upped the ante to $4,000 each, explaining that the two divisions had thirty plainclothesmen each, all of whom were on the pad. They explained that Manhattan South Borough Command would also have to be paid, even though it no longer had a plainclothes squad. Phillips also discussed with the two plainclothesmen the possibility of getting on the pad with PMAD, and the plainclothesmen stated that it could be done, but that it would only be a partial pad, including some but not all of the PMAD plainclothesmen. Phillips made various payments totalling $500 to these officers for their efforts in scouting for suitable locations and making arrangements for the pad.

At about the time all arrangements had been made, Phillips was transferred to the First Division. Because the Commission had the information it wanted and because it was reluctant to pay several thousand dollars, Phillips used his transfer as an excuse for telling the Third and Fourth Division plainclothesmen that he was moving the game to his new division. Evidence gathered during the operation was turned over to the New York County District Attorney's Office and resulted in indictments against four policemen and one civilian.

Phillips, again wearing a transmitter, also approached a plainclothesman whom he knew to be the bagman for the Sixteenth Division in Queens about setting up a game there. This time the game was to be cards rather than dice, because card games have traditionally paid smaller pads than dice games and would fit more comfortably into the Commission's budget. The bagman told Phillips that a card game in the Sixteenth would cost $1,500 to division and explained that that amount covered all the plainclothesmen but only some of the bosses. Phillips then paid the bagman $50 for checking out possible locations. At this point, Phillips' cover was blown, and this particular investigation came to a halt.

In the City's poorer neighborhoods, dice and card games and dominoes are played in the street for money on summer nights. These are generally informal games, played for low stakes, and they do not make pad payments. However, policemen can and do occasionally score the players for $2 and $5.

Comments

The most obvious effect of gambling corruption is the fact that gambling operations all over the City are allowed to operate openly and almost completely unhindered by police action. For most people, who do not regard gambling as a great moral evil, this in itself is not particularly alarming. What is alarming is that plainclothes units serve as an important breeding ground for large-scale corruption in other areas of the Department. Some officers who have managed to stay honest before being assigned to plainclothes are initiated into corrupt practices while in plainclothes units and go on to practice what they learned there for the rest of their tenure in the Department. Others, who have indulged in minor corruption before assignment to plainclothes, learn how to expand their activities.

But perhaps the most important effect of corruption in the so-called gambling control units is the incredible damage their performance wreaks on public confidence in the law and the police. Youngsters raised in New York ghettos, where gambling abounds, regard the law as a joke when all their lives they have seen police officers coming and going from gambling establishments and taking payments from gamblers. Many ghetto people who have grown up watching police performance in relation to gambling and narcotics are absolutely convinced that all policemen are getting rich on their share of the profits of these two illegal activities. While it is certainly not true that all police officers, or even a majority, get rich on gambling and narcotics graft, the fact that a large number of citizens believe they do has a tremendously damaging effect on police authority.

The Department announced in January, 1972, that, as of February 1, anti-gambling enforcement efforts would be concentrated on high-level figures in gambling combines and that low-level runners would no longer be arrested except when complaints were received. In another move to limit opportunities for corruption, the Department also laid down the rule that uniformed patrolmen may no longer make gambling arrests unless a superior officer is present.

The Commission feels that these are eminently sensible reforms insofar as they will tend to limit corruption. However, gambling is traditional and entrenched in many neighborhoods, and it has broad public support. In view of these factors and the severe corruption hazard posed by gambling, the Commission feels that gambling—including numbers and bookmaking—should be legalized. To the extent that the legislature feels that the state should impose controls on gambling, such regulation should be by civil rather than criminal process.

Chapter Five

NARCOTICS

"Police officers have been involved in activities such as extortion of money and/or narcotics from narcotics violators in order to avoid arrest; they have accepted bribes; they have sold narcotics. They have known of narcotics violations and have failed to take proper enforcement action. They have entered into personal associations with narcotics criminals and in some cases have used narcotics. They have given false testimony in court in order to obtain dismissal of the charges against a defendant."

— Donald F. Cawley, Commander,
Inspections Division
Testifying before the State
Commission of Investigation,
April, 1971

Corruption in narcotics law enforcement has grown in recent years to the point where high-ranking police officials acknowledge it to be the most serious problem facing the Department. In the course of its investigation, the Commission became familiar with each of the practices detailed by Chief Cawley, as well as many other corrupt patterns, including:

Keeping money and/or narcotics confiscated at the time of an arrest or raid.

Selling narcotics to addict-informants in exchange for stolen goods.

Passing on confiscated drugs to police informants for sale to addicts.

"Flaking," or planting narcotics on an arrested person in order to have evidence of a law violation.

"Padding," or adding to the quantity of narcotics found on an arrested person in order to upgrade an arrest.

Storing narcotics, needles and other drug paraphernalia in police lockers.

Illegally tapping suspects' telephones to obtain incriminating evidence to be used either in making cases against the suspects, or to blackmail them.

Purporting to guarantee freedom from police wiretaps for a monthly service charge.

Accepting money or narcotics from suspected narcotics law violators as payment for the disclosure of official information.

Accepting money for registering as police informants persons who were in fact giving no information and falsely attributing leads and arrests to them, so that their "cooperation" with the police may win them amnesty for prior misconduct.

Financing heroin transactions.

In addition to these typical patterns, the Commission learned of numerous individual instances of narcotics-related corrupt conduct on the part of police officers, such as:

Determining the purity and strength of unfamiliar drugs they had seized by giving small quantities to addict-informants to test on themselves.

Introducing potential customers to narcotics pushers.

Revealing the identity of a government informant to narcotics criminals.

Kidnapping critical witnesses at the time of trial to prevent them from testifying.

Providing armed protection for narcotics dealers.

Offering to obtain "hit men" to kill potential witnesses.

There is a traditional unwritten rule among policemen that narcotics graft is "dirty" money not acceptable even to those who take "clean" money from gamblers, bar owners, and the like. However, more relaxed attitudes toward drugs, particularly among young people, and the enormous profits to be derived from drug traffic have combined to make narcotics-related payoffs more acceptable to more and more policemen. According to officers in the Narcotics Division, the widespread narcotics corruption in the unit was well known to both the men and their superiors, all of whom tolerated it at least to the extent that they took no action against those known to be corrupt.

Before the Commission's hearings, the Police Department and other agencies had uncovered individual instances of participation by police officers in the narcotics racket. They had also acquired information indicating substantial participation by members of the Department in narcotics operations that extended from street pushing to large quantity distribution.

As former Supervising Assistant Chief Inspector Chief McGovern pointed out in his testimony before the State Commission of Investigation (SCI), narcotics corruption involves "the largest single category of complaints concerning misconduct by policemen" and is not limited to any one division of the Department. In the course of its investigation this Commission looked into many allegations concerning narcotics-related corruption in various parts of the Department and found Chief McGovern's observation to be correct. However, the principal target of the Commission's investigation in this area was the Narcotics Division, which had the primary responsibility for narcotics law enforcement at the local level. At the time of the investigation, the division was a separate unit within the Detective Bureau, and had a complement of 782 men divided into two main groups, each with a different level of responsibility.

The field unit, which consisted of seven groups assigned to various critical locations, was charged with the enforcement of narcotics laws at the street level. Some of these groups worked out of precinct houses and others from independent locations. The field groups generally operated in sub-groups of four men.

The other main unit of the Narcotics Division was the Special Investigation Unit (SIU), to which approximately seventy-five officers were assigned. SIU's responsibility was to initiate long-term investigations of narcotics wholesalers in an effort to apprehend those responsible for high-level drug distribution in the City.

In 1968, allegations of irregularities in the Narcotics Division led to an investigation by the Department's Internal Affairs Division. As a result of this investigation, many members of the division, including almost the entire staff of SIU, were gradually transferred out of the Division. However, three years later, this Commission's study of narcotics-related corruption revealed that both sectors of the Narcotics Division were still pervaded by corruption. Within the past year, there has been a nearly one hundred percent turnover in Narcotics Division personnel, but as the present commander of the Division recently told the Commission, the problem of corruption remains.

Patterns of Corruption in Narcotics Law Enforcement

The most common form of narcotics-related police corruption is not the systematic pad common in other areas such as gambling, but the individual score of money, narcotics, or both, seized at the scene of a raid or arrest.

Extortion and Bribe-Taking

In many cases police officers actively extort money and/or drugs from suspected narcotics law violators. Recently, for example, the motel room of a "dealer" (actually a federal undercover agent who was recording the conversation) was raided by two detectives and one patrolman. They found $12,000 in cash on the premises and demanded that the "dealer" surrender $10,000 to avoid arrest. The "dealer" was finally able to persuade them to leave him $4,000 as getaway money. The detectives later paid a $1,000 finder's fee to another detective who had alerted them to the "dealer's" presence in town.

In June, 1972, a dismissed plainclothesman who had been assigned to the Narcotics Division was convicted in New York County and sentenced to up to four years in prison for his part in an extortion scheme which involved six members of the Narcotics Division. According to testimony at the trial, he and two other police officers contacted a restaurant owner and demanded $6,000, threatening to arrest his daughter-in-law on a narcotics charge unless he paid them. They further threatened to send the woman's two children to a foundling home in the event of her arrest. The restaurant owner paid them what they asked.

Within a few months, the same policeman, along with some other members of the unit, again approached the man and demanded an additional $12,000. The man told them to return in a few days, and in the interim he arranged for police surveillance of the next transaction. The plainclothesman was arrested when he accepted a down payment in marked money.

Two of the Commission's informants in the narcotics area were hard-core heroin addicts who, as registered police informants, were able to witness and sometimes record many instances of police profiteering on the street level. While these informants' credibility is necessarily suspect, there is ample evidence from other sources that the extortion practices they described were common occurrences in the Narcotics Division at the time of the Commission's investigation.

They told of participation in police shakedowns of narcotics "cribs" and said that it was standard practice for an informant to find a location where drugs were being sold in large quantities, and by attempting to make a buy with a large denomination bill, to induce the seller to reveal the hiding place of his cash supply. (Sellers in stationary locations try to keep as little money as possible on their person in order to minimize losses in case of an arrest or shakedown.) On leaving, the informant would arrange to return later to make another buy. On his next visit, as the seller opened the door, the police would crash in behind the informant. If the police felt they could score without risk, they would take whatever money and narcotics were available and let the seller go. If the amount of money was small, they would usually arrest the seller but still keep most of the narcotics, turning in only the amount necessary to charge a felony or misdemeanor as the case might be.

The informants stated that three out of every four times they went out on a raid with plainclothesmen from the Narcotics Division, no arrests were made and scores ranged from a few hundred dollars to as much as $20,000 on one occasion, with the informants getting some money and quantities of drugs as compensation.

The Commission found that, even without prompting from the police, it was quite common for an apprehended suspect to offer to pay his captors for his release and for the right to keep part of his narcotics and cash. This was especially true at higher levels of distribution where the profits to be made and the penalties risked by a dealer were very high. One such case was that of a suspended Narcotics Division detective who was recently indicted in Queens County and charged with taking bribes to overlook narcotics offenses. The indictment alleged that this officer accepted $1,500 on one occasion for not arresting a suspected drug pusher who was apprehended while in possession of $15,000 worth of heroin. There is evidence that on another occasion this detective was paid $4,000 by a different narcotics pusher for agreeing not to confiscate $150,000 worth of heroin. The detective has pleaded guilty to attempting to receive a bribe, and his sentence is pending.

Even after arrest, a suspect would sometimes try to pay the arresting officer to leave him enough money for his legal expenses, or to downgrade the arrest by holding back a large part of the seized narcotics, or to make sure that his case would be a "throw-out" in court. Police officers have accomplished this favor by writing up an ambiguous complaint which did not explicitly link the evidence seized in the arrest to the defendant. For example, an officer's affidavit could aver that narcotics had been discovered not on the defendant's person, but on the ground near his feet. In such a case, of course, the evidence would be inadmissible against the defendant and the case would be thrown out.

The opportunity for an arresting officer to score does not end at the scene of an arrest. As suspended patrolman William Phillips told the Commission in the course of his testimony about similar fixed arrest affidavits in gambling cases, "It's never too late to do business." That is, a police officer who is skillful or experienced enough can write an affidavit which appears to be very strong, but is still open-ended enough to work in favor of a defendant when coupled with appropriate testimony from the arresting officer. For example, an officer could state in his complaint that the suspect threw the evidence to the ground at the approach of the police. Should that officer later testify that he lost sight of the evidence as it fell, the evidence and the case could well be dismissed. The Commission learned that it was not uncommon for defense attorneys in narcotics cases to pay policemen for such favors as lying under oath and procuring confidential police and judicial records concerning their clients' cases.

It was, of course, beyond the scope of this Commission to seek out evidence of narcotics-related crime among agencies and officials outside the Police Department. However, the temptation of a police officer to profit illegally from a narcotics arrest could not be examined completely apart from his awareness or suspicion of corruption among those charged with the prosecution and adjudication of cases he has made. Evidence uncovered by the United States Attorney's Office in Manhattan in a current investigation of bribery by heroin dealers confirms the fact that corruption in narcotics law enforcement goes beyond the Police Department and involves prosecutors, attorneys, bondsmen, and allegedly even certain judges. While this fact does not excuse the illegal conduct of policemen who accept bribes, it does serve to illustrate the demoralizing environment in which police are expected to enforce narcotics laws.

The experience of one Narcotics Division detective who worked as an undercover agent for the U.S. Attorney's Office illustrates the pressures many police officers face after making a legitimate narcotics arrest. In a secretly recorded conversation, an attorney for a defendant in a narcotics case offered the detective various amounts ranging from $15,000 to $30,000 to give false testimony on behalf of his defendant. In an earlier recorded conversation, a co-defendant who had won a dismissal of charges told the detective that he had paid the attorney $20,000 to fix the case.

The belief that an officer's efforts to enforce narcotics law have been or may be nullified by dealings higher up in the legal system has in some instances caused members of the Department to rebel against such corruption. Unfortunately, it seems to be much more common for policemen exposed to such high-level corruption to try to get in on the profits. Such was the case of one Tactical Patrol Force officer who was apparently so confident of the acceptability of bribery that he attempted to arrange for a significant narcotics violator to bribe an assistant district attorney. He later pleaded guilty to bribery and resigned from the force after having served in the Department for eighteen years.

Illegal Use of Wiretaps

An extortion attempt by police officers is sometimes the end product of careful surveillance of a target, often by means of wiretaps. The wiretap is an essential tool in the Police Department's efforts to make cases against narcotics law violators. One state official with extensive experience in the enforcement of narcotics laws told the Commission that he didn't know of a single significant narcotics case prosecuted in the New York State courts without evidence or leads obtained through wiretapping, legal or illegal.

Theoretically, police may not secretly tap a suspect's telephone without a warrant. However, since strict constitutional safeguards and a certain amount of red tape surround the procedure for obtaining a warrant, it was not uncommon for Narcotics Division detectives to monitor and record the conversations of suspects without the required court order.

Since the Police Department has no official record of a wiretap installed without a warrant, no arrest is officially expected. Thus, information obtained by means of illegal taps can be used as easily to extort money and drugs from suspects who have been overheard as to make cases against them. Two Narcotics Division detectives were recently observed by a federal undercover agent as they engineered just such a score. The detectives illegally tapped the telephone conversations of a suspect in order to determine the extent of his dealings in narcotics. They then confronted the suspect with the evidence they had against him and threatened to arrest him unless he paid them $50,000. The suspect acceded to their demand and was given his freedom. The undercover agent, a former member of the Narcotics Division, told the Commission that in his experience the case is not unique.

Stealing Money and Narcotics

A score in the narcotics area is by no means dependent upon a suspect's offer or agreement to pay off the police. Most often a police officer seeking to score simply keeps for himself all or part of the money and drugs confiscated during a raid or arrest. One former member of the Narcotics Division recently assigned to other duties told the Commission that in his experience eighty to ninety percent of the members of the Narcotics Division participated in at least this type of score. While it was not possible for the Commission to verify this estimate, Commission investigators did ascertain that the holding back of money or narcotics contraband is very common and not limited to the Narcotics Division or other special squads.

The Commission learned of several sizable scores made by policemen during narcotics arrests. One such score was described by a plainclothesman in a secretly recorded conversation with Patrolman William Phillips. He told Phillips of an arrest he had made where $137,000 was turned in to the Department while three policemen split an additional $80,000.

Captain Daniel McGowan, then assigned to the Department's Public Morals Administrative Division, testified before the Commission about one matter he had investigated involving the arrest of several people and the confiscation of $150,000. Of this amount, McGowan stated, only $50,000 was turned in, the arresting officers keeping $100,000 for themselves.

Dismissed Patrolman Waverly Logan testified before the Commission about similar stealing, albeit on a lesser scale, by members of the elite Preventive Enforcement Patrol (PEP) Squad. Logan told the Commission that in his experience it was very common for arresting officers to keep confiscated money and drugs for themselves, and he gave many examples of the practice. After one narcotics arrest, for example, Logan and two other patrolmen vouchered $200 and held back $300 to divide among themselves. Later, Logan said, he discovered that one of the arresting officers had pocketed still another $500 which he had seized during the arrest. After another arrest during which Logan had scored $200, he watched from the precinct house window as another patrolman and a sergeant from his squad searched the suspect's car. The sergeant took a black fur coat from the trunk of the car and hid it in his own, while the patrolman walked away with a stereo tape device and several tape cassettes. Other situations described by Logan indicate that theft by police of furnishings and other personal property from premises where a narcotics raid had taken place were not uncommon.

Logan testified that his PEP Squad sergeant taught him the various techniques of scoring, and that such scoring was standard police procedure among his fellow officers. Logan told of one arrest he made where he did turn in all the money and contraband that he had seized. At the precinct station house where he vouchered the evidence, no one would believe that he was turning in the full amount of money confiscated. No matter how much money an arresting officer vouchered, Logan testified, other officers always assumed that he had kept back some for himself. As a result, in Logan's words:

"When you're new, you turn in all the money. But when you're working on the job awhile, you turn in no money. That's been my experience, that you don't voucher no money, or you voucher very little of what you made when a boss is there, and the boss is straight."

At the Commission hearings, Waverly Logan also described the attitude of some members of the Department that even if narcotics bribes are "dirty money," thefts from arrested drug dealers are "clean":

"[T]he general feeling was that the man was going to jail, was going to get what was coming to him, so why should you give him back his money and let him bail himself out. In a way we felt that he was a narcotics pusher, we knew he was a narcotics pusher, we kind of felt he didn't deserve no rights since he was selling narcotics."

This rationalization, certainly a departure from the unwritten rule that not even a "bad cop" would make money in narcotics, was repeated in various terms by other police officers. One former detective in the Narcotics Division told the Commission that money taken from a narcotics dealer or pusher is considered to be "clean" by police officers because no innocent person is directly injured by such a score. Former Detective Frank Serpico testified about the same attitude in hearings before the SCI. "Something that is accepted in narcotics," Serpico said, "is the fact that . . . if you were to make an arrest and there were large sums of money, that the money would be confiscated and not vouchered and the rationale there is the City is going to get it anyway and why shouldn't they." Serpico said that policemen who take money in this way do not worry that the arrested person will complain, because a narcotics team usually consists of four men, and "[t]he feeling is that it is his word against theirs."

Waverly Logan, on the other hand, apparently was bothered by the fact that arrested suspects might complain about having their money stolen by the police. Although he continued to make scores, Logan testified that he began to let suspects go after he had taken their money, so that they would be less likely to complain. This practice was in keeping with the philosophy of scoring taught to Logan by his sergeant: "[W]hen you are scoring a guy, try to leave him happy. If you leave a guy happy, he won't beef, won't make a complaint against you." Logan explained in his testimony that this could be accomplished even after a large amount of money was taken from a suspect by releasing him with enough of his narcotics to get him back into business.

It is clear from evidence assembled by this Commission and by other investigatory agencies that Waverly Logan's experiences and attitude with respect to holding back money and drugs are not unique in the Department. During the SCI public hearings on police corruption in narcotics law enforcement, a former Narcotics Division patrolman who had been convicted for supplying a heroin addict with narcotics to sell on the streets for him was asked to reveal the source of his heroin supply. He testified that one of the ways in which he obtained narcotics was to take it from dope addicts in the street, without making an arrest.

"Q. Was this a common thing in the Narcotics Division?
"A. That's where I learned it from.
"Q. You learned it from other members of the Narcotics Division?
"A. Yes.

*　　*　　*

"Q. Would you say this practice was generally known not only to the patrolmen and detectives, but by superiors?
"A. I would.

"Q. And on what basis do you make that statement?

"A. Being an ex-officer and knowing the routine of the office. It was pretty general knowledge what went on in the streets.

* * *

"Q. In addition to obtaining narcotics in the fashion you just described, were there ever occasions where you would make an arrest but hold back the amount seized?

"A. That is true.

"Q. Was that practice also common with the Narcotics Division?

"A. It was."

Another detective, assigned to a squad in Queens, had been a full partner in a narcotics wholesale enterprise, and testified at the same hearings that when he decided to join the partnership, he discussed with fellow officers the fact that at least part of his heroin supply would come from holding back large quantities of heroin from important narcotics arrests.

In addition to sale at a profit, either directly or through addict-pushers, drugs seized and retained by police officers were put to a variety of illegal uses by police, including payment of finder's fees to police informants and payment to addicts for merchandise stolen to order for policemen. Narcotics retained from prior arrests are also used for "padding," that is, for adding to the quantity of narcotics found on a subsequently arrested person, thus enabling the arresting officer to upgrade the charge to a felony. It is also common to use illegally retained narcotics to "flake" a narcotics suspect, that is, to plant evidence on a person in order to make a narcotics arrest.

Flaking and Padding

Flaking and padding sometimes result from the frustration a police officer feels when he is unable to catch a known narcotics law violator in the actual commission of a crime. An obvious danger is that an officer who can rationalize the illegal arrest of a known narcotics dealer is not far from making easy arrests of persons merely suspected of dealing in narcotics. Traditionally this danger has been magnified by the fact that certain commands in the Narcotics Division required a minimum number of felony arrests per month, usually four, from each officer who hoped for promotion or wished to avoid a transfer back to uniform.

Waverly Logan, in his testimony before the Commission, told of an occasion when he flaked a suspect. He had arrested a suspected narcotics seller and planted four bags of narcotics on him. At the precinct house the prisoner told two narcotics detectives how the arrest had been made. One of the detectives then took Logan aside and carefully instructed him on how to write up the complaint in order to make the case stick.

Former Patrolman Edward Droge explained that padding is sometimes prompted by the fact that smart dealers, who know that the possession of certain amounts of narcotics constitutes a felony rather than a misdemeanor charge, make sure that the quantity of narcotics they carry is somewhat less than the felony amount. When an arrest is made that involves narcotics just short of the felony amount, Droge said, an officer merely has to add a few bags from his own supply. During the SCI public hearings on police corruption, one patrolman testified that padding can also be accomplished by mixing the seized narcotics with adulterants such as quinine and mannitol.

Possession and Sale of Narcotics

Former Assistant Chief Inspector Sydney Cooper, who commanded the Department's Internal Affairs Division and later headed the Special Force established to investigate cases referred to the Department by our Commission, said in a televised interview in August, 1972:

> "We have had cases where allegations were made and the investigations disclosed that policemen became active entrepreneurs in narcotics operations. They were either suppliers of drugs [or] they themselves were sellers of drugs; or they ran shotgun."

The Commission found that police officers were involved in possession and sale of narcotics in a variety of ways, including financing transactions, recruiting informants and addicts as pushers, and share-selling, where the pusher is given drugs on consignment and retains part of the proceeds as payment. In addition, the Commission found it common for police officers to use narcotics as a medium of exchange for goods and services.

The Commission's two addict-informants reported that while acting as registered police informants they had carried on a lively business selling various items to the police for narcotics. Goods sold included guns, liquor, beer, tires, typewriters, clothes, cigarettes, power tools, and other specialty items. The informants stated that in most instances the merchandise was stolen and that the police knew that the items were "hot." On some occasions, the informants purchased merchandise and sold it to the police for narcotics because they could receive more narcotics from the police than the cash expended on the merchandise would have purchased directly. If they had to steal and hock or fence merchandise to get cash for narcotics, the amount of merchandise required would increase four- or fivefold as opposed to selling the goods to police officers for more or less the direct equivalent value in narcotics.

The informants explained that obtaining their narcotics by selling merchandise to police officers greatly reduced their risk. Obviously not only would the police not arrest them for the transaction, but after having committed crimes under police auspices, they would run much less risk of arrest for crimes committed on their own account.

The Commission was able to verify the allegations that merchandise-for-drugs transactions between police officers and addicts were commonplace. The informants, wearing microphones and transmitters, were observed, and in some instances filmed, by Commission agents as police officers approached them and placed their orders. In each instance at least two Commission agents were on hand for surveillance of the transaction, and the conversations between the police and the informants were recorded on tape. The merchandise the informants traded for narcotics was supplied by the Commission.

One plainclothesman, in the middle of a narcotics-for-cigarettes transaction ordered a gasoline powered mini-bike. The informant explained that it was still daylight and that he could not conveniently and easily steal a mini-bike in Central Park until sundown. The officer indicated he didn't care about the informant's troubles in obtaining a mini-bike, he just wanted it and, emphatically, that night. The Commission could hardly have permitted its agents to participate in a robbery or larceny, so, since no funds were available to purchase a mini-bike, that particular transaction was not consummated.

On another occasion, while the two informants were stationed outside headquarters with a bag of merchandise, the Commission filmed and recorded a dozen or more police officers approaching them to ask what was available.

Later the same morning, one patrolman was recorded on film opening the trunk of his car and instructing the informants to put in four bottles of liquor that he was purchasing. The patrolman went into headquarters, came down again, directed the informants to enter his car, and drove around the block. While driving around the block he gave each of the informants a bag containing a white powder which was later found to be heroin valued at about $30. Commission agents observed the two informants leaving the car and immediately took the narcotics from them for analysis.

Among the completed drugs-for-merchandise transactions were several involving whiskey and other alcoholic beverages. In one of these a narcotics plainclothesman gave the two Commission informants a written list specifying thirty-one quart bottles by brand name. He told them to make sure to "come through because I need them for my daughter's wedding shower." The patrolman paid for the liquor with a quantity of white powder containing heroin, starch, quinine, and mannitol.

The police officers who dealt with the informants made little effort to conceal what they were doing. One police officer in uniform met with the informants in a doorway two houses east of the Twenty-Eighth Precinct in Harlem, took from them two large bags containing eight quart bottles of whiskey, and walked back into the station house. He passed the patrolman on guard duty at the doorway and returned shortly to pay the informants with narcotics he said he had just removed from his station house locker. Earlier, when this officer had consummated a similar transaction while in plainclothes and was asked by one of the informants if he wanted the whiskey surreptitiously placed in his car, he grabbed the whiskey and stated, "I am going to walk down the street like I own it."

In all, ten transactions involving the sale of supposedly stolen merchandise to police officers in return for narcotics were recorded by Commission personnel within a period of a few weeks. The police involved included men assigned to the Narcotics Division as well as to local precincts. In addition, approximately twenty additional transactions which the informants said they could arrange were not consummated because of reported changes of plans by police officers, inability to muster sufficient Commission personnel to monitor the transactions properly, or the excessive expense of the items ordered. One scheduled sale was, according to the informants, postponed by the plainclothesman involved because he had to attend a Department anti-corruption meeting.

A police officer who pays in narcotics to have addict-informants steal for him or supply information to him is not far from the realization that he can pay in drugs to have informants push heroin for him.

One witness told the Commission in private that before he had been rehabilitated and took over the leadership of a drug program, he had been a very heavy user-pusher. For a while during this period he had become one of several share sellers for a group of three police officers, two of whom were still on the force as detectives in SIU at the time the witness testified. Although the association had been terminated for more than a year, the former addict said he lived in constant fear of these police officers.

Another similar case which resulted in the conviction of a police officer involved a young woman, the addict mother of several children, who had been arrested on information supplied by her mother and her boyfriend, who hoped she would be treated. The arresting officer, a member of the Narcotics Division, persuaded her to become an informant and continued to supply her with large quantities of narcotics. The arresting officer later introduced her to a "gangster"—actually another member of the Narcotics Division—and together, by threatening to harm her children, they forced her into becoming a share-seller pusher.

Eventually her boyfriend complained to the Internal Affairs Division and an arrest was made. At one point during the investigation, the patrolman kidnapped the victim and held her in captivity while trying to frighten her into refraining from testifying against him.

This patrolman obtained the narcotics he was supplying for sale in part from holding back narcotics seized in arrests and from taking narcotics from addicts in the street without making arrests. As he testified at the SCI public hearings on narcotics-related police corruption, he obtained the balance of the drugs he was pushing from a fellow police officer. The other patrolman asked no questions when he was approached for drugs because "it was a pretty regular thing for one officer to give narcotics to another officer." The patrolman also stated that he had chosen this particular fellow officer to ask for narcotics merely because he knew him better than some of the others, but that he could well have approached many other men in the unit and made the same request.

Several policemen have been investigated and prosecuted in the past three years for their involvement in large-quantity narcotics businesses. In the case of one police officer who was convicted for selling narcotics, it was clear from the evidence that during the period covered by the charges, from the summer of 1970 to December, 1970, he had been a wholesaler of substantial amounts of cocaine. The conviction was obtained largely through the cooperation of another arrested former policeman, who on several occasions had acted as a distributor for him. The evidence included a secretly-recorded conversation in which the defendant discussed the possible effects of his distributor's arrest on his cocaine operation, the possibility of fixing the colleague's case, and the desirability of killing the informant who was responsible for the arrest.

Another police officer, while under investigation by the Police Department and the Federal Bureau of Narcotics and Dangerous Drugs, recently arranged a significant heroin transaction for a federal undercover agent who had been introduced to the police officer as a potential customer. Until his recent arrest and conviction on an unrelated charge of narcotics possession, this patrolman is believed to have been involved in the interstate transport of large quantities of heroin.

One probationary patrolman was recently sentenced to ten years in prison for selling narcotics and to a concurrent five-year term for the possession of a large quantity of narcotics. The patrolman had aroused departmental suspicions because he was often seen in the company of known narcotics addicts. He was finally arrested when he sold fifty bags of heroin to a Police Department undercover agent.

A former Narcotics Division detective, while a member of the force, financed a narcotics wholesale business that dealt in one-eighth kilo quantities of heroin. He obtained some of the heroin he used for resale from an underworld connection, a wholesaler in narcotics.

In the SCI public hearings this police officer testified that he tried to protect his investment by providing armed protection for drug deliveries. He would watch the transactions from a convenient vantage point, he said, prepared to intervene with a loaded weapon in the event of trouble from outsiders, or to intercede with fellow police officers in the event of a threatened arrest.

For his participation in this multi-kilo heroin operation, the officer was indicted in Queens County and charged with conspiracy to sell heroin and with four counts of official misconduct. He pleaded guilty to one count of official misconduct, a misdemeanor, and was sentenced to one year of probation.

Miscellaneous Narcotics-Related Corruption

Policemen have been involved in many other illegal activities connected with narcotics traffic. They have tipped off narcotics dealers to impending arrests and raids and have sold the contents of confidential police files to narcotics suspects. Some police officers have accepted bribes to provide information on the existence, duration, and results of telephone taps, and a few even have collected a monthly fee to guarantee suspected narcotics law violators freedom from taps by the Police Department. In addition, policemen have interceded for known narcotics criminals—both with their fellow officers, and in at least one instance, with an assistant district attorney.

An investigation conducted by local authorities in Brooklyn, which led to the exposure of a narcotics wholesale ring that was responsible for the monthly distribution of 1.5 million dollars' worth of heroin, revealed that a New York City patrolman provided armed protection as the ring made its deliveries.

In at least one case, a policeman has provided rental automobiles for a known narcotics criminal, so that any law enforcement officer suspecting one of the vehicles and checking the license plate would discover only that the car was rented to a police officer.

Members of the Narcotics Division have helped known narcotic violators win amnesty or leniency from district attorneys' offices by fraudulently registering them as police informants and attributing arrests and leads from other sources to these ''informants'' on official Department records.

Captain Daniel McGowan testified before the Commission about another serious instance of narcotics-related police crime. ''[W]e received the information from three separate independent sources,'' Captain McGowan testified, ''that a member of our Narcotics Bureau learned the identity of an East Harlem character who was an informant for the Federal Narcotics Bureau and the allegation was that he passed this information on to the organized crime people in that area, that the informant was subsequently taken upstate and murdered, and the detective was paid $5,000.''

The Commission observed and taped one conversation between a plainclothesman and a registered informant that revealed an especially brutal instance of police misbehavior. The conversation concerned a quantity of heroin seized and not turned in by the officer at the time of an arrest a few days earlier. Since no part of the narcotics had been reported through official channels, the officer would never receive a lab report on the nature, strength, and purity of the narcotics. As the conversation progressed, it became clear that the police officer had given the addict a certain quantity of the untested drugs earlier in the day to test on himself to make sure that it was safe for sale to others. If the drug had been pure heroin, causing the addict to take an overdose, or if it had been a dangerous substance, the addict would have been unlikely to complain even if he had survived.

Comments

It is extremely difficult to estimate the effect of police corruption on the volume of narcotics traffic in New York City. The SCI, upon completing a thorough analysis of the performance of the Narcotics Division in recent years, concluded that in a great number of cases the Department's enforcement effort in narcotics has been completely wasted. However, as the SCI explained in its 1972 Annual Report, this failure was due to a variety of factors besides corruption, including the congestion of the courts and the Narcotics Division's chronic shortage of modern equipment and adequate training and supervision.

In his statement of April 20, 1971, before the SCI, Police Commissioner Murphy insisted that "corruption is not a significant factor either in the incidence of narcotics addiction or in the volume of narcotics traffic." Whatever the validity of his conclusion, Commissioner Murphy correctly pointed out in his statement that the international market structure of narcotics distribution, together with large-scale demand for illegal drugs and the high profitability of narcotics dealing severely limit the ability of local police to deal with the narcotics problem. This would be true even of the most honest and efficient police force.

It is also true, however, that the public depends very heavily on the local police for protection against narcotics-related crime. The role of the policeman in combating this crime is a vital link in the total federal, state, and local response to the narcotics crisis, and this link is certainly being eroded by the growing corruption problem in the Department. The SCI, which observed that the operations of the Narcotics Division in recent years would have been ineffective even in the absence of corruption, went on to say in its Annual Report that "[w]ith the added ingredient of corruption, local enforcement became a tragic farce."

Of course, it is unfair of some City residents to assume that the existence anywhere of conspicuous narcotics trading proves that policemen are either directly involved or are being paid to close their eyes to the illegal activity. Very often, it is not police corruption, but the overcrowding of the courts and the penal system, and the difficult standard of proof required to convict an arrested suspect that are to blame for the apparent non-enforcement of narcotics laws. Nevertheless, there is enough affirmative evidence of narcotics-related police corruption to justify a loss of public confidence in the Department and to diminish the self-esteem of its members. To some extent the public may understand, if not condone, police involvement in so-called victimless crimes such as gambling. But the complicity of some policemen in narcotics dealing—a crime considered utterly heinous by a large segment of society—inevitably has a devastating effect on the public's attitude toward the Department.

As long as society deems it necessary to invoke criminal sanctions in the narcotics area, the Commission believes that the Department must continue to assume responsibility for the enforcement of laws forbidding the sale and possession of narcotics. Of course increased study and attention should be given to ways other than criminal sanctions for dealing with narcotics addiction, but meanwhile, the Department must direct its attention to ways of improving the efficiency and integrity of its anti-narcotics units.

After its year-long study of the operations of the Narcotics Division, the SCI pointed out a number of specific areas in which it felt the Department could improve the effectiveness of its narcotics law enforcement efforts. Among other improvements, the SCI recommended increased supervision and coordination of investigative activities, stricter control of procedures for handling contraband, and the elimination of the quota system as a method of evaluating police performance. The SCI also recommended that the Department's enforcement efforts be directed away from indiscriminate drug loitering arrests and toward making good cases against high-level drug distributors.

In the past year the Department has instituted many salutary changes in narcotics law enforcement, including many of the improvements proposed by the SCI. For example, the Department has to some extent done away with the traditional distinction between SIU and the field units. Now the primary mission of both is to conduct long range investigations leading to the arrest of those responsible for drug distribution at the highest levels. Investigations are to be closely directed and coordinated from headquarters—a change which should result in less free-lancing by individual teams of investigators and therefore less opportunity for officers to exploit an arrest or raid situation for their own profit.

With an influx of new sergeants into the division, the ratio of supervisors to investigators has dropped to one to six. Thus each investigator will be under closer supervision in the field. This should lessen the opportunity for scoring by investigators. It should also provide a police officer's superiors with a method of rating his field performance that is more dependable and certainly less subject to abuse than the discredited quota system. Sergeants are now expected to accompany their men on important arrests, and in some cases, to make the actual arrest and take custody of the seized narcotics. New handling and reporting procedures have been designed to make it much more difficult for an officer who has confiscated narcotics to avoid turning them in to the Department.

When a police officer keeps for himself a portion of confiscated narcotics he is not always acting from corrupt motives. The Department's practice in the past of not providing money to pay informants, who usually are addicts themselves, created great pressure on police officers to use seized narcotics to pay for information. Money is now being made available for paying informants and this temptation, which often can be the first step to more serious illegal behavior, should be reduced as a result.

These and other improvements represent an important step in making narcotics graft less accessible to police officers. But as Chief Inspector William T. Bonacum, the commander of the Narcotics Division, recently told the Commission, such changes are meaningless unless the desire of his men to score in the narcotics area can be eliminated. To this end, Chief Bonacum has been conducting regular anti-corruption meetings with his men to keep them aware of the dangers of corruption and to instill in them the desire to make their division corruption-free. In addition, he meets regularly with individual members of the division to discover their problems and to keep them personally apprised of division policies. A complete change in attitude from the toleration of corruption that the Commission found to be prevalent in the division is necessarily a long-range goal. In the meantime, the Department can help to suppress narcotics corruption by dealing effectively with corruption in other areas, where it is usually considered less serious. Unchecked corruption anywhere in the Department creates a climate of permissiveness that makes it easier for a police officer to overcome his natural reluctance to become involved in narcotics traffic.

Chapter Six

PROSTITUTION

> "Q. Do the police ever bother you?
> "A. Not here, get off . . . Not here.
> Are you kidding? Are you for real?
> No way, honey. No way."
>
> — Recorded conversation between a
> Commission investigator and the
> hostess of a prostitute bar.

In its investigation into prostitution, the Commission was able to find little hard evidence of regular payments to police for protection from arrest. It did find specific evidence that some madams occasionally pay police officers on a one-time basis, and considerable circumstantial evidence that police protection on a regular basis is available to bars and nightclubs acting openly as the base of operations for large numbers of prostitutes.

The investigation into possible police connections with prostitution was focused mainly on the East Side of Manhattan from 40th Street to 80th Street, from Park Avenue to First Avenue, which takes in parts of the Seventeenth and Nineteenth Precincts. The principal factor in selecting this area was that it afforded a convenient view of several different forms of prostitution, namely brothels, independent call girls, streetwalkers, and prostitutes who work openly out of bars. Investigators interviewed prostitutes and madams, infiltrated and conducted surveillances of brothels and prostitute-bars, and used confidential informants who were sometimes equipped with electronic recording equipment.

Police Attitudes Toward Accepting Payoffs from Prostitutes

Prostitution in New York, while widespread, is unequivocally illegal and would seem to be a likely target for corrupt police officers.

However, it is an unwritten rule among policemen that taking money from prostitutes is unduly risky. Patrolman Phillips testified that the advice he was given by older officers when he joined the force was "never to take money in narcotics, prostitution, or involving weapons." He conceded that the rule has broken down concerning narcotics, but that for the most part it still holds concerning prostitutes. When asked why it was considered a bad idea to get involved with prostitutes, he explained the prevailing attitudes of policemen toward prostitutes, "[W]ell, first of all, prostitutes are known to be dangerous people to deal with. They are unreliable and they give people up. People [policemen] shy away from them." This conventional wisdom, coupled with the fact that other more lucrative sources of payoff money were available, apparently acted as a brake on police involvement with prostitution.

Brothels

Although the Commission encountered several brothels in the course of its investigation, its efforts focused on one in particular which seemed fairly typical in its operations. The madam of the establishment was a foreign national who had operated her business at varying East Side locations over the preceding two years. She employed from two to ten prostitutes and a maid who served drinks to customers.

Commission investigators held a number of interviews with her, during which she described several episodes in which she said she had paid off policemen in the past. To protect her operation from police interference, the madam said she utilized several precautionary measures. She had an arrangement with the building doorman to notify her through a series of buzzer rings of any suspicious police activity in the vicinity. She used a free-lance chauffeur to pass payments to individual police officers to head off impending raids. And, lastly, through her boy friend, she cultivated a friendship with a sergeant who she claimed served as her unofficial contact man within the Police Department and who allegedly agreed to warn her of any raids he knew about but couldn't head off.

The madam said that the friendly sergeant told her on January 18, 1971, that a lieutenant in the "vice squad" knew about her operation, was planning to arrest her, and that the lieutenant wanted $1,000 for calling off the arrest. The sergeant told her that he thought the lieutenant would settle for $500, which she gave him for transmittal to the lieutenant. She said she believed the sergeant gave the money to the lieutenant either that evening or the next day.

Six weeks later, according to the madam, a free-lance limousine chauffeur of her acquaintance called to tell her that there were two uniformed police officers downstairs in her building, but that he knew them and for a payment of $200 to each officer could stop them from coming up and arresting her. The chauffeur went up to the madam's apartment, she gave him the money, and the officers went away. She said that the payoff was witnessed by one of her girls and by the building doorman.

The following evening three plainclothesmen entered the madam's apartment and arrested her. She was charged with a felony for operating a house of prostitution, a charge which could have led to her deportation.

A month later, the establishment was raided for a second time. Plainclothesmen confiscated the madam's client and cashbooks and demanded $400 for their return, which the madam paid. The charges against her were reduced to a violation.

At this point, apparently tired of being raided, the madam designated an associate of hers to explore the possibility of obtaining regular police protection. Unbeknownst to her, this associate was working as an undercover informant for the Commission and wore a transmitter during most of the subsequent conversations, allowing Commission investigators to substantiate the following account.

The informant was introduced by a third party to Patrolman William Phillips (starting the chain of events that led to his being uncovered by the Commission). Phillips negotiated with the informant and the madam, and they were able to agree on a figure of $1,100 a month to be paid by the madam for protection of her operation, with the money to be distributed among plainclothesmen at precinct, division, and borough levels. Phillips told her that this arrangement would provide a 98% guarantee of protection against arrests and raids. To cover the remaining 2%, a code was established whereby the police would notify the madam in advance of any pending raid by calling up and making an appointment for "Mr. White from Chicago."

During the same period—and also documented by undercover tape recordings—the madam asked Phillips for help in gaining a dismissal of the felony charge she faced as the result of her first arrest for running a house of prostitution. If convicted, she would have been subject to deportation as an undesirable alien, as in fact she ultimately was. She spoke to Phillips and asked him if he could help her. Phillips agreed to get in touch with the arresting officer in the case and try to arrange for him to alter his testimony. After considerable bargaining, Phillips persuaded the madam to pay $3,500 and the arresting officer to accept $2,500, with Phillips keeping the remaining $1,000. The madam paid $1,500 to Phillips before the trial, and Phillips passed some of the money on to the arresting officer, who arrived late for the trial, after the madam's attorney had made a deal with the prosecutor whereby the felony charge was dropped and the madam pleaded guilty to a violation for disorderly conduct. Since the arresting officer had been of no help, the madam balked at paying the $2,000 she still owed, and Phillips eventually settled for $1,000, of which he gave half to the arresting officer.

In this last incident, it is noteworthy that the arresting officer never approached the madam asking for money and that he was drawn in only after she approached him through Phillips.

The madam told the Commission that she knows of two other madams who had paid off the police in the past. Another madam, running a similar operation, told Commission investigators that during a ten-month period she had paid plainclothesmen twice in amounts of $1,000 and $800. She said that she finally changed her location to avoid paying. Other madams interviewed by Commission investigators denied ever having been asked by policemen for money, but they did say that they charged half price to members of the force, which would in itself assure a certain amount of police protection.

The latest dodge used by brothels to avoid police interference is that of masquerading as massage parlors. According to the owner of one such parlor who was interviewed by a Commission attorney, a customer pays the massage parlor a fee for his massage and then makes whatever private arrangements he chooses with the "masseuse." However, the owner also said that he hires streetwalkers as his masseuses, which must have some effect on the nature of the massages offered. The set-up is a very private one, similar to that of private call girls, and as such is not a likely target for police shakedowns.

Prostitute Bars

There are several bars in the midtown area which the Commission found acted as bases of operations for large numbers of prostitutes. Most were operated very openly, in a manner similar to one described by Patrolman Phillips:

"I had observed [one bar] for about half an hour—forty-five minutes—and I saw the same woman go in and out with two different men . . . I informed [the sergeant] of what I had observed . . . and he said, 'Well, don't worry about it. I don't think it's anything. It's a real busy bar.'

"And later I found out through my own information that the place was a large call girl operation . . . There is no way that this place could operate without paying somebody. It was just too wide open."

Owners of such bars are extremely vulnerable to police interference, since they run their business at fixed addresses which are very visible to the public and to the police. In addition, if a bar owner were convicted of promoting prostitution, or even permitting it, he would lose his liquor license. The investigation concentrated on two particular bars, but no hard evidence of police payoffs was found.

In the first of these bars, girls sat at tables in twos and threes. When a customer entered, he was approached by the hostess and directed to a table. If she approved of him as a customer, she would direct one of the girls to join him. All contacts between male and female customers were directed strictly by the hostess or bartender. After one or two drinks, the couple would leave and go to one of the better hotels in the area. The rate was a minimum of $50, plus the cost of drinks consumed and, in some cases, a non-existent dinner.

The manager of this bar never admitted paying off the police but the hostess confidently stated that she was not worried about being arrested. Such assurance in view of the notoriety and openness of the operation leaves room for the possibility of a police fix, although it could be simply a case of police inaction.

The manager of a similar operation freely admitted that prostitution was the most lucrative part of his business, and that without it he would have to close his bar. Again, the Commission obtained no admissions or direct evidence substantiating police involvement. Yet, the bar was a notorious operation which was the subject of 100 police visits within a six-month period, although none of these resulted in the issuance of a single summons.

Call Girls and Streetwalkers

Call girls work very privately from their apartments, accepting only known or recommended customers by phone appointment. They are the least conspicuous of all prostitutes and consequently the least vulnerable to police interference. The Commission did hear allegations of payments made on a haphazard basis by call girls to individual policemen, but these allegations were unsubstantiated.

The Commission found no evidence that police officers shake down streetwalkers, although we heard numerous allegations—from policemen as well as prostitutes—that policemen often arrest women they assume to be prostitutes without obtaining any evidence that the women are actually soliciting. Before an officer can make a legally valid arrest of a prostitute, she must solicit him in explicit terms. Because most streetwalkers simply approach prospective customers and ask, "Want a date?" then discuss price, a legitimate arrest is difficult to make. Instead, officers will often just pick up women loitering in the target area and later claim in court that they were solicited for explicit sexual purposes. Such arrests are resorted to particularly when public pressure mounts to "clean up" one area or another. Streetwalkers are the most overt of all prostitutes and would seem to be the most vulnerable of all to police interference. However, such interference takes the form of arrests rather than shakedowns. One reason for this may be that streetwalkers carry very little money with them, turning their earnings over almost hourly to their pimps, and thus would not be very profitable sources of payoffs. A more likely explanation is the fact that streetwalkers are considered unstable, slovenly, disagreeable characters, many of whom are addicts, and even very dishonest police officers are probably loathe to deal with them. In addition, the relatively mild sanctions of the law make arrest only an inconvenience for them.

Comments

Whether or not prostitutes regularly pay off the police, it is clear that current police practices have had little effect on curtailing illegal prostitution. Prostitutes operate openly and are likely to continue to do so. Although the Commission's investigation turned up little hard evidence of extensive or organized corruption of police by prostitutes, the Department itself recognizes prostitution as a definite corruption hazard. In other jurisdictions attempts have been made to solve the problem by legalizing prostitution but that step has had mixed success and involves social judgments beyond this Commission's purview. At this time, the Commission can offer no alternative to police enforcement of the anti-prostitution laws, with all its incumbent problems.

Chapter Seven

CONSTRUCTION

"It is virtually impossible for a builder to erect a building within the City of New York and comply with every statute and ordinance in connection with the work. In short, many of the statutes and rules and regulations are not only unrealistic but lead to the temptation for corruption."

So said H. Earl Fullilove, Chairman of the Board of Governors of the Building Trades Employers Association of the City of New York, in testimony before the Commission on October 29, 1971, summing up a situation which has led to extensive graft in the construction industry. The Commission found that payments to the police by contractors and subcontractors were the rule rather than exceptions and constituted a major source of graft to the uniformed police. It must be noted that policemen were not alone in receiving payoffs from contractors. Much larger payoffs were made to inspectors and permit-granting personnel from other agencies.

The Investigation

In its initial investigation into corruption in the construction industry, the Commission came up against a stone wall. Sixteen veteran job superintendents and two project managers interviewed at construction sites solemnly denied that they had ever paid off the police or known anyone who had. Similar denials were made under oath by other construction people and by three patrolmen and their precinct commander, who were subpoenaed by the Commission. Later, in private talks with members of the construction industry, quite a different story began to emerge. From information obtained in these lengthy, off-the-record interviews, the Commission was able to piece together a detailed picture of corruption in the construction industry.

Although several of these sources were unusually helpful to the Commission in private talks, only one agreed to testify extensively in executive session (and then only under the cloak of anonymity) and none would testify at the public hearings. Their testimony could at no time be compelled, because the Commission lacked the power to obviate claims of Fifth Amendment privileges by conferring immunity. However, it was arranged that the construction industry would be represented at the public hearings by Mr. Fullilove, whose association is made up of 800 contractors and subcontractors, including industry giants as well as smaller companies.

Speaking for his membership, Mr. Fullilove said, "Many—if not most—people in the industry are reluctant to appear at an open hearing and to testify on these matters. Our members feel that unless the entire situation can be remedied in one fell swoop, it's a tremendous burden on a member to become a hero for a day and then suffer the consequential individual harassment." He then went on to detail the laws and ordinances leading to police harassment and consequent graft. This information was corroborated and buttressed by the testimony of Patrolmen William Phillips and Waverly Logan.

Reasons for Police Corruption in Relation to Construction

Corruption is a fact of life in the construction industry. In addition to extensive payoffs contractors make to police and others in regulatory agencies, there is evidence of considerable corruption within the industry itself. Contractors have been known to pay owners' agents to get an inside track on upcoming jobs; subcontractors pay contractors' purchasing agents to receive projects or to get information helpful in competitive bidding; sub-subcontractors pay subcontractors; dump-truck drivers exact a per-load payment for taking out extra loads they don't report to their bosses; and hoist engineers get money from various subcontractors to insure that materials are lifted to high floors without loss or damage. In this climate, it is only natural that contractors also pay the police.

The heart of the problem of police corruption in the construction industry is the dizzying array of laws, ordinances, and regulations governing construction in the City. To put up a building in New York, a builder is required to get a minimum of forty to fifty different permits and licenses from various City departments. For a very large project, the total number of permits needed may soar to 120, 130 or more. These permits range in importance from the initial building permit down through permits required for erecting fences, wooden walkways and construction shanties, to seemingly petty ones like that required whenever a track vehicle is moved across a sidewalk. "This [latter] regulation is often violated," Mr. Fullilove told the Commission, "because it is tremendous inconvenience to obtain a one-shot permit to move a bulldozer over a five-foot stretch of sidewalk." In practice, most builders don't bother to get all the permits required by law. Instead, they apply for a handful of the more important ones (often making a payoff to personnel at the appropriate agency to insure prompt issuance of the permit). Payments to the police and inspectors from other departments insure that builders won't be hounded for not having other permits.

Of the City ordinances enforced by the police which affect construction, most relate to use of the streets and sidewalks and to excessive dust and noise. Ordinances most troublesome to contractors are those which prohibit double-parking, flying dust, obstructing the sidewalk, or leaving it strewn with piles of sand and rubble, and beginning work before 7:00 a.m. or continuing after 6:00 p.m. (This last is for the protection of neighborhood residents already subject to eleven legal hours a day of construction noise.)

Most large contractors seem to regard all of the ordinances mentioned above and many of the permit requirements simply as nuisances which interfere with efficient construction work. Thus, they are willing parties to a system which frees them from strict adherence to the regulations.

Police Enforcement of Laws Regulating Construction

Although building inspectors are responsible for enforcement of regulations concerning construction techniques, the responsibility for inspecting certain permits and enforcing the ordinances outlined above lies with the police. The police officers charged with this responsibility have always been faced with a particularly tempting opportunity for corruption. The Department has attempted, since the Commission hearings, to lessen the opportunities by cutting back on enforcement. It has ordered its men to stop enforcing all laws pertaining to construction, unless pedestrians are endangered or traffic is impeded. If a patrolman observes a condition which affects pedestrians or traffic, he is to call his superior to come to the site and take whatever action is needed. Nevertheless, pending a revision of the laws to make them more realistic, they cannot go entirely unenforced and whoever is given the job will meet the same pressures found by the Commission.

Traditionally, construction enforcement was the function of one foot patrolman in each precinct called the "conditions man" who concentrated on construction enforcement. At the time of the investigation, a growing number of precincts had abolished the post, leaving the responsibility for construction enforcement to other officers, such as "summons men" who had broader responsibilities for issuing summonses in other areas. Foot patrolmen and those in patrol cars were also empowered to go onto any site in their sectors to check for violations. In any case, the patrolman whose duty it was to enforce construction laws was, at the time of the investigation, required to make periodic checks of all construction sites in the precinct to make sure that they 1) had the proper permits, 2) conformed to the limitations of those permits, and 3) adhered to all City ordinances not covered by the permits. If he found any violations, he was supposed to issue a summons. Department regulations provided that he make a notation in his memo book whenever he visited a construction site and maintain a file at the precinct with a folder for each construction job in his jurisdiction, containing copies of all permit numbers for the site and a record of all civil summonses it had received.

In practice, the Commission found, officers responsible for enforcing ordinances relating to construction simply kept pro forma files and pretty much let the job go at that. Examination of conditions men's memo books in the Twentieth Precinct, where there were between twenty and fifty construction projects underway at one time, indicated that a grand total of thirty-nine visits were reported to have been made to construction sites over the two-year period from March, 1969, to March, 1971, with over half those visits recorded as having been for the purpose of copying down permit numbers. The patrolmen whose notebooks were examined admitted under oath that they did not follow Department regulations in getting permit numbers from new sites or in making entries in their memo books every time they entered a site. In short, the Commission found that these patrolmen had not been doing their jobs properly, were aware that they weren't, and knew that their work would not be reviewed by senior officers.

These rules were designed to facilitate control of corruption. Where the rules were ignored by supervisors, the spread of corruption was almost inevitable.

Patterns of Police Corruption in Construction

The most common pattern of police payoffs in the construction industry, as described to the Commission by police officers and by contractors and their employees, involved payment to the sector car of a fixed monthly or weekly fee, which varied according to the size of the construction job. Occasionally, the sergeants would also have a pad, and in larger jobs, the precinct captain sometimes had one of his own. In addition, all construction sites, no matter how small, were found to be vulnerable to overtures from local foot patrolmen.*

---

* One small contractor told how it's done: "Put a five dollar bill in one pocket, a ten in the other. Fold it up real small. Size up the situation and pay accordingly. You can pass it in a handshake if necessary. It really isn't. You know the touch is on as soon as he . . . walks on the job to see your permit and questions it."

In a small job like the renovation of a brownstone, the general contractor was likely to pay the police between $50 and $150 a month, and the fee ascended sharply for larger jobs. An excavator on a small job paid $50 to $100 a week for the duration of excavation to avoid summonses for dirt spillage, flying dust, double-parked dump trucks, or for running vehicles over the sidewalk without a permit. A concrete company pouring a foundation paid another $50 to $100 a week to avoid summonses for double-parking its trucks or for running them across a sidewalk without a curb cut. (Concrete contractors are especially vulnerable, as it is essential that foundation-pouring be carried on continuously. This means that one or more trucks must be kept standing by while one is actually pouring.) Steel erectors paid a weekly fee to keep steel delivery trucks standing by; masons paid; the crane company paid. In addition, all construction sites were approached by police for contributions at Christmas, and a significant number paid extra for additional police patrols in the hope of obtaining protection from vandalism of building materials and equipment.

In small contracting companies, payments were generally negotiated and made by the owner; larger firms often had an employee whose sole job was to handle negotiations with agencies which regulate construction. This man, called an expeditor, negotiated and made all such payments, both to the police and to inspectors and permit-granting personnel from other agencies. In either case, when work was started on a new site, arrangements were made with the local police.

One contractor, whose experiences were fairly typical, spoke at length with Commission investigators and later—with promise of anonymity—testified before the Commission in executive session. He was a small general contractor who worked on jobs of less than one million dollars. He started his own company in the early sixties with a contract for a small job in Brooklyn. During the first week of construction, a sector car pulled up to the construction site and a patrolman came onto the site, asking to see the permits for demolition, sidewalk construction, etc. He looked over the various permits and left. The following day, another sector car came by, and one of the patrolmen issued a summons for obstruction of the sidewalk. The contractor protested that he had the necessary permit and was in no way violating the law. "If we don't work together," the patrolman told him, "there will be a ticket every day." When the contractor asked how much "working together" would cost, he was told, "$50 a week." The contractor testified that he balked at this, claiming that his was a small operation and that he couldn't afford such payments. He said he would prefer to operate within the limitations of his permits and go to court to answer any summonses he might receive.

The following day, the contractor received another summons for $100. Two days later, he was approached again and told that it would be cheaper to pay off the police than to accumulate summonses. "We decided for our own good to make that $50 payment and not maintain our hero status," he said. He continued to make payments of $50 a week to a patrolman from the sector car for the duration of the construction work, which lasted about one year. His site was never again inspected by the police and he received no more summonses.

This contractor further testified that he was approached by the police, and paid them, on all the jobs he did in various City precincts. On none of these was he ever served with a summons. On his last job, in 1970, when he was in financial difficulties which eventually led to bankruptcy proceedings, he was, as usual, approached by the police for payoffs. Pleading insolvency, he refused to pay and used various ruses to avoid payment. He again began receiving summonses for violations—the first that had been served on him since he started paying the police.

This contractor stated that in addition to paying the police he has also made payments to personnel from the Department of Buildings, other divisions of the Housing and Development Administration, the Department of Highways, and such federal agencies as the Department of Housing and Urban Affairs and the Federal Housing Administration.

Another builder, the owner of a medium-sized contracting company which does work for such clients as Consolidated Edison, the New York Telephone Company and the Catholic Dioceses of New York and Brooklyn, told Commission investigators that his company had paid off the police on every construction job it had done in the City, including the six or eight jobs in progress at the time of the interview. He told the Commission that he paid the police from $50 to $100 a week for each job he had in progress, and that payments were made by his expeditor, whose job it was to obtain permits and pay off police and others. He went on to say that his company frequently negotiated the amount of payment with the precinct commander either at the building site or at the local precinct.

A reliable informant who was intimately connected with this builder told the Commission that the builder's payoffs were in fact much larger than the $50 to $100 he claimed. The informant also reported that the expeditor handled all negotiations for payoffs, then reported to officers of the company, who gave him the appropriate amount out of petty cash. At a later date, the expeditor submitted covering expense vouchers indicating travel or entertainment expenses. During the time this informant was giving information to the Commission, he observed a sergeant approach a foreman at one of the company's construction sites in Queens and threaten to write out a summons for burning refuse. The foreman then told the sergeant that he couldn't see going to court over it and would give him $20 to forget about it. The sergeant said he would have to discuss it with his boss and left the site. That afternoon, the sergeant returned to the construction site with his precinct captain, who advised the foreman that there were "a lot of violations around." He said he wanted to speak to someone about "taking care of it" (a clear reference to the expeditor), and would return on the Tuesday afternoon following. At this point, the informant's role was discovered and the Commission was not able to find out how big a payoff the captain had in mind, although a three installment $2,500 payoff which the informant said was arranged with a building inspector a few days earlier indicates that it would have been sizable.

Comments

The current system of laws and ordinances relevant to construction is badly in need of overhaul. Many ordinances now on the books make construction unduly difficult and create bountiful opportunities for graft. The needed review should preferably be undertaken by members both of the industry and of regulatory agencies.

A start has been made in this direction. In June, 1972, *The New York Times* ran a series of investigative articles which described in detail corrupt practices in the construction industry in the City. In response to the newspaper's allegations, a State Senate committee chaired by Senator Roy Goodman held six days of hearings, which resulted in a plan to have industry leaders, legislators, and the appropriate City commissioners review the tangle of City and state laws governing construction, with a view to eliminating those laws which are unrealistic or unnecessary and which lead to corruption. Industry groups have studied the laws and are expected soon to submit recommendations to the appropriate City commissioners.

One other important reform is needed. Builders in special situations may have a legitimate reason for violating ordinances. However, there is currently no procedure whereby such relief may be afforded. A publicly-recognized means for waiving regulations where necessary and appropriate should be established.

As outlined earlier, the Department has curtailed police enforcement of ordinances relating to construction. The Commission favors this step and feels that, insofar as possible, police officers should be relieved of responsibility for enforcing laws in any area under the jurisdiction of regulatory agencies—in this case, the Department of Buildings, other divisions of the Housing and Development Administration, and the Department of Highways, among others.

We recognize that this approach will not in itself eliminate corruption but may simply transfer it from the police to other agencies. But we we believe that corruption in other agencies—undesirable as it is—has far less impact upon the body politic than corruption among the police.

The progression found again and again in the course of our investigation, from the acceptance by a police officer of petty graft to more serious corruption, makes it desirable to remove as many sources of such petty graft as possible. By eliminating the opportunity for petty graft, the Department can perhaps change the current attitude that such graft is an accepted part of the police job—an attitude which makes it easier for a police officer to accept or solicit graft of a more serious nature when the opportunity presents itself. Moreover, policemen are more likely to pursue vigorously a corrupt public official who is not one of their own.

Moreover, as a simple matter of efficiency there is no justification for using the police, with all their powers and prerogatives, in the enforcement of many minor regulations.

A promising method of curtailing construction graft which the Department has yet to use on a broad scale, would be a campaign to arrest contractors who offer bribes to policemen. The recent use in the Bronx of police undercover agents posing as regular policemen has led to the arrests of such would-be bribers. Carrying this technique one step further, Department anti-corruption personnel could, without advance warning, require a police officer to don a concealed transmitter and, under surveillance, give a summons to a construction foreman in his area of patrol with whom he may or may not have had corrupt dealings.

Chapter Eight

BARS

In late 1970 and early 1971, the Commission conducted a concentrated investigation into police involvement with drinking establishments. It found that payoffs from bars licensed by the state to sell liquor, along with those from construction firms, were the most common source of illegal outside income to uniformed policemen, and that unlicensed premises, operating completely outside the law, were paying substantial amounts to plainclothesmen and detectives.

Like the construction industry, the business of selling liquor by the drink is governed by a complex system of state and local laws, infractions of which can lead to criminal penalties, as well as suspension or loss of license. Thus licensees are highly vulnerable to police shakedowns. The licensed premises most commonly solicited for payments were found to be lucrative bars, such as popular singles bars and dance halls, and establishments which played host to ancillary illegal operations, such as bars which catered heavily to prostitutes and their customers, to drug pushers and addicts, to gamblers, or to homosexuals soliciting partners. Payoffs were also made by establishments operating completely outside the law, such as bars which served liquor without a license, or after legal hours, and "juice joints"— informal unlicensed spots which sell liquor by the bottle after midnight or on Sundays, when liquor stores are legally closed.

Although police officers receive free meals, drinks, and Christmas presents from legitimate restaurants, Commission investigators did not turn up evidence that such establishments were solicited by policemen for regular payments to avoid summonses.

At the time of the Commission's investigation, the responsibility for inspection and supervision of licensed premises was the duty of patrol sergeants in each sector. In October, 1971, the Department took these duties away from uniformed policemen and turned them over to plainclothesmen and detectives. However, there are some indications that the system of shakedowns and payoffs has continued, with plainclothesmen and detectives taking over where the uniformed force left off.

The Investigation

When the Commission began its investigation it was aware that one area in which it was likely to find patterns of systematic and widespread police corruption was the enforcement of laws relating to bars and restaurants licensed to sell liquor by the drink. Over the years, there had been periodic scandals involving bar payoffs to police officers. On at least two occasions, these had been triggered by the discovery of policemen's notebooks listing amounts due monthly or biweekly from licensed premises to various police officers. And the Commission itself had received complaints that such payments were in fact being made. Moreover, bars are especially vulnerable to pressure from corrupt police officers because of the wide range of regulatory statutes to which they are subject, some of which are anachronistic and others overly vague.

The Commission undertook to ascertain whether these allegations of corruption with respect to bars were true, and if so, to determine the extent and nature of that corruption. The Commission decided to focus its investigation on the Nineteenth Precinct on the East Side of Manhattan and the Sixth Precinct in the West Village. The Nineteenth Precinct was chosen because of its convenient location and high concentration of bars (it contains over 100 bars and restaurants), and its selection is not meant to imply that corruption there was any worse than in other precincts. In fact, as Patrolman Phillips testified, "The Nineteenth is not a big money precinct." The Sixth Precinct was chosen for its large number of completely unlicensed bars.

In conducting their investigations, Commission investigators sought information from a variety of sources. Thus, in the Nineteenth Precinct they followed officers to bars and noted the frequency of their visits, interviewed owners, managers, and bartenders, used confidential informants, and generally observed activities in and about the premises. Based upon these investigations, it became evident that the allegations of a systematic pattern of police corruption in connection with licensed bars and restaurants were substantially accurate. Furthermore, it is significant that these patterns changed abruptly, when, two months after the investigation in the Nineteenth had begun, the police became aware that Commission investigators were in the area. At that point, the officers who had previously been observed barhopping ceased such activities and warned bar owners and bartenders that, if they were questioned, they were to tell Commission investigators only that police sergeants came in occasionally to check licenses.

These police efforts to conceal the previously observed patterns had some measure of success. When the Commission held its executive hearings, it subpoenaed police officers responsible for bar inspections and directed them to bring with them their financial records and memo books covering the period of surveillance. Bar owners, managers, and bartenders were also subpoenaed along with their account books. Without exception, both police and bar personnel denied any knowledge of payoffs made to policemen by bars, and some even went so far as to deny having had various meetings and corruption-related conversations which had been observed, and in some cases overheard, by investigators.

In the Sixth Precinct in the West Village, the Commission used similar techniques of surveillance, undercover work, and interrogation of owners, employees, and informants to gather information about payoffs to police from both licensed bars and the large number of openly-operated unlicensed bars in that precinct. Here, too, the Commission's investigation confirmed the accuracy of allegations of systematic patterns of police corruption.

Patterns of Police Payoffs by Licensed Bars

As discussed in Chapter Fourteen, virtually all bars were found to provide free food and drinks to policemen and also made Christmas and vacation payments to police.

In addition, investigators found that many bars doing a substantial volume of business customarily made regular biweekly or monthly payments to the police. During the Commission's investigation such payments were usually initiated by the sector patrol sergeant who, bar owners said, would pay a visit to the premises and point out various violations or suggest that he could always flush the soap down the toilet and write out a summons for "no soap in the men's room." The next step would be negotiations as to how much the bar owner would pay—a sum to be split among the sergeants to insure protection from summonses. Finally, an agreement would be reached, a pad established, the down payment made, and from then on for as long as he stayed in business, the bar owner continued to pay. If the bagman was retired, promoted, or transferred, a new one soon took his place.

Although pad money was almost always paid to sergeants in the areas under investigation, other officers received payoffs from bars on a less regular basis. Radio car patrolmen picked up $5 to $10 apiece from certain bars on weekend nights when bar crowds were heaviest and trouble (and violations) most likely, and some captains were reported to have contracts with the busier bars.

In one bar, Commission investigators were mistaken for detectives, and the owner told them, in a tape-recorded conversation, that he had recently paid the precinct captain. As a result of that incident the precinct captain, now a deputy inspector, has been brought up on departmental charges of unlawfully accepting $300 and then attempting to persuade the bar owner not to testify against him.

According to information received by the Commission, pad payments made to sergeants began at $60 a month, and ascended to a high of $2,000 a month reportedly paid by one large establishment in the Village. In smaller bars, the pick-up was generally made once a month, usually on or near the first, and in larger ones biweekly on the first and fifteenth.

Behavior of supervising patrol sergeants in the Nineteenth, who were responsible for licensed premises inspections, was consistent with a pattern of biweekly and monthly payoffs to them by bar owners. Duty schedules in the precinct were arranged so that the three sergeants who were alleged to act as bagmen were always assigned to different shifts. They turned out to be a bar-hopping lot. The sheer volume of their visits to bars was out of all proportion to law-enforcement problems posed by licensed premises.

The most glaring example was one sergeant who invariably showed up in one bar or another ten minutes after going on duty and ordered a V.O. on the rocks, then proceeded to go from bar to bar for the rest of his tour. His pattern of visits, like that of the other two alleged sergeant-bagmen, changed sharply on the first and fifteenth of the month, when payoffs were collected, in that he went to more bars than usual and spent less time in each. On the first of one month, Commission investigators observed the sergeant make the following ten visits to eight different bars, of which only two visits were recorded in his memo book:

Investigators' Observations		*Sergeant's Memo Book Entries*
Time	*Bar*	
4:35 P.M.	Rowan's	1620-1730 [4:20-5:30] Patrolling 1st, 2nd, 3rd Aves.
4:40	Dangerfields	
5:30	Muggs	
8:00	Uncle Charlie's	2000 [8:00] Brandy's B&G no viol. observed
8:12	Brandy's	
8:20	Merry Ploughboy	2020 [8:25] Ploughboy Pub
8:35	Sam's	2030-2100 [8:30-9:00] Patrolling
8:40	Tittle Tattle	
9:05	Tittle Tattle	
11:00	Uncle Charlie's	

In the four months from July 1, 1970, through November 2, 1970, this sergeant recorded a total of at least eighty-five official visits to bars.* In the same period he did not file a single licensed premises inspection form or issue a single summons. When questioned before the Commission and confronted with the disparity between his actual and recorded visits to bars, the sergeant attempted to explain his unreported bar visits by saying that he went into bars simply to use the toilet. He claimed he had to do this frequently because of a "urinary condition," which, however, he had never reported to the Department.

As in other precincts, honest enforcement of the law in relation to bars seemed to be the exclusive province of certain foot patrolmen. For example, one bar noted for permitting open gambling, drug-dealing and prostitution, and for staying open after legal closing hours, received ten summonses in one seven-month period, all issued by patrolmen.

In addition to ordinary pad payments, other opportunities for payoffs also arose. Fairly typical is the experience of one bar owner in the Twentieth Precinct on Manhattan's Upper West Side, who was approached by the police for payoffs in March of 1972. At this time, supervision of licensed premises had been taken away from uniformed sergeants and turned over to detectives and plainclothesmen, and the incident indicates that this organizational change may have had little impact on the basic operation of the system.

Four detectives entered this man's bar one night, announcing that they were there to inspect the premises, which they proceeded to do. After searching the men's room, one detective produced a small aluminum foil package which he said he had found in the men's room, and

---

* As might be expected of someone who spent so much time in bars, the sergeant's memo book entries became increasingly illegible as the night wore on, deteriorating to an undecipherable scrawl toward the end of a tour. Eighty-five represents the number of entries relating to bars that Commission investigators were able to read.

which he alleged contained cocaine. He told the bar owner that he was "in trouble," and that this incident would have to be written up and reported to the State Liquor Authority (SLA). The detectives then left, but a half-hour later, a patrolman known to the bar owner appeared and said he had seen the detectives writing up papers in the station house. He said that he would talk to the detectives and "see if anything could be done." It was clear that he was talking about a payoff. Later in the week, the patrolman telephoned the owner and told him he had arranged a meeting between the two of them and one of the detectives, to take place three days later in a neighborhood bar.

At this point, the incident became highly atypical because the owner got in touch with the Commission, which, no longer having an investigative staff, contacted the Police Department's Internal Affairs Division, which arranged to supply the bar owner with $100 in marked money and to cover the meeting.

At the meeting, the detective asked for $500 for changing his report on the bar so that the licensee wouldn't get in trouble with the SLA. The owner said he had only $100 with him, which the policemen took as partial payment, after which they left the bar and walked straight into the hands of IAD. Both the detective and the patrolman have been indicted for receiving a bribe.

Another kind of score situation develops whenever there is a fight in a licensed premises, or any other disturbance which leads to arrest. All arrests made in bars must be reported to the SLA, which takes a dim view of the kind of activity which leads to arrest (fighting, for example), and which may revoke a bar owner's license on the grounds that he is running a "disorderly house." At the very least, if the SLA receives a report of an arrest in a bar, it will hold a hearing to determine the licensee's culpability.

So, while bar owners frequently need police help to break up fights or get rid of obstreperous drunks, they have a strong interest in making sure that these things are not reported to the SLA. And the police are only too happy to oblige. For a fee which commonly ranges from $200 to $400, police officers will either not report a fight at all or will report that it took place on the street in front of the bar instead of inside. They will also make the arrest outside. Such a procedure insures that no records are sent to the SLA, and the licensee is off the hook.

Patterns of Police Payoffs by Unlicensed Bars

The Commission's investigation of unlicensed bars centered in the Sixth Precinct in the West Village, primarily one seventeen-square block area which is dominated during the day by the Gansevoort Meat Market. At night it becomes a haven for homosexuals who are drawn by the large number of completely illegal, unlicensed bars which cater to them. These establishments have been identified by local and federal law enforcement agencies as being owned or controlled by members of organized crime, and they are the scene of substantial illegal activity.

The unlicensed bars in the Village (usually euphemistically called "after-hours clubs" because they stay open long after the 4:00 a.m. legal closing time for licensed premises) are located in sizable lofts which accommodate as many as 700 men at a time. These bars generally consist of a large open space containing a bar and dance floor, and a connected "sex room" or "orgy room" where men practice homosexual acts on each other.

The Commission found that many of these unlicensed bars made payoffs to division plainclothesmen and detectives who were charged with enforcing laws against them, to insure that the bars would be allowed to operate virtually unhindered by police action. The payments were substantial, ranging up to $2,000 a month for the largest and most lucrative club. The understanding between bar owners and police was that occasional token arrests would be made to keep up a facade of police alertness, but that the arrests would be handled in such a manner that they did not seriously disrupt business. Arrests were generally limited to a handful of minor employees, and were made quietly, so that customers were not harassed or intimidated. Seizure of liquor generally consisted of police taking two or three half-empty bottles for evidence and leaving the main supply intact.

Despite their completely illegal status, the Sixth Precinct's after-hours clubs operated so openly—even blatantly—that their existence was obvious even to the most casual passerby. On weekend nights, Commission investigators saw long, often noisy, queues of patrons lined up outside the clubs, waiting to get in. Numerous citizen complaints were received by the First Division, uniformed officers filed endless suspected premises reports, and on occasion complaints were forwarded from the SLA. Yet division personnel took little action. When plainclothesmen and detectives were sent to check on after-hours clubs, they usually filed reports indicating that they had observed no illegal activity.

At the time of the Commission's investigation, the largest after-hours club in the Sixth Precinct occupied the entire third floor of a block-long building on West 13th Street. The street floor of the same building housed a licensed bar, also catering to homosexuals, which was under the same management as the after-hours club. This club, like most others in the neighborhood, was operated openly. On weekend nights, large numbers of patrons lined up in the street outside the club to wait for the elevator to the third floor.

According to an informant, the owner of this bar paid plainclothesmen from the First Division $2,000 a month for being allowed to operate, with the understanding that no substantial action would be taken against the club, but that it would have to be "raided" occasionally. The club was indeed "raided" seven times in twelve months, with the raids consisting of plainclothesmen entering the premises and quietly arresting a handful of minor employees (porters, doormen, and the like) and seizing a few half-empty liquor bottles for evidence, all without disturbing the regular operations of the club or embarrassing its patrons. According to a witness at one of the raids, even this was too much for the manager, who yelled at one of the plainclothesmen during a raid, ''You dirty —————, after I just gave you $2,000 and you go pull this ———! I have shoved so much money down your throat and you raid me the next day!'' The witness added that the plainclothesman looked embarrassed and said nothing.

During this club's existence, the First Division received many citizen complaints about it, and additional complaints were forwarded from the SLA. Also, numerous uniformed sergeants from the Sixth Precinct filed suspected premises reports. Yet plainclothesmen from the division sent down to look into the complaints generally reported that the club was closed or that they were refused admittance.

A review of Police Department records reveals that, several days after the club was opened in mid-April of 1970, a uniformed sergeant filed a suspected premises report. Over the next six weeks, plainclothesmen sent to investigate either reported the club closed or said they had been refused admittance. On June 6, 1970, plainclothesmen finally entered the club and made several token arrests. From June 6 to June 17, they made five visits, reporting each time that the club was closed. Another raid was made on June 18. However, the police handled the raids with enough discretion to avoid interfering with the club's operations, as was evidenced by the fact that the club leased additional space, doubling its size, eleven days after the June 18 raid. Over the next two months, despite the filing of suspected premises reports by uniformed sergeants, plainclothesmen from division claimed they could find no violations. Over the following five months, they made four raids, claiming in between raids either that the club was closed or that they were refused admittance. (Despite the numerous reports of being refused entrance to the club, the division at no time attempted to get a search warrant.) During the periods when division plainclothesmen claimed that the place was closed, uniformed police and Commission investigators observed it open. And during periods when plainclothesmen claimed they were refused admittance, Commission investigators had no trouble getting in.

Eventually, the Investigation Unit of Patrol Borough Manhattan South was called to investigate. Among other things, their report on the matter cast considerable doubt on plainclothesmen's claims that they were refused admittance. The investigating officers' report stated, "The officers while entering and leaving the premises were not asked for membership cards; nor was there any evidence of security either at the door nor inside the premises proper."

After the presence of Commission investigators in the area was publicized, a reliable informant told the Commission that supervisory police officers advised the owner of the club to close down "until the heat is off," which he did. At the time of the investigation, the owner of the club had reportedly already signed the lease on new space around the corner and refurbished it as an after-hours club at a cost of $40,000.

Another unlicensed club notable for the number of policemen who frequented it, both in and out of uniform, operated equally openly and with little police interference. Arrests at this club were exceedingly amicable. On one occasion, a Commission informant was on the premises when a raid took place. Plainclothesmen mentioned to the doorman on their way in that there would be a raid that evening, and that they needed two people. They then went on upstairs to the club and ordered drinks. When they had finished drinking, they said, "Okay, let's go," and walked out with the doorman, one of the bartenders, and two half-empty bottles of liquor. A former employee who had been arrested several times said that all the raids followed the same pattern, with arrested employees being taken to court the following morning, where they pleaded guilty to "disorderly conduct."

As with most of the after-hours clubs, suspected premises reports filed on this one by uniformed men were largely ignored at division level. During one month, five reports were filed. Plainclothesmen took no action on the first four, then, after the fifth, paid a visit one night at 1:00 a.m., when they reported the bar closed. However, a uniformed sergeant who passed by two and a half hours later reported it open and operating.

Not all uniformed officers were so diligent about filing suspected premises reports, though. For example, Commission investigators observed six different patrol cars cruise past the club one night between 3:00 a.m. and 5:00 a.m. During this period, large numbers of patrons were entering and leaving, yet not one suspected premises report was filed—perhaps because uniformed men saw little point in filing reports which they knew would be ignored.

In some cases, uniformed police officers shook down afterhours clubs. One owner of such an establishment told the Commission the following story, which was later corroborated by another source. Shortly after his bar opened, the local precinct captain paid a visit and asked the owner if he was running an after-hours bar. The owner admitted he was, whereupon the captain produced a neatly typed list of payments the owner was to make to the police for the privilege of operating. Listed were captains, lieutenants, sergeants, and sector car patrolmen, with the amount to be paid to each.

Afterhours bars were not the only unlicensed premises found to make systematic payoffs to the police. Officers Phillips and Droge both testified that they, their fellow patrolmen, and in some cases, their supervisors, had accepted regular payments from bottle clubs and "juice joints."

Bottle clubs are drinking places, supposedly open only to members who bring their own liquor. In fact, most bottle clubs are open to anyone, and they sell liquor by the drink. Because they posed as private clubs, these establishments were exempt from regulation by the State Liquor Authority until 1969, when a law was passed requiring bottle clubs to register with the SLA and to obey the laws applicable to public taverns, including the curfew rules. As of late 1972, not one of the City's hundreds of bottle clubs had applied for a license from the SLA, each apparently preferring its informal "licensing" arrangements with the local police. An informant who had operated a bottle club in Brooklyn in the late sixties told the Commission that he had made biweekly payments of $30 to two sergeants, and had also made regular payments to two detectives assigned to the Youth Squad. After he stopped making payments, his club was raided and cash and liquor confiscated.

Juice joints, which are essentially unlicensed and untaxed package stores operating out of hallways or private apartments, sell liquor and wine by the bottle when licensed liquor stores are closed. Patrolman Droge testified that the daily payoffs from juice joints in one precinct where he had been assigned amounted to $10 per sector car from each establishment. The sergeants in that precinct, Droge testified, usually made their own contracts with the proprietors of juice joints.

If a juice joint is very conspicuous, an accommodation arrest may occasionally be necessary, as Patrolman Phillips explained in his testimony before the Commission. Phillips described an incident involving a very active and conspicuous juice joint in Harlem, where Phillips and his partner made an arrest one Sunday morning at 9:00 a.m. The hallway where the liquor was being sold was full of cases of whiskey, rye, gin, and wine. Phillips testified:

> "So we told him [the proprietor], 'We're going to arrest you for selling liquor in violation of the ABC laws.' So he says, 'Well, I can't go, you have to take my wife. I'm too busy.' So he says to his wife, 'Sweetie, get dressed, you're taking a pinch.'

> "So his wife got dressed and packed a little lunch and we took his wife. We also took a few hundred dollars and took liquor for evidence. So his wife went to court and pleaded guilty and [paid] a small fine and she walked out."

Comments

The most visible evidence of police toleration of illegal conditions in and around bars at the time of the investigation were the long lines of double- and triple-parked cars outside bars along the East Side avenues. Patrons of the bars were instructed to put matchbooks or menus from the bars on their dashboards. These acted, in effect, as parking permits. Patrolmen would walk along the lines of illegally-parked cars, looking at the dashboards and issuing summonses only to cars without matchbooks or menus. The bars themselves were of course immune from summonses for violations of the various laws, and those bars which permitted open prostitution, drug-pushing, gambling, and soliciting by homosexuals were left alone to pursue their lucrative operations. Unlicensed premises were permitted to operate openly, subject only to occasional token arrests.

More serious was the effect of police corruption with respect to licensed and unlicensed bars on overall law enforcement efforts. In the Nineteenth Precinct, Commission investigators were struck by the visible lack of police patrols. During the six-week period of intense surveillance, investigators rarely saw a police car on patrol west of Lexington Avenue (almost all of the bars in the precinct are east of Lexington). According to the FBI index of serious crimes for the period covering the investigation, the Nineteenth Precinct ranked fourth highest of the seventy-eight precincts then in the City in the number of crimes reported, and the third lowest in the number of arrests per 100 reported felonies. Furthermore, a high percentage of the crimes committed in this precinct, like robbery, larceny of $50 and over, and auto theft, take place outdoors, where a strong police presence would act as a powerful deterrent.

The Department has taken steps to restore uniformed men to more productive tasks by ordering that no uniformed men are to enter bars except in emergencies or for meals. This step was apparently directed not merely at corruption but also at reducing public perception of it by shifting responsibility to non-uniformed men. Plainclothesmen may enter bars only in answer to specific complaints, or to take their meals. The change in policy has apparently had limited effectiveness in curtailing bar-related corruption, as illustrated by the incident related above, in which four detectives shook down a West Side bar shortly after the change went into effect.

The laws regulating drinking establishments are so numerous and so all-encompassing that virtually every licensed premise is guilty, at least sporadically, of technical violations. Drinking places are licensed by the State Liquor Authority, which is also empowered to revoke or refuse to renew licenses, and they are subject to regulation under numerous laws including the Alcoholic Beverage Control (ABC) Law, the Administrative Code, the Building Code, and the Health Code.

The New York City Administrative Code prohibits dancing in any bar that doesn't have a cabaret license, a regulation that has led to the issuance of at least one summons to a bar in which a patron was stepping in time to the music as he put coins in a juke box. Under §106 of the ABC Law, no licensed premises may have a "screen, blind, [or] curtain" covering any part of any window on the premises; under the same section, booths, partitions, and swinging doors are also prohibited. Other commonly violated provisions of the ABC Law are those 1) prohibiting lighting too dim to permit the reading of a newspaper; 2) requiring separate sanitary facilities for men and women (violated by very small bars and by those patronized solely by men); 3) stipulating that for every three feet of bar there must be at least one seat at a table.

A licensee may be issued a summons if he "suffers or permits" certain activities among his patrons over which he may, in fact, have limited control: A bar is violating the law if its patrons use "indecent, vile or vulgar" language or if they are "disorderly." Some of the laws police officers are called on to enforce in relation to licensed premises are sound in principle but are so vague and ill-defined that they lend themselves to abuses in practice. Bars are prohibited from serving persons "under the influence of liquor," but the law in no way defines "influence." Does one drink create influence? Three? Five? In enforcing this provision of the law, the police have established no objective standard and use no objective tests, such as those given to motorists suspected of drunken driving. To confuse the issue even more, the law states that a bar is in violation if a drink is served to someone who is "apparently" under the influence. Of the nuisance laws, those most commonly mentioned by bar owners are Health Department ordinances requiring that kitchen garbage cans be covered at all times and that there be soap in the men's room.

The Commission concluded during its investigation that the interests of both the police and the public would best be served by divesting the Police Department of responsibility for enforcing these laws except in response to specific complaints. The Department has effected this change in policy, which has diminished the number of bar visits and thus cut down the opportunities for police shakedowns. The police should be removed still further from enforcing minor ordinances affecting bars by shifting such responsibility to other agencies like the SLA or the Health Department. Any corruption which may exist in such agencies is a lesser evil than corruption among policemen for the same reasons set forth above with respect to the construction industry.

Chapter Nine

SABBATH LAW

The Commission found that the New York State Sabbath Law provided the basis for one minor but widespread form of police graft. The Sabbath Law, which regulates the sale of food and other necessities on Sunday, is a complicated statute with many provisions which are routinely violated by food stores open on Sunday. The Commission found that some police officers took money from proprietors of such businesses in return for not issuing summonses for violations.

The Sabbath Law contains many provisions which, while they may have been logical at one time, seem now to have little rhyme or reason. In theory, the law provides that only necessities may be sold on Sunday; however, the law defines as "necessities" such items as beer, drugs, newspapers, flowers, gasoline, souvenirs, and cemetery monuments. Certain foodstuffs may be sold on Sundays, others may not, and still others may be sold only at certain hours. For example, the proprietor of a delicatessen may sell bread, milk, and eggs at any hour on Sunday, but he is restricted to selling prepared or cooked foods before 10:00 a.m. or between 4:00 and 7:00 p.m. Thus, he can legally sell an egg at 12:00 noon, but not egg salad. Police officers are empowered to issue summonses for violations of such provisions of the Sabbath Law, but in practice, many officers were more likely to demand $2 or $5 for not issuing a summons.

Patterns of Payoffs by Food Store Owners

One group of stores most vulnerable to police who threaten to issue summonses for violations of the Sabbath Law were delicatessens and bodegas, which are seven-day-a-week Spanish grocery stores. Bodegas were doubly vulnerable, since their proprietors frequently do not speak English fluently, were unfamiliar with the maze of provisions in the Sabbath Law, and were unlikely to know where to go to complain about shakedowns.

Every Sunday, the Commission found that many delicatessen and bodega owners paid police from $2 to $10, or the equivalent in merchandise—usually cigarettes, cold cuts, canned goods, or six-packs of beer. In effect, these payoffs amounted to a license to stay open on Sunday. Proprietors who were unwilling to pay were plagued with numerous summonses for violations of the Sabbath Law and sometimes even for unrelated violations.

On Manhattan's Upper West Side, many large supermarket chain stores stay open on Sundays, apparently unhampered by police action, although the Commission has no knowledge of any payoffs made by them except in return for daily escort service to the bank.

Payoffs to avoid summonses for violations of the Sabbath Law were collected by either the foot patrolman or the patrolmen assigned to the sector car. Thus, the total amount a police officer could make on a given Sunday depended upon the sector to which he was assigned, since one sector might have had a great many delicatessens or bodegas and another very few.

Department Response

In December, 1970, following an experiment begun in the Bronx, the Police Department issued an order to all police officers not to enforce the Sabbath Law unless a specific complaint was received or a flagrant violation was observed. In such instances, the sergeant on duty in the sector was to be responsible for correction of the violation. Two associations of bodega-owners, who had cooperated with the Commission in this investigation, said that incidents of shakedowns by police officers dropped dramatically after the new order went into effect. However, this policy has not been so successful in other areas. Shortly after the announcement of the policy change, *The New York*

Times made a survey of stores in the Times Square area which were technically in violation of the law for selling nonessential items on Sunday. Proprietors reported that the new directive had changed nothing: Although none admitted ever having been asked for a bribe, many proprietors were reported as saying that they were being served with two to four summonses each Sunday—just as they had before the Department's directive.

Comments

The effects of payments made by store owners to police for non-enforcement of the Sabbath Law are the same familiar effects of most police graft: increased public cynicism about the police and lowered police efficiency. The present Sabbath laws should be repealed as they have been in a number of states. To the extent they are retained, enforcement should not be a police function.

Chapter Ten

PARKING AND TRAFFIC

One of the pettiest but sometimes most annoying forms of police corruption involves policemen taking money in return for not issuing summonses for illegal parking or for moving violations. Generally, payoffs to permit illegal parking were made to police officers on a regular weekly or monthly pad basis, most often by businessmen wishing to park their trucks, delivery vehicles, or private automobiles illegally, or to protect their customers' illegally-parked cars. Payments to the police by motorists seeking to avoid summonses for moving violations, on the other hand, were scores, which are necessarily of a catch-as-catch-can nature.

Although the Commission felt traffic payments were but a minor part of police corruption and chose not to devote any sizable investigative effort to the matter, it received a flood of complaints from citizens indicating that traffic payoffs are a subject of wide interest. And the staggering number of illegally-parked cars passed over by policemen issuing summonses bears silent witness to the prevalence of selective enforcement.

Patterns of Payoffs by Motorists

New York City has a system of stringent parking regulations, combined with extremely high parking fines, and the two taken together offer strong temptations to corruption. In most of midtown Manhattan, there is no parking or standing permitted between 8:00 a.m. and 6:00 p.m., and violators' cars may be towed away. Once a car has been towed off by the police, getting it back involves paying a $50 towing charge in addition to the amount on the summons, which is usually $25.

Enforcement of the parking laws is primarily the responsibility of officers assigned to sector cars in each precinct and of the citywide

Parking Enforcement Squad. These officers sometimes collected regular pad payments from people whose businesses would be hurt if they or their customers received parking tickets. One example was the payoffs made by bar owners to police to insure that patrons' cars could double- and triple-park with impunity. Other payors included construction companies and businesses which must make pick-ups and deliveries in congested areas like midtown Manhattan, which includes the garment district where streets are customarily choked with delivery trucks. In addition, some smaller companies used unlicensed or otherwise unqualified drivers during rush seasons and were therefore doubly susceptible to police demands for money.

Many companies carried on their books accounts entitled "Traffic Expense" or "Delivery Expense," which covered illicit payments to the police. In the case of one company whose books were inspected by the Commission this amounted to regular entries of several hundred dollars a month.

An employee of one major trucking firm, which did not pay off the police, told the Commission that his company paid between $48,000 and $60,000 a year in parking fines. By way of contrast, a Commission informant reported that another company, a large air freight concern, paid the police $15,000 a year—a staggering amount, but a substantial saving over the amount paid in fines by the other trucking company.

The Commission was inundated by allegations of parking pads at a less exalted level, of which the following are examples:

— The owner of a vending machine company in Queens told the Commission he paid the local sector car $5 a week so that he could park his truck in front of the shop.

— An ambulance service paid $10 a week to four patrolmen so that it could double-park ambulances in front of its office, according to a complainant who had audited the company's books.

— A university official received bills from a limousine company, which included a surcharge of $2 per car. When he called the company to question the bill, he was told that the police in Manhattan regularly demand money from limousine drivers waiting to pick up clients, and that the company added a $2 charge on all calls to Manhattan to cover this expense.

— A Greenwich Village storekeeper, who refused to make weekly payments to a local sergeant who approached him, complained to the Commission that he received summonses regularly for parking his truck on a sidewalk where other businessmen's trucks were parked with impunity.

— The owner of a chain of six parking garages near Madison Square Garden told a Commission consultant that he had been paying the police $100 per garage per week—a total of $600 a week—until the Commission's public hearings began. At that point, he said the police raised the price to $800 a week on the grounds that it had become more dangerous for them to overlook violations.

— Numerous informants, including at least two cab drivers, reported that yellow cab fleets paid in return for being permitted to park their cabs on "no parking" streets and sidewalks.

The public's resentment of the parking problem is aggravated by the fact that the police are among the City's worst offenders, routinely parking their personal cars in "no parking" zones, including tow-away areas, under circumstances indicating that no job-related reason exists. Policemen's justification for ignoring parking ordinances is that the City has agreed to "make every effort to provide parking spaces" for policemen, but that there are not an adequate number near the station houses.

In the case of moving violations, as opposed to illegal parking, police corruption takes the form of scores. In New York State, repeated moving violations can result in loss of license. Because of this, motorists, particularly those whose livelihood depends on having a driver's license—like taxi drivers, truck drivers or salesmen—are often eager to pay officers to overlook violations, real or imagined. The ten dollar bill folded in a license is a common but impossible-to-prove fact of life, the extent of which can only be speculated upon.

If the motorist made no overture, the policeman sometimes would. One example of this occurred in the Bronx in August of 1970. Two policemen in a radio car stopped a motorist who had just made a U-turn and told him that they would overlook the violation if he "showed his appreciation." At this point, the incident became highly atypical when the motorist, claiming that he had no money with him, made a date for a subsequent meeting with the officers and reported the incident to the borough commander. The meeting was held and $15 was exchanged. As a result, both officers were convicted of official misconduct, and one of them was also convicted of receiving a bribe.

An even more picayune attempt at soliciting money from a motorist was made on a member of the Commission staff one afternoon in Queens, when her car's motor died in heavy traffic. A passing radio car stopped and the policemen in it offered to push her car to the nearest gas station for $5. She politely declined and the officers just as politely wished her luck and drove off.

Another kind of traffic-related corruption involves straightforward payment for services rendered. An investigation conducted by the Department of Investigation into several rental car companies revealed that they made regular payments to Police Department personnel who provided them with daily copies of the Department's stolen-car lists including the names and addresses of the cars' owners. The companies would then solicit the owners' business, offering them special rates. Records reflecting this practice were received from the Department of Investigation which, faced with Fifth Amendment claims by car rental officials, was unable to make any criminal cases.

The Commission also received several complaints, which tended to corroborate each other, that members of the Hack Bureau of the Police Department, which regulates taxis and taxi drivers, charged drivers and owners under-the-table fees. The schedule of payments was reported to be $20 for seeing that violations were overlooked, $2 for insuring that taxis passed inspections, and $15 to expedite the transfer of medallions. Reportedly, employees of one insurance company which specializes in insuring taxis instructed owners to put $15 in a sealed envelope and hand it to the lieutenant in charge when they went to the bureau to transfer a medallion.

Comments

Under current laws, in order to facilitate the movement of traffic, no parking whatsoever is permitted at certain hours in areas like midtown Manhattan, which includes some streets which have extremely light traffic. This is clearly unrealistic, and gives the police something of an excuse for enforcing the laws only sporadically and ineffectively.

Parking laws are generally designed to serve valid public purposes, such as facilitating traffic flow and insuring access to hydrants, and should be enforced for the public good, regardless of their unpopularity. Where the laws are unreasonable—for example, the prohibition against all parking and standing in certain areas—they simply invite violations and give the police an excuse for enforcing them only selectively and ineffectively.

The Police Department has claimed that parking enforcement must be selective, because they simply don't have the manpower to ticket all the illegally-parked cars in the City. That may or may not be true, but in any case it is clear that police performance in this area could be dramatically improved.

If the laws were changed to make them more realistic than current ones, part of the parking problem and its attendant corruption would be solved. Another part could be solved by announcing a crackdown on illegally-parked cars and really holding sergeants accountable for the performance of their men, as the Department has announced it is trying to do in the Neighborhood Police Teams. If the Department really means business, a sergeant will be held responsible for controlling illegal parking in his sector and subject to discipline if he allows it to get out of hand. He, in turn, can be expected to prevent the men under him from taking payments for not enforcing parking ordinances.

As for payments to police officers for overlooking moving violations, the Commission feels that motorists are often the instigators of such bribes and should be arrested. If the Department vigorously pursues its policy of arresting those who offer money to police officers, the practice will be much diminished. If such a policy is pursued, the Department should make every effort to obtain corroborative evidence —such as tape-recordings—that a bribery attempt was indeed made.

A more subtle effect of police corruption and consequent inefficiency in enforcing parking regulations is the cynicism engendered in the citizenry when they see police automobiles parked next to signs reading "No PARKING ANY TIME—TOWAWAY ZONE" in one block, and then encounter policemen towing away civilian cars a block away. This situation could be somewhat alleviated simply by adding the legend "POLICE VEHICLES ONLY" to signs in front of precinct houses.

Chapter Eleven

TOW TRUCKS

When an automobile accident occurs and a car sustains enough damage to require the services of a tow truck, patrolmen at the scene may receive payments from the tow-truck driver. This practice, as uncovered by the Commission's investigation, has remained virtually unchanged since 1960, when a series of articles in the now defunct *New York Journal-American* exposed the same pattern. As a result of that scandal, several dozen police officers were transferred and reprimanded and a deputy inspector was suspended from the force, but the practice of tow-truck drivers making payoffs to police officers was found to have continued.

Reasons for Payoffs by Tow-Truck Companies

Towing wrecks is not in itself lucrative enough to warrant payoffs to the police. In fact, the charge for towing cars is regulated by law and generally would not even cover the cost of the customary payment to police.*

However, repairing wrecks, especially badly damaged recent-model wrecks, is an extremely profitable business, and since the garage to which such wrecks are first towed generally gets the repair business, the competition for towing damaged cars is fierce among the 650 licensed towing companies in the City.

This competition takes the form of a great race among tow-truck drivers to be the first to arrive at the scene of an accident and sign up the customer. To get there first, some tow trucks career through City streets, often disregarding stop signs, one-way signs, and red lights. Some companies also seek to gain an edge over their competitors by installing illegal police-band radios in their trucks so that they can be first on the scene, sometimes reaching accident sites even before the police.

---

* The rate for towing cars is $5 for preparing the car for towing and $4 for the first mile plus $1 a mile thereafter.

The Commission found that, for wreckers who paid off, the police usually overlooked such violations of the law. They also overlooked the operator's using high-pressure sales tactics on owners who were sometimes injured, dazed or drunk, in spite of the fact that towing companies are prohibited by law from soliciting business at the scene of an accident. On occasion, policemen even interceded when a tow-truck driver was having difficulty signing up a recalcitrant driver. They would then warn the driver that he was liable to a summons for obstructing traffic or that if the vehicle was not towed away, it might be vandalized during the night by spare-parts scavengers. Many companies insist on getting the owner to sign an authorization for the repair work while at the scene. In this case also, a policeman might be instrumental in touting the attributes of the particular tow-truck company involved. One such instance reported to the Commission was the case of a driver who refused to let the towing company sign him up on the spot. His position changed quickly when the policeman reminded him that he could be issued summonses for drunken driving and for driving without a license.

For these services, the Commission found that the two radio car patrolmen whose car was directed to the scene by the police dispatcher commonly received $20, although they sometimes picked up more later if they went to the garage and found that the towing company did indeed get authorization for an expensive repair job. On occasion, when a police officer saw an accident before it had been broadcast over the police radio, he would go to a pay phone and call a tow-truck company himself, in which case he received $20, $30 or more from the company.

The Investigation

In December, 1970, the Commission received a complaint from a tow-truck operator named George Burkert that he and others were being shaken down by the police. He agreed to help the Commission gather evidence to confirm his allegations under an arrangement whereby he would never offer money to policemen and would stall those who asked him for money, telling them that he needed to get it from his boss, and then he would set up a subsequent meeting. Afterwards, he would notify Commission investigators, who would equip him with a transmitter, observe the rendezvous and monitor and record all conversations. Under this arrangement, clear evidence was gathered of a number of payoffs to police officers.

At the first of these incidents another driver, who worked the day shift for the same garage as Burkert, was stopped by police officers while he was towing a wrecked new car in the Fifth Precinct in lower Manhattan. The officers apparently asked the driver for $30. The tow-truck operator, who knew that Burkert was working with the Commission, told the officers that he had no money with him and made arrangements for them to meet with Burkert the following night.

Burkert, wearing a transmitter and observed by Commission agents, drove in his tow-truck to the rendezvous point, where he found a police car waiting for him. After he stopped his truck, an officer from the car came over to him and, after some desultory conversation, Burkert handed him $30, which he accepted.

A month later, when Burkert responded to an accident in Long Island City and received permission from the owner of the car for the tow job, he was approached by an officer who wanted to be ''taken care of'' on the spot. Burkert explained that he would have to speak to his boss and the police officer arranged to telephone him later. The officer did call and set up a meeting, at which time Burkert, again wired and observed, gave him $10, an unusually low sum, in an attempt to elicit some conversation about amounts. The only such conversation that followed consisted of the officer referring to Burkert's boss as ''a stiff.''

On a third occasion, when Burkert was approached by police as he was preparing to tow a car, he again set up a subsequent meeting and kept the date, accompanied as usual by a microphone and two Commission agents. At the meeting he told the police that he didn't know if his shop was going to be given authorization to make repairs on the automobile, and no money changed hands. The officer apparently resented not being paid off and issued a summons to Burkert the following day. Through another policeman, word was passed to Burkert that the resentful officer wanted $100 from the driver "to be friends." Burkert met with the officer and, in a conversation which was, as usual, recorded by Commission agents, negotiated the $100 friendship payment down to $25, which he paid to the officer.

On still another occasion, Burkert was approached at the site of a tow job by a police officer asking for money. The customary arrangements were made for a meeting the following night at a location suggested by the officers: the corner of 67th Street and Lexington Avenue, next to the Nineteenth Precinct station house. Shortly after the tow truck arrived on the corner a police car pulled up and a sergeant asked Burkert, "You got it?", whereupon the driver handed him $30.

This meeting took place during a shift change at the precinct, at which time there were a large number of policemen milling around on the sidewalk. The meeting was filmed in its entirety by a hidden camera, as well as being observed and recorded by Commission agents.

The patrolmen who took the payoff saw the film truck and later telephoned Burkert to give him a cover story to use in the event of an investigation. (The patrolman said the story had been concocted with the aid of the precinct's PBA delegate.) This and subsequent telephone calls made to discuss the matter were recorded by Commission agents who arranged to be with Burkert when the calls were made. During the conversation Burkert pointed out that the corner where they exchanged the money may not have been the best place for the meeting:

> Burkert: ". . . That was kind of a bad spot for you to tell me to meet you in the first place."
> Officer: "What, over there?"
> Burkert: "By the precinct, where there's cops all over the place?"

Officer: "The cops are nothing. You know what we should have done? We should have taken you right into the station house."

Burkert: "The cops are nothing?"

Officer: "Well, that's the easiest. Cops you never worry about."

These instances and other similar ones monitored by Commission investigators certainly indicate that shaking down tow-truck drivers was a prevalent practice in New York, and one that was tolerated even by officers not themselves involved.* Both Patrolman Phillips and Patrolman Droge testified that they had received payments from towing companies in circumstances similar to those outlined above. Their testimony also corroborated the amounts and methods of meeting to receive payments that the Commission found in its surveillances. In addition, Patrolman Droge testified that the police harass trucks belonging to companies which don't pay by strict enforcement of the laws regulating tow trucks. Patrolman Logan testified that, although he had never received payments from tow-truck operators, he knew of the practice.

Comments

When police payoffs are made by towing companies, those companies are left free to harass and browbeat motorists who have been involved in accidents, often signing them up at the scene for repair work which will be billed at rates inflated at least enough to cover the payoffs.

A second result of such payments is that the immunity from traffic summonses conferred on certain tow-truck drivers allows them to drive around the City in a manner dangerous to other motorists and pedestrians.

The business of towing automobiles is one where adequate and reasonable laws and regulations are already in effect. Curtailing the practices outlined above is simply a matter of police will and diligence.

* Burkert was indicted, following the hearings, by a federal grand jury to which he had repeated testimony about an experience occurring before his involvement with the Commission relating to an incident involving alleged harassment by police officers in connection with some traffic tickets. In July, 1972, his trial ended in a hung jury. The retrial is pending.

Chapter Twelve

RETRIEVING SEIZED AUTOMOBILES FROM THE POLICE

The Commission found that payoffs were being made to policemen assigned to the Property Clerk's office and to the Police Department's automobile storage yards by field representatives of one of the nation's largest automobile finance companies. The payments were made for "information and assistance" in gaining release of automobiles which had been seized during the commission of crimes and held as evidence. The automobiles involved were ones on which the buyers had stopped making payments, and which the finance company was seeking to repossess.

The company also made $5 and $10 payments to policemen on patrol for assistance in recovering automobiles from the streets, mainly in ghetto neighborhoods.

Payments to Policemen at City Auto Storage Yards

The legal methods available to a finance company seeking to gain custody of cars in City pounds are elaborate and can be extremely time-consuming if followed to the letter of the law. And, since most cars finance companies seek to repossess are expensive late models which depreciate rapidly, there is a substantial dollar saving in repossessing them as quickly as possible. This saving more than covers the cost of bribing personnel at the storage lots for expediting matters.

Roughly a third of the sixty or so employees in one finance company's repossession unit were former New York City policemen. The company's files, which were subpoenaed by the Commission, indicated that money had been paid to policemen for aiding in the recovery of twenty-one out of thirty-nine cars retrieved from City pounds in an eleven-month period. The amounts paid ranged from $25 to $100, with most payments in the neighborhood of $45 to $55, for a total of $1,267.50. In nineteen of the twenty-one cases, the payments were made by one ex-police officer, who was described by his boss as a specialist in getting cars out of the pounds. The most common reasons given for the payments in company records were "Assistance" or "Information and Assistance," although one came right out and said "Reward." Another benefit which the company received in return for its payments was that the usual City storage charges of $5 per day were often waived. One note made to explain a $100 payment reads, "Car was impounded by NYC Police and stored since Dec. 11th at $5.00 per day—for a total of $385.00—was able to secure car with assistance and release without paying the storage of $385.00 for the sum of $100.00." In another incident, when $100 was paid, the company saved some $1800 in storage charges: "Obtained this release to get car from the Pound where it was stored for about a year (without storage charges)."

Because witnesses invoked the Fifth Amendment, the Commission could get no direct testimonial evidence that all or even part of the money listed in company records was ever actually paid to police officers. However, the former manager of a City branch of the company testified in executive session that he had found that the only way to get cars back quickly in New York was to pay the police to expedite recovery of the cars. He said that the payments had risen since 1965, when he first came to the City and made about twelve payments of $3 to $5 himself, to the current figure of around $50. The current manager of another City branch also admitted knowledge of the practice.

The Commission found no evidence that other large automobile finance companies made similar cash payments to the police. One reason for this may be that the company which did pay off has a more lenient policy toward financing cars bought by residents of poor areas and, consequently, has more unpaid-for cars seized as evidence in criminal cases.

A sergeant who was at one time in charge of the Brooklyn Automobile Storage Yard was recently found guilty of accepting $50 from a citizen to expedite recovery of his car. This charge in no way involved a finance company but it does indicate that the finance company we investigated was not alone in paying police to hasten recovery of automobiles from the yards.

Payments to Precinct Patrolmen

According to a Commission informant employed by the automobile finance company in question, all automobile finance companies in the City paid $5 or $10 to patrolmen, sergeants, and lieutenants at the precinct level for help in locating a car they sought to repossess and for standing by while their agent broke into the car and drove it away (an activity which might well have attracted the police if they had not been notified that the agent was from a finance company and entitled to repossess the car for nonpayment).

On other occasions, agents of the repossession unit paid a token sum to police officers to overlook the fact that they did not have the proper papers drawn up for repossession.

In a third situation, repossession agents sometimes need to trespass onto private property (a driveway or a parking garage) in order to repossess a car, and in this case they have been known to pay police officers to overlook the fact that they did not have the necessary papers. In one such instance, two repossession agents had snapped the lock on a car and were preparing to drive it away when the car's owner appeared. He called the police, and when several officers responded, the owner demanded that they arrest the repossession agents. The agents were taken to the precinct house and a call was made to a retired policeman employed by the repossession unit. He went to the precinct house and reportedly paid five hundred dollars to the lieutenant on duty, after which the agents were released and no charges were pressed against them.

Comments

As is the case with respect to many businesses where paying police is customary, the custom can be substantially curtailed, if not stopped, if the businessman is willing. During the Commission's executive hearings into this matter, a letter went out over the signature of an executive vice-president of the finance company which paid police at the auto storage yards. It was sent to all the company's field representatives and instructed them that payments to government officials "are not to be made under any circumstances."

Chapter Thirteen

INTRADEPARTMENTAL PAYMENTS

According to every police officer who cooperated with the Commission, it was common practice for policemen to make payments to each other for services rendered, ranging from the payment of a couple of dollars for typing up arrest reports to the payment of hundreds of dollars for choice assignments.

In any large organization a certain amount of favoritism is bound to exist, but generally it does not progress to the point where favors are routinely bought and sold, as was the case in the Police Department. A likely explanation for intradepartmental gratuities is that the system permitted officers assigned to desk jobs to share in the profits realized by those in the more lucrative outside jobs. For example, as Officer Phillips explained, when a plaincothesman vouchered many thousands of dollars found in a raid, the officers at the precinct assumed that he kept back a goodly sum for himself and expected a tip of at least a few dollars. This practice wreaked a genuine hardship on honest officers, who had to pay out of their own pockets to get things typed. The Commission heard numerous allegations of police officers paying other officers to handle routine work. In the course of the various investigations, investigators encountered considerable specific evidence of this practice, of which the following are typical.

Payment for Paperwork: Police duties often involve a good deal of paperwork, ranging from evidence vouchers, complaints and arrest reports, which must be filled out in special form with numerous copies, to requests for departmental recognition. Sergeant Durk told the Commission that it was standard practice, citywide, for an arresting officer to pay $5 to the desk officer and $2 or $3 to the clerical man for each gambling arrest. On the arrest of a prostitute, payments were $2 to the desk officer and $1 to the clerical man. When an arresting officer brings in evidence connected with an arrest, it must be vouchered, which in the case of a large number of bills means that the serial number of each must be listed—obviously, a laborious process—and the desk officer's assistant, who is called the 124 man, is given the job. According to Sergeant Durk, the 124 man was also given a couple of dollars to expedite matters.

When a police officer feels he has done an outstanding bit of police work, he will often put in a request for a departmental citation, which must be typed up in a special form. Patrolman Droge testified that it was customary for the clerical man to receive $5 for this service, but he pointed out that the clerical man "probably would type it up for you whether you gave him $5 or not, but it would certainly be expedited if $5 were included." However, he went on to tell of the first time he gave a request for recognition to a clerical man to be typed, when he had been on the force only six weeks and had not yet learned that the clerical man should be tipped: "When I handed in the scratch copy with no $5 . . . there was no recommendation. There was no interview. It was never sent in."

Payment for Temporary Assignments: The roll call man in each precinct is in charge of making temporary assignments, designating men to fill in for others who are on vacation, out sick, or in court. He was routinely paid $5 or so by patrolmen in exchange for plum assignments, particularly for lucrative ones like riding in a sector car. Patrolman Phillips paid one roll call man $25 for a week's assignment to an unmarked car, and both Droge and Logan stated that the practice of paying for temporary assignments was a common one. Payments were also made for getting one's choice of days off and of vacation dates. Phillips testified that the roll call man in a busy precinct could make $200 a month in this way.

Payment for Permanent Assignments: The Commission heard numerous allegations from policemen that in some precincts, police officers bought permanent assignments from the administrative lieutenant for various amounts, commonly $500. Some officers were confident that lieutenants on occasion would split this money with precinct commanders.

The Commission also heard numerous unsubstantiated rumors that appointment as a detective could be bought for a price which ranged from $500 to $2,000. While working for the Commission, Patrolman Phillips at one point contacted a policeman serving as a high police official's chauffeur to discuss the possibility of buying his way into detectives. While wearing a transmitter, Phillips held several conversations with this patrolman, who told him that the usual price was $500, but that since Phillips had once been a detective and had been demoted, the price for him would be $1,000. The proposed transfer could not be pursued because it would have conflicted with Phillips' other undercover activities.

Buying Medical Discharges: The Commission received several allegations that in the past police officers have bribed certain police surgeons to certify that they were permanently disabled, making it possible for those officers to retire early and receive all or part of their pensions. One doctor, a former police surgeon who has been retired for twenty years, told the Commission that surgeons took such kickbacks when he was in the Department, and that he believed the practice still to be in existence. The Commission was unable to corroborate these allegations.

A number of high-ranking police officers have in recent years received disability retirements only to take civilian jobs as arduous as those they left. Officers who retire with disability pensions, who later get paying jobs, may technically have their pensions reduced or eliminated. However, an officer at the Pension Unit told the Commission that this is never done—a policy which might encourage fraudulent disability retirements. This practice is, of course, not necessarily the result of bribery.

An encouraging sign that current attitudes may be better than those reported in the past was the action of the current chief surgeon who, when serving as a police surgeon in late 1970, turned in a patrol-man for attempting to bribe him, and the patrolman was suspended without pension.

Sale of Information: Patrolman Phillips testified that police officers would on occasion sell each other information to be used in blackmailing criminals. This most often happened among plainclothes-men, when one of them had information on a criminal outside his jurisdiction, in which case he would sell the information to another plainclothesman who had jurisdiction, and the plainclothesman who had bought the information would then use it to make a score.

On one occasion, Phillips reported to the Commission that he had just been approached by two plainclothesmen who used an illegal wire recorder to bug pay telephones in an effort to get information on gamblers. When they had the information, they would threaten the gambler with arrest and score him. In this fashion, the officers had obtained information on a bookmaking operation outside their division and were seeking to sell it to Phillips. Under Commission surveillance, Phillips bargained with them about buying the information and about buying recording equipment from them. Since the Commission's investigation was drawing to a close the deals were never consummated.

Comments

Payments like those made to the clerical man, roll call man, desk officer, and the 124 man (the desk officer's assistant) should be easier to eliminate than corruption on the street because they take place in the station house in full view of many supervisory officers, and because the amounts are usually small.

The practice of buying assignments poses a more serious and difficult problem, but one which the Department's announced policy of accountability could go a long way toward solving. The commander of a precinct is directly responsible for the assignment of his men, and where the commander is both honest and conscientious the problem need not arise.

Chapter Fourteeen

GRATUITIES

By far the most widespread form of misconduct the Commission found in the Police Department was the acceptance by police officers of gratuities in the form of free meals, free goods, and cash payments. Almost all policemen either solicited or accepted such favors in one form or another, and the practice was widely accepted by both the police and the citizenry, with many feeling that it wasn't corruption at all, but a natural perquisite of the job.

Free Meals

The most universally accepted gratuity was the free meal offered to policemen by luncheonettes, restaurants, bars, and hotels. Despite the Commission's announced lack of interest in investigating instances of police free meals, investigators found it impossible to avoid noticing such instances while going about their private affairs or while engaged in investigating more serious matters.

Early in his administration Commissioner Murphy took a strong stand with respect to such freeloading and stirred up a good deal of animosity among rank and file policemen by inveighing against even a free cup of coffee.

The Commissioner's position was somewhat undermined by his handling of what was undoubtedly the most highly publicized free meal served to a New York policeman in recent years. Assistant Chief Inspector Albert Seedman—in March of 1972 when he was under active consideration for the post of Chief of Detectives—hosted a dinner for his wife and another couple at the New York Hilton. The bill for dinner, which came to $84.30 including tip, was picked up by the hotel. When the check for this meal was discovered by Commission investigators during the course of a routine investigation, a Commission attorney immediately brought it to the attention of Seedman, who had in the meantime been appointed the Chief of Detectives. Chief Seedman then explained that the hotel management had invited him to dine in return for performing a security check for the hotel—a service normally provided by the police at no charge. This information was turned over on a confidential basis to Commissioner Murphy, who relieved Chief Seedman of his command pending an inquiry.

A week later the Commissioner released a statement outlining a version of the affair which was significantly different from the one Chief Seedman had given our staff attorney. While he originally had ascribed the free meal (including tip) to an invitation from the hotel in specific recognition of services rendered, the statement released by the Commissioner indicated that he had gone with his friends to the hotel fully expecting to pay for the meal, had simply made "no fuss" when the management failed to present a bill, and had covered his embarrassment by leaving a "large tip." Having accepted Chief Seedman's revised version of the affair, Commissioner Murphy restored him to command of the division, announcing that he had committed no "serious wrongdoing".

This incident had a significant effect on the already cynical attitude of many policemen. It was difficult for police officers to take seriously Commissioner Murphy's stern warnings against receiving "any buck but a pay check," when they apparently did not apply to one of the Commissioner's top aides. Several police officers commented wryly to Commission investigators that at last a meaningful guideline had been established for free meals: "It's okay—up to $84.30."

In fact, of course, the average patrolman was found to eat nowhere near that well. Free meals were indeed available to almost all policemen throughout the City, but patrolmen rarely dined in style. Every patrolman knew which establishments on his beat provided free meals, and these were the places where he lunched each day. Uniformed

policemen generally ate modest-priced meals in cafeterias, luncheonettes, restaurants, bars, or in the employee cafeterias of hotels.
Commission employees observed countless uniformed patrolmen eating
in such establishments, then leaving without paying and sometimes
without even leaving a tip. Most often, no bill was even presented.

Many thousands of free meals were consumed by policemen each
day and the sheer numbers created problems for the most popular
eateries. Some luncheonettes which did a particularly heavy police
business either offered a discount or charged policemen a token fee,
most commonly $.50.

It was not only the policeman on patrol who felt that his lunches
should be provided free. Numerous examples were reported to the
Commission of officers in the station house sending radio cars to local
restaurants to pick up meals for police officers whose duties prevented
them from getting out on the street.

Nor were take-out orders always limited to food. Patrolman
Phillips testified that it was not uncommon for policemen assigned to
a radio car to pick up a "flute"—a Coke bottle filled with liquor—
which they would deliver to the station house. In most instances,
however, take-out orders involved the same sort of low-priced meals
obtained by police officers on patrol. The Commission obtained a list
used in one precinct house apparently setting out the dates on which
certain eating places were to be approached for sandwiches, pizza,
and other food to go.

The owner of one home-delivery food business which sold $2.00
fried chicken dinners found that his dinners were so popular with
the police in his local precinct that they were ordering eighty to ninety
dinners a week from him. This was substantially cutting into his
profits, so he decided to start charging the police a nominal price of
$.50 per dinner. This angered the police, who began issuing summonses
to his delivery cars on every trip they made, resulting in $600 in sum-

monses in one week. The owner called the Police Commissioner's office and explained his problem, and soon afterwards, he stopped receiving summonses. However, he had already dropped the $.50 charge per dinner.

Not all patrolmen were as restrained as the general run, and some were observed eating in rather fashionable establishments. Two patrolmen in particular confronted Commission investigators with a situation difficult to ignore by pulling up nightly to the back entrance of a fairly high-priced downtown restaurant located directly under the windows of the Commission's offices. The officers were served in their car by a uniformed waiter with a tray and a napkin draped over one arm.

Non-uniformed officers generally ordered less modest meals than uniformed patrolmen. Plainclothesmen, detectives, and high-level officers, who worked in civilian clothes instead of the conspicuous blue uniform, patronized a much wider selection of restaurants than the uniformed force, including many clearly in the luxury category. And the meals they ordered were often grandiose compared with the cafeteria-style food favored by uniformed men.

William Phillips, when assigned as a detective in a midtown precinct, regularly patronized, with other detectives, the very best restaurants, where he received gratis what he called ''electric-chair meals.'' He reported that as he sipped the last drop of brandy after an enormous feast all he could think was ''pull the switch, I'm ready to go!'' Free meals of this sort, which in Phillips' case could add up to hundreds of dollars in one week, obviously presented a more serious but much less frequently encountered problem than the hot dog traditionally demanded by a patrolman from a vendor.

The owner of one of New York's finest French restaurants reported to the Commission that he was approached by policemen demanding free dinners. When he flatly turned them down, they took retaliatory action: The restaurant was located on a street where parking was illegal before 7:00 P.M., and the police began showing up every night at 6:55 to tow away cars belonging to patrons.

The Commission discovered that there was a certain etiquette among police officers concerning free meals in restaurants. In most precincts an officer could not eat free in a restaurant on another man's beat without first getting his permission. Officers also tried to time their free meals for restaurants' slow periods, to avoid taking up tables which might otherwise be used by paying customers. And thoughtful policemen in at least one precinct installed a wall chart containing a box for each eatery in the precinct, where officers made an appropriate entry every time they had a free meal, the idea being to keep track of the police traffic and spread the burden fairly. Also, some restaurants offered free meals only to officers in a position to do them a favor in return. At one luncheonette in the Bronx where a Commission attorney was dining with his wife, the waitress took a patrolman's order for food to go, then went to the manager and asked, "We don't charge him, do we?" The manager took one look at the officer and said, "You can charge that bastard as much as you like. It's only the ones from the Forty-Seventh [that we take care of]."

Hotels

The Commission's interest turned to hotels after a former hotel security officer came in with hotel records indicating that at least one hotel was paying off police in free meals, free rooms, and cash payments at Christmas. Commission investigators then interviewed security officers and general managers at ten major hotels in the City, all of whom flatly denied giving gratuities in any form to the police.

The Commission's next step was to subpoena personnel and records reflecting police gratuities from seven large hotels, two of which were among those questioned earlier. The result was a paper flood of meal checks, meal tickets, room records and hotel logs. An initial examination of these records showed that large numbers of policemen—as well as other public officials—were receiving gratuities from hotels, chiefly in the form of free meals. This practice was described in detail by security directors and managers who this time were subpoenaed for testimony under oath.

The pattern of free meals that emerged was similar to that the Commission had found in independent restaurants, with patrolmen generally eating in the hotels' employee dining rooms, coffee shops, or less expensive restaurants, and higher-ranking officers ordering lavish meals in the hotels' more expensive restaurants.

Records from several of the hotels showed that they each fed as many as 300 to 400 meals a month to policemen in their employee dining rooms, mostly to patrolmen in uniform. The value of these meals was usually under $2.00 each. To get free meals in the employee dining rooms, the policemen generally went to the security office, where their uniforms—or in the case of non-uniformed officers, their shields —served as identification. They were either asked to sign the meal checks or hotel logs with their names and ranks or were given meal tickets to be turned in in the dining rooms. When the names given in the hotel checks and logs were checked against the precinct rosters, a sizable percentage of them proved to be false (including two uniformed officers identifying themselves as Whitman Knapp and Sydney Cooper, who was then chief of the Department's anti-corruption force).

In these same hotels, higher-ranking officers (sergeants, detectives, inspectors, lieutenants, captains, and one chief inspector) ate in the hotels' better restaurants, ordering the most expensive items on the menu, with the tab rarely coming to less than $20 per person in the larger midtown hotels. And the volume was substantial: over $500 a month at most hotels checked and $1,500 a month at the Statler-Hilton.

Hotels also were found to provide free rooms to police officers upon request. The ostensible reason for this was usually that the officer lived out of town and had to be in court early the following morning. In practice, however, policemen often took rooms when they were neither on official business nor scheduled to make a court appearance the following day. Occasionally, a group of them would book a free room for an afternoon in order to watch an important ball game on the TV provided by the hotel.

Free Drinks

In the course of its investigation into bars, Commission investigators could not help but observe numerous uniformed police officers imbibing free drinks—both on duty and off. Bar owners and policemen also told the Commission that it was common practice for bars to offer free drinks to policemen.

As discussed above in Chapter Eight, three patrol sergeants in the Nineteenth Precinct regularly spent their entire tours going from one bar to another. While the behavior of patrolmen was less extreme, there was plenty of drinking on duty and off by them, too, with no evidence of any attempt by superiors to stop it. One example of a superior's laisser-faire attitude occurred in the presence of Commission investigators at an East Side bar. Three patrolmen, in uniform and on duty, were in the bar, one drinking a mixed drink, one a beer, and one coffee. The uniformed sergeant for the sector, who was on patrol and theoretically responsible for supervising the patrolmen, entered the bar, stayed for five minutes, then left. The patrolmen continued to drink during and after his visit.

Christmas Payments

Payments to police at Christmas by bars, restaurants, hotels, department stores, and other retail businesses have long been a police tradition. Although the Department has made efforts to halt the practice, at the time of the investigation it still continued. A particularly rigorous campaign was waged against the practice in December of 1971, with the reported result that officers collected their Christmas gratuities in January, after the campaign was over.

Christmas money was usually collected in a fairly organized fashion. Early in December, lists were made up at many precinct houses, division headquarters, and squad rooms, on which were entered the names of all the businesses in their jurisdiction from which the police expected Christmas payments. The list was then divided up among the various officers, each of whom was to go to the businesses on his list and collect. He either collected a flat fee to be divided up later at the station house by participating officers, or he presented a list, broken down to include the various officers.

Patrolman Phillips described how Christmas graft was collected when he was a detective in the Seventeenth Precinct some years ago:

"Well, Christmas was an organized operation, and the squad clerical men had the master Christmas list, which was kept locked up at all times. Each detective at Christmas time was given a list of between ten and fifteen establishments. The money was all brought in. It was divided equally among all the detectives in the squad. The lieutenant and sergeant had their own Christmas list. They did not participate in ours."

When asked how long the master list was, Patrolman Phillips said, "it was quite a long list, ten or fifteen yellow pages . . . [it contained] every hotel, almost every bar, every cabaret, and other business establishments in the Seventeenth Precinct." He said that the Christmas pad came to $400 or $500 per man in that precinct, not counting individual payments, which usually added another $200 or so. Phillips also reported that specific amounts were set aside for transmittal to higher ranking supervisors, right up to the Chief of Detectives. The Commission was unable to verify whether the money was actually transmitted.

The Christmas lists presented to hotels in particular were quite detailed, giving amounts to be paid to police officers of all ranks, up to and including the borough commander and Chief Inspector. (Again, the Commission obtained no direct proof that these monies were ever actually received by the officers named on the lists.) One Christmas list obtained from a large hotel set forth specific amounts to be given to each of the detectives assigned to the squad with jurisdiction over that hotel.

While lists of this sort reflected a practice as widespread as it was long-standing, the lists themselves could not always be accepted on face value since, as in the case of the detective list, they often reflected proposed rather than actual payments. During the Commission hearings the lieutenant in charge of the detective squad mentioned above requested and was given the opportunity to testify that he had never received the payment reflected on the list and the hotel personnel who provided the list acknowledged that not all payments on it were actually accepted.

The giving of gratuities to high-level police officers was a common practice. Former Chief Inspector Sanford Garelik acknowledged in executive testimony before the Commission that, as a field commander, he had received gratuities from businessmen with whom he came in contact in the course of his duties. Instead of returning these gifts or asking that they not be sent, he stated that he attempted to respond by giving return gifts of equal value.

Free Merchandise and Other Gifts

A number of merchants gave policemen gifts for services rendered and free merchandise. These included such items as free packages of cigarettes solicited by policemen from tobacco shops and grocery stores, free bags of groceries from retail stores, free service at dry cleaners and laundries, and free goods from factories and wholesalers. In his public testimony before the Commission Patrolman Droge stated that in one precinct in which he had served, police officers had used their tours to make the rounds of a bread factory, a frankfurter plant, and an ice cream plant, among others, stocking up on goods to take home. "I recall one police officer," said Droge, "who felt that if he didn't go home with a bag of groceries, then his tour wasn't complete."

Tips for Services Rendered

Policemen often accepted or solicited payments for services performed during their tours of duty. Some of these services were legitimate parts of their jobs, like guarding foreign diplomats, for which they should not have been tipped, and others were services which should have been performed by private guards rather than by City-paid policemen, like escorting supermarket managers to the bank.

Foreign consulates, many of which have City policemen assigned to guard them, have been known to offer gratuities to the police in various forms. Some would send cases of whiskey and champagne to precinct houses. Others made gifts of gold watches and money to various police officers.

When City marshals served eviction notices, they would notify the police, and when a car responded, the marshal paid $5 to the patrolmen in the car for handling the eviction.

When managers of many supermarkets and liquor stores were ready to take the day's receipts to the bank, they called the local precinct house and asked that a patrol car be sent over. The policemen in the car would then give the manager a ride to the bank, for which they received "anywhere from a couple of packs of cigarettes to $4.00."

Proprietors of check cashing services, who open up shop in the morning with large supplies of cash on hand, frequently had standing arrangements to have a patrol car waiting outside each morning when the proprietor came in.

Proprietors of burglarized stores and factories, if they arrived at the scene before the police did, paid $5 a man to each officer who showed up. However, if the police arrived first, they often helped themselves to merchandise.

Since our investigation, the Department has issued an order requiring that, when patrol cars manned by patrolmen reach the scene of a burglary before the sergeant gets there, the cars must be inspected by the sergeant before they leave the scene. Although this sounds like a sensible reform, a precinct commander and other police officers told the Commission that they felt the required procedure was demeaning and unlikely ever to be followed, as it would result in the public spectacle of a police supervisor searching for evidence of theft by patrolmen.

Comments

Almost to a man, legitimate businessmen questioned by the Commission about why they offered gratuities to the police claimed that they did so "to promote good will." Almost all expected to receive either extra or better service than that given to the general public, and many expected the police to overlook minor illegal acts or conditions.

Restaurants and bars expected police who dined and drank free to respond promptly if they were ever called in an emergency and to handle such calls with more discretion than usual. If the police ever had to arrest a man in one of the hotels which offered free meals and Christmas money, the management could be fairly confident that instead of charging into the dining room in the middle of dinner and making the arrest in full view of all the diners, the police would probably make the arrest much more discreetly.

Another benefit to bars, restaurants, and hotels was that patrons were allowed to park and double-park illegally in front of their establishments.

In many instances it is unfair to infer that payments of a gratuity necessarily reflected a shakedown by the police officer involved. A bar owner, restaurateur, or other businessman is usually most happy to have a police officer in or near his premises, and in a good many situations, payments—particularly Christmas gratuities—were made simply because the police officer became friendly with the local merchants in his patrol area. Gift giving, however, was very rarely a reciprocal matter in the sense of friends exchanging gifts on an equal basis. If, as in the case of some high-ranking officers, a return gift was made it was always in response to an original overture by someone who usually stood to gain by the presumed good will.

The fact is that the public by and large does not regard gratuities as a serious matter. While some may be offended by the occasionally arrogant way in which some police officers demand what they consider to be their due, most people are willing to allow a police officer who spends long hours providing protection for an area to stop in for a quick free meal or cup of coffee at an eating establishment which enjoys the benefit of his protection. Indeed, an investigation of hotels in New York conducted a few years ago by the New York County District Attorney came up with essentially the same evidence as that found by the Commission of hotels providing free meals and a prosecutorial judgment was apparently made not to pursue the matter even though criminal violations were involved.

Officers who participated in Ethical Awareness Workshops recently sponsored by the Department have reached an interesting conclusion. They felt that no police officer should ever accept a gratuity of any sort. Their reasoning was twofold: One, that even a series of small gratuities—like cups of coffee—would, in certain instances, affect an officer's performance of his duty, and two, that acceptance of gratuities is demeaning to a professional police officer. However, it is doubtful whether such standards could reasonably be imposed throughout the Department.

The general tolerance of gratuities both by policemen and by the public gives rise to the question whether some system should be developed whereby gratuities are specifically condoned as long as they are not excessive. At the time of our investigation, there was a *de facto* tolerance of such gratuities, and if the Department could institutionalize this approach by establishing realistic guidelines setting out what is and is not permissible it could at least remove the illegal atmosphere which may operate to condition policemen for more serious misconduct. Admittedly, the problem of drawing a line is a difficult one. If the Department should decide to permit policemen to accept free meals and goods, the Commission urges that all such gratuities be reported in memorandum books or on Daily Field Activity Reports, which should be reviewed daily by supervisory officers. Supervisory personnel could then be held responsible for insuring that such privileges were not abused.

Some areas do seem susceptible to an official regulatory approach. For example, there would seem to be no reason why the practice of hotels providing free rooms to police officers could not be officially sanctioned. If an officer is forced to work late hours in any area of the City far from his home and is expected to be on duty or in court early the following morning, it does not seem unreasonable that he be provided with a hotel room, on a space available basis, with the expense being paid for by the City. If such rooms are provided they should be duly reported and, where possible, approved in advance as part of a regular system.

Assuming that hotel and restaurants actually do not wish to provide free meals and rooms to police officers, it has been demonstrated that they are not forced to. At the time of the Commission hearings, under the glare of publicity, many of the big hotels announced that they would no longer provide such services.

Chapter Fifteen

MISCELLANY

The Commission had neither the time nor the resources to investigate thoroughly all corrupt practices allegedly indulged in by police officers. In some areas where the hazards of corruption appeared to be great the Commission's investigators were unable to gather adequate evidence. Other allegations involved acts which were either so petty or so individual in nature that full-scale investigations were simply not warranted. Some types of corrupt behavior not corroborated by the Commission were widely talked about in the Department as well as in some sections of the community and have officially been recognized by the Department as corruption hazards. Others have been the subject of criminal prosecutions.

The Commission was not able, for one reason or another, to identify most of the matters discussed in this chapter as definite patterns of corruption. These matters must nevertheless be mentioned since some of them clearly present grave corruption hazards and, in any event, it is a serious matter even when the only evidence of a particular type of corrupt behavior is the commonly accepted belief among police officers that it exists.

Loansharks: Although the Commission did not find conclusive evidence of police corruption involving loansharks, in the course of its work it came across numerous allegations of police collusion with loansharks and the nature of the business is such that corruption would seem to be an obvious hazard. Some policemen apparently shake down loansharks on a haphazard basis and others have been known to work for loansharks in various capacities, ranging from referring to potential borrowers to roughing up slow payers.

Officer Phillips told the Commission that he had been "friendly" with two loansharks and, while working under the supervision of the

Commission, he received intermittent payments of $10 and $20 from them.

Another patrolman, currently under indictment in the Bronx, was described by Bronx County District Attorney Burton Roberts as "a $100-a-week collector for a loanshark operation." He faces perjury charges for allegedly giving a grand jury false testimony about his connection with the loansharks. Another patrolman in the Bronx is currently under indictment for allegedly operating a loanshark ring with two civilian partners. He faces usury and assault charges stemming from a beating he reportedly gave to a customer who owed $120 and $100 loan.

DOA's: In police terminology a "DOA" (dead on arrival) is a corpse requiring official police action. Patrolman Phillips and others told the Commission that, when police officers were called upon to handle DOA's, they would sometimes go through the victim's pockets and steal anything of value. Likewise, when called to a house or apartment where someone has died, the police have been known to burglarize the premises if the deceased had been living alone. Similar burglaries have taken place after police officers escorted someone to the hospital, who turned out to be dead on arrival. In such cases, officers would take the dead person's keys and let themselves into his apartment, then take anything of value. Patrolman Phillips told the Commission that old people who die in the City frequently keep large sums of money hidden in their homes, apparently not trusting banks. He went on to say that thefts from DOA's in such circumstances have amounted to several thousand dollars.

The Department has recognized theft from DOA's as a corruption hazard and now requires that a complete inventory of property taken from a DOA be made by one officer at the scene. The inventory must be initialed by a superior officer and all the property inventoried must "be vouchered immediately, entered in the blotter and then placed in the property locker for safeguarding."

Hijacking: Various informants told the Commission that truck hijackings almost always received police protection in one form or another. The Commission was told that various policemen were sometimes alerted ahead of time to a scheduled hijacking. If they had not been notified ahead of time and were attracted to the suspicious unloading, hijackers would attempt to buy them off on the spot.

Auto Theft Rings: In the past few years, several instances have come to light of individual police involvement with auto theft rings. One of these dovetails with allegations received by the Commission that police officers sometimes ride shotgun for such outfits. The others involve payments for protection of such rings.

In September of 1970, the Bronx County District Attorney announced the indictment of two patrolmen and several civilians on larceny and conspiracy charges. The district attorney alleged that the patrolmen had acted as guards during the theft of late model automobiles, using their jobs and patrol car as covers.

In another auto theft case involving policemen who did not work as guards, the Bronx County District Attorney announced the indictment of five police officers and several civilians in June, 1971. Of the five officers, four (two sergeants, a detective, and a patrolman) were indicted for their part in shakedowns of the ringleader. The fifth officer, a patrolman, was indicted for his activities as an auto cutter, which entailed dismantling the stolen autos for resale as parts. In a third auto theft case, the Queens County District Attorney announced the indictment of several individuals, including two detectives. It was alleged that the detectives, acting as agents for members of the ring, offered $2,000 to two other police officers not to arrest four alleged members of the ring. The detectives pleaded guilty to the charges.

Police Theft from Burglarized Premises: Several police officers told the Commission that it was common practice for policemen responding to burglarized premises to steal items the previous thieves had left behind. The Department recognizes burglarized premises as a corruption hazard, and calls police theft at the sites "compound burglaries." At the Commission's public hearings, Patrolman Droge and former policeman Waverly Logan both testified that several cars would customarily respond to burglary calls, including calls about burglaries outside their sectors, and would steal the merchandise they were charged with guarding. Logan described what happened at a shirt factory where he and his partner answered a burglary call:

> "Me and my partner went in the back of the building [where] a door was open. We went in. There was about six or seven radio cars out front. A lot of cops was inside. Everybody was stuffing clothes down their pants, in their shirt, up their sleeves. Everybody looking fat because they were stuffing so much clothes in their pants. And my partner was telling me that the owners usually take it out on their income tax. Usually declare—say—more was stolen than was actually taken. Or they would take it out on their insurance."

Commission agents, while conducting a surveillance of an after-hours bar after midnight, stumbled upon a flagrant example of what appeared to be a compound burglary. The agents noticed an unoccupied police car parked next to a meat packing company where a door was ajar. They soon saw men in police uniforms emerge from the packing company carrying large, paper-wrapped packages which they loaded into the car. In the next few hours, four other police cars (the entire motor patrol force for one-half of the precinct) responded to the site. Police officers from four of the five cars were seen putting packages from the company into their cars. The fifth car, assigned to the supervising sergeant, stopped by briefly, but no packages were loaded into it. The investigators later observed some of the patrolmen transferring the packages into two private automobiles, which were parked near the station house and turned out to be registered to one of the patrolmen involved and to an officer sharing a car pool with another. Two of the participating officers have been indicted by a New

York County grand jury for perjury resulting from their testimony in executive session before the Commission.

Court-Related Payoffs: The Commission was told about numerous kinds of payoffs which affected the outcome of court cases. The most common court-related payoffs were those made to policemen to change their testimony so that a case was dismissed or the defendant acquitted, as discussed in the chapters on narcotics and gambling.

Another common payoff—really a gratuity—was that given to the "bridgeman" (a court attendant) by policemen and lawyers in order to have their cases called quickly so they didn't have to spend hours waiting. Patrolman Phillips testified that police officers tipped the bridgeman $2 to call a case ahead of others scheduled before it, and that lawyers tipped $5.

A fortunately more unusual court-related payoff was that made to influence a judge. Before Phillips was caught by the Commission, he had arranged for a man accused of possession of a stolen $250,000 check to make contact with a lawyer who claimed he could bribe any of several judges. The man was represented in these negotiations by a Commission informant wearing a transmitter. The lawyer asked for $10,000 to fix the case, saying he could give an 80% guarantee of acquittal. The lawyer received an initial payment of $4,500 before the informant's transmitter was discovered by Patrolman Phillips and the negotiations broken off. The Commission has no way of knowing the truth of the representations made by the lawyer, who fled the country after being discovered.

The Garment Industry: Members of the garment industry were reported to pay off the police on a regular basis, primarily to avoid summonses for illegally-parked delivery trucks and for obstructing the streets and sidewalks with garment racks.

Peddlers: Six informants, including four peddlers, complained to the Commission that peddlers were forced to pay the police or receive summonses, which could lead to fines of up to $100. Payments were reportedly made either daily or weekly and ranged from $5 to $10. The owner of a fleet of fifteen hot dog wagons was reported to have paid police $5 per wagon per day. Ticket scalpers operating near Madison Square Garden allegedly paid police $10 per day.

Polling Places: According to a highly-placed aide to an elected official and several police officers, at the beginning of Election Day both the Democratic and Republican party captains in some election districts habitually gave $5 and $10 to the policemen on duty, indicating that the money was for food and coffee, although party poll watchers always provide free food and coffee to the officers. Since such payments were made by both parties, their apparent purpose was to ensure equal treatment and lack of harassment.

Pistol Permits: The Commission received several allegations that applicants for pistol permits have made payments to the appropriate precinct captain in order to get permits. The fee was usually reported to be $100, requested by the clerical officer to expedite approval of the application for a permit, with the understanding that the money would be passed on to the precinct commander.

One man who has a pistol permit told the Commission that when he applied for it at the local precinct, the clerical man told him that the fee for the permit was $20, but that he would have to pay another $100 for the captain when approval came through. He made the payment to the clerical man, and said he was later able to confirm that the captain did, indeed, receive the money.

Another Commission informant, who was a police officer before he was dismissed from the force, told the Commission that in every precinct he had worked in it was common knowledge that applicants had to pay the commander in order to get a pistol permit.

A New York City gun dealer confirmed that one must pay $100 to the precinct commander to get a pistol permit, and added that gun dealers must make payoffs to the Police Department's Pistol License Bureau when renewing the various permits required for operating a gun business in the City. He said that the official costs for the necessary licenses amount to about $150, but that the actual costs total between $400 and $450 a year. He also reported that he paid an extra $100 every January to a bagman from the Pistol Bureau. He said that these costs are not reflected in his books, and he doubted that other gun dealers' books would have such entries.

Although the Commission, in its limited investigation into pistol permits, was unable to develop hard evidence of payoffs, it heard enough allegations to warrant the conclusion that some applicants for permits probably make payments to the police in excess of the legal $20 fee. However, the Commission interviewed thirty other pistol permitees, whose names were selected at random from several hundred applicant files subpoenaed from the Police Department, and every one of them denied making extra payments.

Under current procedures, the Department's Pistol License Bureau in deciding to grant or deny a pistol license relies heavily on the recommendation of the relevant precinct commander, who must interview each pistol permit applicant. Since the commander's recommendation is weighed so heavily, those commanding officers desiring to shake down applicants are in an excellent position to demand payment in return for a favorable recommendation.

However, the Department has identified its current procedure for granting pistol permits as a corruption hazard, and is in the process of completely revamping the system. By January, 1973, the entire pistol-licensing program will be centralized under the direction of a City agency.

Sale of Information: Companies doing background checks on job applicants have, in the past, paid police officers for looking through Department records to determine whether the applicants had criminal records, and for supplying copies of these records. In 1971, following an investigation by the Department of Investigation, nine policemen and fourteen corporations were indicted in New York courts for participating in the sale of records of this kind. The nine officers (four detectives and five patrolmen, most of whom worked for the Bureau of Criminal Identification) were found to have received from $1.00 to $2.50 for each name they processed. Some processed relatively few names while others operated in volume. One detective was found to have performed checks for at least seven companies for over fifteen years, netting more than $15,000 a year for this service.

The corporations indicted included a number of private detective agencies and two airlines. They were quick to point out that the information they paid for was a matter of public record, theoretically available to anyone. However, it is available to the public only in the form of court records, which would necessitate a long, laborious search in various court files to check for information on just one person. Instead, they paid police officers to supply them with copies of the Department's yellow sheets, which are lists, filed by name, of all arrests and dispositions of individuals arrested by the police.

Fortune Tellers: The Commission heard numerous allegations from Gypsies and others that some policemen, particularly detectives assigned to the Pickpocket and Confidence Squad (PP&C), received payments from Gypsy confidence artists who swindle people who come to them for advice, particularly the elderly. In return for the payoffs, officers did what they could to insure that the swindlers would not be apprehended and arrested.

The most common of the Gypsy confidence games is the Gypsy blessing, usually perpetrated by self-styled Gypsy "spiritual advisors" on lonely elderly women who seek their advice. After several visits, they are usually told that the cause of their problems is a "curse" which someone has placed on their money. These women are told that the curse can be removed only by the Gypsy blessing, and they are advised to bring their money in to be blessed. When the money is brought in, the advisor sews it up in a special bag, which is switched for an identical bag containing paper. The victim is told to put this bag away in a dark place like a bank vault for a specified time—often two years—and warned that if she should open the bag before the time is up the money will vanish. The Commission was told that such thefts range from a few hundred dollars to as much as $40,000.

When the victim finally realizes that her money has been stolen, she reports it to the local precinct, which in turn refers her to PP&C. At PP&C, the victim is invited to look through a file of photographs of known Gypsy confidence artists and a detective is assigned to the case.

Informants told the Commission that detectives in PP&C sometimes received 15% of Gypsy blessing scores from Gypsy contact men who acted as liaisons with PP&C. This fee insured that the swindler's picture would be removed from the Gypsy mug shot file, and that any investigation into the matter would be inconclusive.

One victim of the Gypsy blessing scheme went not to the police but to the Bronx District Attorney's Office after being bilked out of $1,200 by a palmist. The D.A.'s Office chose to handle this case themselves rather than turn it over to the PP&C Squad who are supposed to be experts in Gypsy crime. At the direction of an assistant D.A., the victim returned to the palmist with $265 in marked money, which the palmist wrapped in a handkerchief and switched with a similarly wrapped bundle. At this point, two detectives from the D.A.'s Office stepped in and arrested the palmist. The palmist and her husband then returned most of the victim's money and offered to bribe the detectives, who pretended to be interested. The group then went to another location to meet the palmist's father and collect the bribe. When the money was offered, the palmist's husband and father were also arrested.

In one such case, restitution was alleged to have been arranged by two precinct detectives. After the victim complained to them, they purportedly arranged through a Gypsy contact man to have $6,000 restored to her. An interesting facet of this case is that neither of the detectives ever filed a report of the crime either with the precinct or PP&C.

When Commission investigators inspected PP&C's Gypsy rogues' gallery, they found that photographs were kept loose in metal trays similar to those used for filing inventory cards. Even on cursory examination it was evident that numerous photos had been removed from the trays and that such removal was a simple matter, since the pictures were arranged in haphazard fashion with no numbering system.

Chapter Sixteen

INDIVIDUAL MISCONDUCT UNCOVERED BY THE COMMISSION

Although the Commission was primarily concerned with exposing patterns of corrupt behavior, inevitably, our investigation uncovered evidence of numerous individual acts of corruption involving police officers and members of the public, narcotics addicts, gamblers, and a variety of other criminals. The large number of such instances, uncovered by a small staff in a limited period of time, gives some indication of the magnitude of corruption in the Department at that time.

Following the Commission's public hearings, the Department set up the First Deputy Commissioner's Special Force to follow up on matters developed in the Commission's investigation. This unit examined all of the Commission's cases and allegations which were not already under investigation by district or federal attorneys.

The Special Force undertook to look into 310 cases involving 627 police officers, against whom allegations were serious enough to warrant investigation. They retained 102 cases and referred another 196 cases to the Internal Affairs Division of the Department for investigation. Twelve cases have been referred to the intelligence unit of the Department.

To date twenty-six police officers and fourteen civilians have been indicted by various federal and state prosecutors in cases originated by the Commission. Of these, two policemen and one civilian have pleaded guilty and one policeman has been acquitted. The indictments of twenty-three policemen and thirteen civilians have not yet come to trial.

Thirty-four police officers (including twenty-four of those indicted) have been suspended and fifty-seven (including those indicted or suspended) have been brought up on departmental charges. One of these has resigned. Other investigations are still pending.

A breakdown of the instances of corrupt behavior discovered by the Commission reflects incidents of specific criminal activity involving 164 individuals which were uncovered during Commission investigations or were confirmed by Commission investigators.* Of these, sixty-six were police officers and ninety-eight were civilians. The incidents included minor corruption, sales of narcotics, bribe-giving, bribe-receiving, and extortion. One incident involved an effort to fix a murder case. Forty-one additional police officers were found to have participated in actions which constituted violations of departmental rules and regulations.**

Incidents of corruption amounting to criminal violations involving 301 individuals were reported by credible witnesses having direct knowledge of the corrupt transactions, although these were not independently confirmed by Commission investigators. Some of these incidents were described in public testimony by such witnesses as officers Phillips and Droge and former officer Logan, who detailed the numerous occasions on which they participated in extortion, bribe-taking, and other crimes. Other incidents were reported by such people as a contractor who declined at the last minute to testify at the public hearings but who had testified in closed hearings to numerous petty but continuous payoffs he was obliged to make to policemen in various precincts to avoid harassment.

Similar information was obtained with respect to thirty-one police officers who committed violations of departmental rules and regulations.

---

* This does not include thirty-six police officers whose names appeared on the Christmas gratuity list of one hotel, most of whom were said by hotel officials to have accepted the gratuities.

** This does not include the names of 660 police officers who appeared as guests on restaurant checks of various midtown hotels, and in hotel logs as occupants of free rooms during the period of the survey.

In addition to information actually uncovered by Commission investigators or reported by witnesses whom the Commission staff could determine to be credible, alleged incidents involving 810 individuals, 286 of whom were police officers, were reported by sources whose credibility the Commission had no opportunity to evaluate. These were in addition to the 1,700 complaints received from the public.

Mere numbers of corrupt acts are not as significant as the patterns of behavior which they reflect. The number of people caught and convicted for participating in any type of criminal activity is always a small fraction of those actually involved. It is difficult to make arrests and even more difficult to satisfy standards of proof necessary for convictions with respect to many crimes which, nevertheless, are quite apparently being committed on a large scale. For the Commission's purposes, tape-recorded conversations in which corrupt police officers discussed their activities with undercover agents were invaluable even though such evidence is, under current law, insufficient to establish guilt without further corroboration. Using criminal convictions to measure the extent of police corruption is particularly worthless because the transactions are necessarily secret and those involved in them are extremely unlikely to complain.

SECTION THREE: ANTI-CORRUPTION EFFORTS

Chapter Seventeen

THE SERPICO-DURK STORY: A MISHANDLED CORRUPTION COMPLAINT

In 1966 and 1967, Sergeant David Durk and Patrolman Frank Serpico took specific information of serious police corruption to a number of highly-placed individuals both in and out of the Department in an attempt to get someone to start an investigation. Their experiences illustrate some of the deficiencies, in attitude as well as procedure, in the way such complaints have been handled in the past by City officials as well as by the police.

Serpico's and Durk's allegations centered chiefly around two separate series of events involving Serpico, which took place in 1966 and 1967. Both involved first-hand accounts of corruption given by Serpico, in the first instance to a police captain assigned to the City Department of Investigation and in the second to members of the Police Department, an assistant to the Mayor, and the Commissioner of Investigation.

The Commission explored the way Serpico's charges were handled, both in executive session and in the second set of public hearings held in December, 1971. Both times, police and City officials who played significant roles in the events under investigation were called to testify under oath and gave sometimes conflicting recollections.

Ninetieth Precinct Incident

According to Serpico and Durk, in August, 1966, in the Ninetieth Precinct, a patrolman handed Serpico an envelope containing $300 which the patrolman said was Serpico's share from a gambler named "Jewish Max." At the suggestion of his friend Durk, then assigned to the Department of Investigation, Serpico went with Durk to Captain Phillip Foran, head of the Department of Investigation's investigative squad, with whom they had an off-the-record chat, with the understanding that Serpico's identity would be protected. Serpico did not want to be a witness against the patrolman who had given him the money because he feared he might become an "outcast" in the Department.

Serpico and Durk testified that Serpico told Foran about the incident and showed him the envelope containing the money. They said Foran told Serpico he had two choices: He could go to the Commissioner of Investigation who would send him before a grand jury, after which he might well wind up "in the East River"; or he could forget about the incident. Serpico and Durk felt Foran was not making a threat, but simply giving them practical advice. As for the money, the three officers agreed that Serpico should turn it over to his supervisory sergeant after explaining how he got it, which he did. There is no record of the sergeant making an official report of the matter or turning over the money to anyone else.

In executive session, Captain Foran denied making the statements attributed to him by Serpico and Durk and said he had never been shown any envelope or told that Serpico had received any money. According to Foran, Serpico told him only about a possible future payoff and he said he had recommended that Serpico act as an undercover agent with a transmitter so that police action could be taken after the payoff was received. Foran said Serpico had refused to wear a wire as he feared he might become an outcast.

The foregoing incident was presented to a Brooklyn grand jury in 1970. Serpico, Durk, Foran and Serpico's sergeant all testified and no indictment was returned. In 1972 Foran was tried on departmental charges and fined thirty days' pay.

Seventh Division Incident

In 1966, while Serpico was serving as a plainclothesman, he learned that he was about to be transferred to the Seventh Division in Bronx County. Because Serpico was worried about possible corruption in the Seventh, an acquaintance, Inspector Cornelius Behan, offered to speak to the administrator of the division, Deputy Inspector Phillip Sheridan.

Sheridan told Behan that, as far as he knew, there was no corruption in the Seventh. Behan passed the information on to Serpico, who was transferred in late December. In Serpico's first month in the Seventh Division, however, another plainclothesman offered Serpico a $100 share of a score, told him that a division pad existed, explained how it was organized, and introduced him to a known gambler who offered him money. Serpico refused the money and reported these and other similar incidents to Behan early in 1967. Serpico testified that Behan was "shocked." Behan told Serpico it was his duty to come forward with specific information about the individuals involved so that action could be taken. Serpico was hesitant to do this, but wanted to get out of the Seventh Division. Behan offered to help arrange a transfer and told Serpico he would relay Serpico's information to First Deputy Commissioner John Walsh, who was in charge of the Department's anti-corruption efforts.

Behan met three times with Walsh. Referring to notes taken at around the time of the meetings, he testified that he had recounted Serpico's charges of corruption, as well as Serpico's desire to be transferred. Behan said that Walsh wanted Serpico to stay in the division for the rest of his one-year tour and that, at the first two meetings, Walsh asked Behan to continue to meet with Serpico and attempt to persuade him to come up with specific information. Walsh testified that he did not recall being told of any corruption at the first two meetings. But, after Behan's note-assisted testimony was read to him, he said he would not dispute Behan's account of what had been said at the meetings. Serpico, who testified that he had given Behan specific information in January, 1967, testified that Behan reported to him that Walsh wanted him to keep gathering information. Serpico expected to receive instructions and guidance from Walsh, but no one from Walsh's office contacted him.

Behan testified that in April, 1967, Serpico for the first time gave him specific information including names of officers involved in the division pad. Behan testified that he told Serpico at that time that, since he was now willing to divulge specific information, he should deal directly with Walsh. Behan told Serpico he would no longer act as liaison.

Behan then met with Walsh for the third and final time and recounted the substance of Serpico's information. Walsh thanked him and said he would be in touch with Serpico, and Behan so reported to Serpico. However, Walsh never attempted to reach Serpico or to follow up on his charges. There is no indication that anything was done about the charges until six months later when Serpico brought them to the attention of his division commander. "I intended to see Serpico," Walsh testified. "Yes. That I failed to see him—that was my mistake and I say so."

Walsh testified that despite the serious nature of Serpico's charges, he spoke to no one else in the Department about them. Howard R. Leary, Police Commissioner at the time of these events, testified that he had never been informed of the charges by his First Deputy Commissioner and did not learn of them until Serpico's division commander precipitated an official investigation.

In addition to his contacts with Inspector Behan, Serpico had been keeping Durk abreast of his experiences. Durk, in turn, had discussed them in informal meetings with Jay Kriegel, an Assistant to the Mayor whose duties included liaison work with the Police Department. Durk was a personal friend of Kriegel's who, as a patrolman, had contributed ideas regarding police matters to the Mayor's 1965 campaign. Since then Durk had been assigned to the Department of Investigation and he and Kriegel often met and discussed police problems. Kriegel testified that he saw Durk frequently and valued his opinions highly. Durk's own superior, the chief of the Department of Investigation's investigative squad, was appointed after Durk recommended him for the post.

Durk told Kriegel about Serpico's allegations and relayed Serpico's complaint that, although he was supposed to be working undercover for Walsh, Walsh had never called him and, as far as Serpico and Durk knew, no investigation had been started.

Durk and Serpico met with Kriegel on a confidential basis with the understanding that Serpico's identity would be protected. Durk and Serpico testified that the meeting had occurred in the spring of 1967, but Kriegel recalled it as being in summer or fall. Serpico told Kriegel about his experiences in the Seventh Division, of his reporting them to the First Deputy Commissioner, and of his frustration that apparently no one was taking action. Durk and Serpico both testified that they prodded Kriegel to get the Mayor to launch an investigation of Serpico's charges of corruption and of the reasons why they were being ignored by the Department. They said Kriegel told them he would look into the possibility of taking such action and also would try to find out why Walsh had not called Serpico.

According to Durk, Kriegel told him several weeks later that any investigation would have to wait until the end of the summer because the administration did not want to ''upset the cops.'' Durk assumed this meant that the administration was worried about trouble in the ghetto, and did not want to antagonize the police, whose help might be critical. Kriegel denied making any such statement.

Kriegel's testimony before the Commission in executive session with respect to his meeting with Durk and Serpico varied from the testimony he later gave in the Commission's public hearings.

In executive session Kriegel recalled that Durk and Serpico had come to him for the purpose of having him bring to the attention of the Mayor serious and specific charges of corruption which had been reported to Walsh and about which nothing had been done. Kriegel testified that he was impressed with the importance of the information and had spoken to the Mayor about it, indicating to him both the allegations of corruption and the dissatisfaction of Durk and Serpico (whom he did not mention by name) with the way in which the allegations were being handled by the Department. Kriegel did not remember the Mayor's response with respect to the alleged mishandling of the complaints but acknowledged that it was a very serious problem which the Mayor could legitimately discuss with Commissioner Leary although Kriegel would not presume to do so himself.

In his public testimony, Kriegel stated that Durk and Serpico had never claimed that nothing was being done about Serpico's charges but had merely complained about the "pace" of the investigation, a charge he had discounted in the light of Walsh's reputation as an aggressive corruption fighter. He said that he now recalled that he had not reported this complaint to the Mayor but had mentioned only the allegations of corruption and the fact that they had been reported to the Department. Under these circumstances the Mayor would have had no reason to interfere with a police investigation which, as far as he knew, was effectively under way. Although the Department's apparent inaction was the heart of Durk's and Serpico's allegations, and Kriegel again confirmed the two officers' expressed desire to have their charges made known to the Mayor, Kriegel testified that he chose not to tell the Mayor because he believed the Mayor would have gone directly to the Police Department and followed up on the charges, thus revealing Serpico's and Durk's identities. He did not, however, ask Durk and Serpico if they were willing to take that risk in order to have their information passed on to the Mayor and, although he continued to see Durk regularly, never told him that the Mayor had not been given the full story.

Kriegel testified that he did not thereafter say anything to the Mayor about Walsh's alleged delay in investigating Serpico's charges even when the investigation had finally begun and the Mayor could routinely have inquired about it without revealing that he had first learned of the situation from Serpico. Kriegel explained that it would have been inappropriate for the Mayor to interfere in an ongoing police investigation.

The only other action Kriegel took in the matter was to advise the Mayor to "spend more time with the Police Commissioner" on corruption matters.

In their search for someone willing to take action, Serpico and Durk went on May 30, 1967, to Commissioner of Investigation (now New York Supreme Court Justice) Arnold Fraiman, also with the understanding that the meeting was confidential and that Serpico's identity would be protected. After hearing Serpico's allegations, Fraiman suggested that Serpico wear a transmitter to obtain evidence, which Serpico refused to do. Serpico's position was that he would be willing to work undercover only if he were officially assigned to an anti-corruption unit. The three men then decided to bug the Seventh Division plainclothes surveillance truck, a plan which later turned out to be technically unfeasible. Serpico was again urged to wear a transmitter and again refused.

Durk testified that he approached Fraiman several times to ask what was being done about Serpico's allegations, and that Fraiman first refused to talk to him and later discounted Serpico's information, saying Serpico was a "psycho." Fraiman denied this and said he had never doubted the truth of Serpico's charges. However, his office did not pursue the matter and he did not refer Serpico's information to any other agency, although Fraiman had previously testified that cases not followed up by his staff were routinely referred to the appropriate district attorney's office.

Action was finally taken on Serpico's charges in October, 1967, when he went to his division commander, Deputy Inspector Phillip Sheridan, as Behan had urged him to do in the first place. Sheridan informed his supervisors, including Walsh, and an investigation was begun by personnel assigned to division and borough commands. Although Serpico still refused to work as an undercover agent, he provided information which led to the arrest of a gambler whose testimony, augmented by Serpico's, led to departmental charges against nineteen officers, ten of whom were also indicted by federal or county grand juries or both. In subsequent Bronx County proceedings three officers were convicted of criminal charges and one pleaded guilty to a violation. Three were acquitted and one was given conditional discharge. Federal cases against eight officers are pending. In addition, forty-two civilians have been indicted.

Conclusions

Although Walsh, Kriegel and Fraiman all acknowledged the extreme seriousness of the charges and the unique opportunity provided by the fact that a police officer was making them, none of them took any action. No serious investigation was undertaken until some months later when Serpico went to his division commander. No general evaluation of the problems of corruption in the Department was undertaken until *The New York Times* publicized the charges two years later, at which time the Mayor initiated the chain of events which led to the appointment of this Commission.

First Deputy Commissioner Walsh, whose reputation in the Department was that of an implacable corruption fighter, inexplicably took no action whatsoever for at least six months. Commissioner Leary and Chief Inspector Sanford Garelik, who met regularly with Walsh and discussed, among other things, problems of corruption, testified that they were not even informed of the incident. Departmental deficiencies which made possible this state of affairs are discussed in

Chapters Eighteen through Twenty, along with an evaluation of the steps since taken by Commissioner Murphy to correct them.

While it is not clear to what extent Durk's and Serpico's charges were passed on to the Mayor, it is clear that the Mayor's office did not see to it that the specific charges made by Serpico were investigated. No effective actions were taken to find out why the Department had delayed investigating the charges, or to explore the broader significance of a situation which indicated widespread corruption among the police.

Similarly, the Commissioner of Investigation failed to take the action that was clearly called for in a situation which seemed to involve one of the most serious kinds of corruption ever to come to the attention of his office, and which seemed to be precisely the sort of case his office was set up to handle. Conditions in the Department of Investigation which hamper its ability to investigate police corruption cases are discussed in Chapter Twenty-One.

Chapter Eighteen

DEPARTMENTAL MACHINERY FOR INVESTIGATING CORRUPTION

In the past a number of administrative defects precluded effective investigations of police corruption in New York City and indicated a lack of adequate planning by the Department's top management. Specifically, the Department's machinery for detecting and investigating police corruption was fragmented and even when unified was not given official standing, adequate records, or adequate manpower. In addition, the Department often failed to use appropriate and effective techniques of investigation.

Today many of these deficiencies are being corrected. The Department's investigative apparatus has been unified organizationally, staffed appropriately, and encouraged to use more effective investigative techniques. While it is too soon to assess the impact on corruption of many of the changes that have been made, there are encouraging signs of progress.

Past Deficiencies

Organizational Fragmentation: As reported by the International Association of Police Chiefs in 1967, the various units charged with searching out misconduct within the Department and with maintaining internal discipline, efficiency and integrity were widely dispersed, poorly coordinated, undermanned and, in many instances, so misdirected that they were almost totally ineffective in rooting out corrupt policemen. Simply to call the roll of the anti-corruption units at that time is to indicate how diffuse and unsystematic the Department's anti-corruption efforts were. At the top of the organization there was a separate First Deputy Commissioner's Investigating Unit and a Police Commissioner's Confidential Investigating Unit which were involved in the control of the Department's activities in the area of public morals and personnel security. At the next level there was a Chief Inspector's Investigating Unit which had related and overlapping responsibilities with the first two; the Patrol Bureau had an Inspections Unit; the Detective Division had an Evaluation and Analysis Unit; and there were two principal intelligence units in the Department at the time, the Bureau of Special Services (BOSS) and the Central Investigations Division (CID), both in the Detective Division. In addition, there also existed a Personnel Investigation Section in the Personnel and Administrative Services Bureau which investigated police candidates. Lastly, there was a Gambling Enforcement and Inspection Review Board.

To correct this organizational fragmentation, the various units charged with searching out misconduct within the Department and with maintaining internal integrity and efficiency were brought together in an Inspection Services Bureau (ISB). Command of this Bureau was vested in the First Deputy Commissioner.

At the time of its creation in 1967, the ISB included in its structure the various kinds of units generally agreed upon as necessary for effective anti-corruption work: an Internal Affairs Division (IAD) to investigate complaints or other evidence of misconduct; an Inspections Division to monitor and evaluate the performance of the various commands on a regular basis; an Intelligence Division to gather information about organized crime, including its ties to policemen; and a Public Morals Administrative Division whose function was to monitor plainclothes enforcement of anti-gambling and anti-vice laws.* However, until Commissioner Murphy took over the Department, the ISB lacked the authority and resources necessary for its job.

Lack of Authority: According to the testimony of former First Deputy Commissioner John Walsh, the order establishing the ISB was

---

* The Public Morals Administrative Division has now been removed from the ISB and shifted to the new Organized Crime Control Bureau.

never promulgated, and the Bureau therefore operated without official standing. Thus, the First Deputy Commissioner did not have the authority to examine the records of either the Detective Bureau or the Patrol Bureau without first seeking permission from the Chief of Patrol, the Chief of Detectives or the Chief Inspector or by requesting specific authorization from the Police Commissioner.

Obtaining records from the Patrol Bureau apparently posed no problem to ISB. Detective records, however, were a different story. Former Commissioner Walsh testified that when he received a complaint concerning corruption within the Detective Bureau:

> ". . . we conducted an investigation without going near any of the records we have to get if we have to get the permission of the Detective Bureau."

Walsh pointed out that this hampered his operations. In fact, during the pre-Murphy years the First Deputy found it almost impossible to get information from the Detective Bureau, which maintained two of the Department's most sensitive intelligence files. One of the least edifying episodes in departmental history occurred one evening a few years ago when the head of the Internal Affairs Division, charged with investigating all allegations of corruption, attempted an after-hours look into the Detective Bureau's files at the request of the First Deputy Commissioner. He was caught in the act by the Chief of Detectives, who had been tipped off to the raid, whereupon the two middle-aged lawmen exchanged a non-lethal blow or two. The chief of the IAD promptly retired, leaving the Chief of Detectives still sole master of his own files. Of course, by applying to the Commissioner, the First Deputy ultimately obtained access to the detective files.

Lack of Manpower: Between 1967 and the beginning of the Murphy administration, ISB's manpower was kept at a level that virtually made it impossible to do its job effectively. The manpower of its various components actually shrank after ISB was organized.

At one point the Inspections Division was down to eighteen men. IAD suffered a manpower cut of roughly fifty percent in 1966 and was left with forty-five men. Just one investigation of the kind IAD classifies now as ''medium,'' that which consumes from 300 to 1,000 man-hours, could occupy a third of its personnel full time for an entire week. Intelligence had twenty-two men to keep track of the members of the five organized crime families operating in New York City and the relations between 30,000 policemen and the City's professional criminals.

Inadequate Investigative Techniques: For what appears to have been a combination of reasons, the investigative work of all the ISB's units tended to be of low quality. First, its top officers clung to a case-by-case approach, instead of looking for patterns of corruption. The Internal Affairs Division did not actively seek to uncover corruption but instead reacted to complaints brought to it. This reactive posture contributed to an official underestimation of the extent and indeed the very nature of police corruption. Second, because of adherence to the ''rotten apple'' theory, the Department did not utilize investigative methods such as turning corrupt policemen and allowing a known corrupt situation to continue over a period of time in the interest of rounding up all offenders. This was clearly brought out in testimony given in the Commission's executive sessions. Both former First Deputy Commissioner Walsh and former Supervising Assistant Chief Inspector and also former Chief of ISB Joseph McGovern testified that whenever ISB was satisfied that they could prove the guilt of a particular patrolman, that patrolman was immediately arrested or departmental charges and specifications were brought against him. As noted by Mr. Walsh:

''. . . I worked on the theory that, once a policeman puts out his hand and accepts some type of corruptive money, that he is no longer a man of his own soul: He is always under the thumb of that person because, as long as he is a member of the Department, that person can hold him to it.''

Lack of Coordination in Assignment of Investigations: According to personnel in ISB at that time, another reason for the low quality of ISB's work was that former First Deputy Commissioner Walsh and his principal aides seemed to have been so accustomed to operating in highly personal ways that they found it difficult to abide by the ISB's division of functions. They continued to do what they always had done and assigned each investigation, regardless of where the organization chart said it belonged, to the investigator they personally felt should handle it. The result was that there was no coordination, or even shared knowledge, among ISB's branches operating on the same case.

Disorganized Records: An extremely serious probem discussed in the Commission's Summary and Principal Recommendations is the physically diffuse and disorganized condition of the Department's personnel records.

Other records were found by Commission investigators to be in a similarly disorganized state. Files were maintained on "known gamblers" and "combines" to provide information on, respectively, individuals and organized groups engaged in criminal gambling operations. These files were woefully out of date and incomplete. Moreover, on more than one occasion, by the time Commission investigators could complete the procedures necessary to examine these files in connection with a specific investigation the files had been stripped of pertinent information. Adequate procedures did not exist even to determine what belonged in a particular file, and material could be removed from a file without leaving any evidence that it had ever been there.

The conditions found in the personnel, known gambler, and combine files were typical of most of the Department's operational files. Although police records systems rarely measure up to the standards maintained by business organizations, New York has even lagged behind other police departments in making reforms. For instance, not until recently had any attempts been made to computerize or even modernize crime and arrest report data, criminal histories, wanted and missing persons files, stolen vehicle and property files, and warrant files. The maintenance of vast and disorganized manually maintained files hampers all Department investigations, including those into corruption.

Improper Attitudes: The inefficiency and lack of proper coordination in the Inspectional Services Bureau are to blame in some measure for the ineffectiveness of the Department's anti-corruption efforts in recent years. However, there are indications that there was also some reluctance on the part of top level police personnel to undertake investigations that might have led to exposure of widespread corruption inconsistent with the official line that corruption was limited to a few "rotten apples." Certain evidence uncovered by the Commission tends to support the inference that this attitude was a factor in the Department's failure to expose the nature and extent of its corruption problem.

An example is the untouched file of specific and serious allegations against New York City police officers that was found by Commission investigators in the course of an early investigation into narcotics corruption. The allegations, which concerned seventy-two officers, had been referred to the Department by the Federal Bureau of Narcotics and Dangerous Drugs (BNDD) during a fourteen-month period beginning in April, 1968. Two of the reports in the file were very vague, and on their face, contained no very useful intelligence. One report clearly exonerated the named detective. The remaining sixty-nine reports alleged various types of police misconduct, ranging from association with known narcotics criminals to murder. Thirty officers were alleged to have accepted bribes or extorted payments for the release of apprehended suspects. Five officers were alleged to have purchased stolen goods from a notorious fence. Twenty-seven separate allegations, implicating fifteen different officers including a captain, reported the direct involvement of these men in the sale of narcotics.

Although the Commission found evidence that the existence and contents of this file were known to the supervisors of the Inspectional Services Bureau, nothing—as far as the Commission was able to ascertain—was ever done about the allegations until our investigators came upon the file in the late fall of 1970. The Department's official explanation for its neglect of the file is contained in a memorandum written by First Deputy Commissioner William H. T. Smith in February, 1971, after a meeting with the Director of BNDD. The memorandum explained that Smith's predecessors had been bound by an unofficial gentlemen's agreement with BNDD officials not to investigate the allegations until the BNDD had completed its related prosecutions and the various federal informants could be made available to the Department. According to the memorandum, there was an understanding that the file was to be used by the Department only for intelligence purposes until BNDD lifted its restriction. However, the federal inspectors who intitially referred the allegations to the Intelligence Division told the Commission that they did not remember any such understanding. They said that while several cases were subject to restrictions, such restrictions were imposed on a case-by-case basis. There was, they said, no blanket restriction covering the entire file. According to one BNDD official, there had only been seven cases which involved federal informants whose anonymity was critical to ongoing investigations, or which were related in some other way to federal investigations in progress. In at least thirty-six of the cases, there seems to have been no reason to refrain from a thorough departmental investigation.

Even if there was a misunderstanding in the Department of BNDD's purposes in relaying the reports to the Department, the fact remains that the Department was given reason to suspect that some of its members were extortionists, murderers, and heroin entrepreneurs and made no attempt to verify these suspicions or dispute them. At the very least some attempt should have been made to follow up on the information by keeping in touch with BNDD to stay abreast of progress in these cases.

There are other incidents that came to the attention of the Commission that are not conclusive in themselves, but that may offer an insight into the attitude of the Department's supervisors toward exposing corruption. On April 30, 1970, two BNDD inspectors met with the Chief of the Narcotics Division. At this meeting, serious allegations against nine members of the Narcotics Division were revealed and discussed in detail. According to the federal inspectors' memorandum of this meeting, the Chief stated that he was grateful for the information and that he would discuss it with his superiors in an effort to decide which avenue of investigation should be pursued. However, no departmental action was ever taken on these allegations.

When this former Chief of the Narcotics Division testified under oath before the Commission in executive session in December, 1970, he repeatedly denied having been told by BNDD inspectors that some New York City policemen were selling narcotics. He finally did admit that he recalled having met with the federal agents, but he denied that anything significant had transpired at the meeting. At the request of the Commission, the former Chief turned over his notes from the meeting to two Commission agents who accompanied him to his office at the close of his testimony. The notes contained the names of four of the officers discussed at the meeting, as well as the names and aliases of some narcotics criminals who allegedly acted as middlemen for police officers who sold heroin. The Commission did not pursue the investigation of these matters further because to do so would have focused attention on SIU and jeopardized the undercover work of Detective Leuci.

The Commission discovered one further piece of evidence relating to the Department's attitude toward exposing corruption. In the files of the Internal Affairs Division, Commission agents found a request from BNDD for assistance from the Department in an operation which might have led to the exposure of certain police officers believed to be involved in the sale of narcotics. The request had been forwarded by Deputy Inspector John Norey, commander of the Intelligence Division, to First Deputy Commissioner Walsh, who in turn sent it to Supervising Assistant Chief Inspector John McGovern, then the commander of IAD and Walsh's right hand man in corruption investigations. The request was never acted upon. Instead, it was filed with an attached coversheet with two notations written on it in the hand of Chief McGovern. One note reads "I want to get our men out of that." The other, apparently referring to instructions from the First Deputy Commissioner, says, "Norey 11/19/69—IDC doesn't want to help the feds lock up local police. Let them arrest federal people." The Commission was unable to establish that these words did express the sentiments of the First Deputy Commissioner. Deputy Inspector Norey and Chief McGovern both told the Commission that they did not recall Walsh ever saying such a thing to them. Nevertheless, the fact is that such a statement was written down, and cooperation with federal agents was not forthcoming.

Correction of Deficiencies

Some of the deficiencies cited above in the Department's anti-corruption efforts have been corrected. There are additional changes which the Police Commissioner has indicated he is planning or studying and some which this Commission has recommended.

Increased Manpower: With respect to the simple matter of manpower, there were in April, 1972, seventy-five men assigned to the Inspections Division, 135 to the Internal Affairs Division, and 366 to Intelligence. That last figure represents in large part the intelligence units that were moved into ISB from the Detective Bureau and does not signify that all these intelligence people are working full time against corruption. On the other hand, the IAD figure does not include the 167 full-time anti-corruption people who man the new Field Internal Affairs Units within each of the seven patrol borough commands and each of the special commands: Detectives, Technical Services, Special Operations, Traffic, Criminal Justice, Personnel, OCCB, Administration, and Community Affairs.

New Investigative Approach: The Field Internal Affairs **Units,** all but the two or three smallest of which are headed by captains, are at the heart of the Murphy administration's program to handle both local corruption hazards and particular indications of corruption among specific policemen. In line with the administration's conviction that command responsibility and accountability are a prerequisite for a well-managed Department, it is placing the onus upon commanders for keeping their commands corruption-free.

Responsibility for investigating corruption has always—in theory at least—rested with commanders. But as former First Deputy Commissioner John Walsh testified, reports submitted at six-month intervals from field commanders about corruption in their units always indicated the absence of corruption. Today, all complaints or other indications of corruption which the Department receives are sent to IAD. However, IAD itself now investigates few of them: only those that cross command lines, that promise to lead to investigations lasting many months, that involve officers of the highest rank, that concern particularly sensitive aspects of police work, or that concern situations within the ISB itself. All others—the great majority—are forwarded to the commands involved for investigation by their Field Internal Affairs Units, with IAD keeping record of the referral.

The commanders of the Field Units have been instructed to classify the complaints they receive as either "for full investigation and report," "for investigation and file," or "for information only," and to notify IAD of the classification within 72 hours. They are required to complete investigations in the first category within four months and send the full investigative report to IAD. Investigation in the second category must be completed within one month and the findings sent to IAD. Information in the third category must be evaluated within ten days and the conclusions sent to IAD. This would amount to no more than the discredited old system of every unit investigating itself if there had not been established within

IAD at the same time a new Staff Supervisory Section with a complement of thirty-three men, whose function is to provide technical advice and help to the Field Units and, more to the point, monitor their investigations. It does this in a number of ways. It studies and evaluates the Field Unit's investigative reports and passes along its comments. If it is really dissatisfied, it re-investigates on its own. If it has reason to feel that a field investigation will be perfunctory, it conducts a parallel investigation. Parallel investigations are also conducted at random as spot checks on the Field Units.

It is still much too soon to say whether this Field Unit system will work. Its success depends on how well the Staff Supervisory Section performs, and it has been in operation only since March of 1972. However, it is not too soon to say that the only long-range safeguard against widespread corruption in the Department is the willingness and ability of individual commanders to eliminate it. The Field Unit program, perhaps at the short-range sacrifice of a few cases, appears to be one promising way to inculcate such willingness and ability. In any case, the sheer number of investigations that are called for each year makes it imperative that some of them be conducted, for better or for worse, by the field. In 1971 IAD received 2,779 complaints of corruption in addition to whatever evidence of corruption it turned up on its own.

Many of the 2,779 complaints were all but impossible to respond to: anonymous letters along the lines of, "Every cop in Coney Island is a crook"; or phone calls with such information as, "There's a black haired plainclothesman in the Bronx who takes bribes." Even so, IAD was able to investigate only 367 of these complaints.* Sixteen of its investigations were "heavy," which means over 1,000 man-hours; ninety were medium; eighty-seven were under 300 man-hours, or light, and 174 were apparently so light as not to require classification. In

---

* IAD conducted a total of 532 investigations in 1971; 405 involved corruption and 127 involved misconduct. One hundred and sixty-five of these investigations were self-initiated.

addition, the figure of 2,779 complaints included 160 that were either IAD carry-overs from the preceding year or sent to the field for checking out. It is likely that, as the Field Units get to work and as the Department's credibility in anti-corruption work rises, people who were previously reluctant to come forward will do so and the annual total of complaints will increase.

Whatever its obvious hazards, vesting primary responsibility for all but the most serious corruption investigations in the commands concerned appears to be the most rational way for the Police Department to deal with the problem on more than an emergency basis.

Of particular interest in connection with the field unit approach is the operation of the Field Control Division of the Organized Crime Control Bureau (OCCB), whose sole function is to monitor the activities of the plainclothes enforcement units in the field. The Field Control Division, whose headquarters is separate from those of the OCCB's other divisions to minimize the social contacts of its carefully selected members with other OCCB personnel, has investigations and inspection groups that both respond to complaints and rumors and generate their own inquiries. Its files contain up-to-date photographs and various identifying data about every man in plainclothes, so that it can begin its inquiries without going for records to any other part of the Department.

The commander of the Field Control Division also has responsibility for the Field Associates program that is one of Deputy Commissioner William McCarthy's principal innovations. A field associate is a regularly assigned member of the Public Morals or Narcotics Divisions who has volunteered for the additional duty of keeping his eyes open for evidence of misconduct in his unit and reporting such evidence to the Field Control Division. This plan has already met with some success. It was the work of one of the field associates which led to important indictments recently returned in Bronx County where three detectives and five patrolmen were indicted for involvement in narcotics-related corruption.

The intent of this program was made clear by the statement of one top-ranking official of the OCCB. "We had a system where any policeman could do anything in front of any other policeman. We're trying to end that." Given the conditions in which plainclothesmen work, it is questionable whether this program, or any imaginable program can completely stamp out corruption among them. Opportunities to score gamblers and narcotics traffickers will always be abundant, and some policemen will always succumb to the temptations of taking advantage of them. But at least the Department can create a climate in which a plainclothesman will not be under constant pressure by his peers to join them in their corruption.

Improved Investigative Methods: Not only have organizational changes been made but a beginning has been made in getting rid of former inadequacies in the investigative approach. The Department's methods in the recent investigation in the Thirteenth Division in Brooklyn, with its startling results of criminal indictments against twenty-four plainclothesmen and ex-plainclothesmen and departmental charges against one dozen more, was a sharp break with the way the Department had previously handled such matters. In that investigation, a corrupt situation was allowed to continue for many months so that as many participants as possible could be identified. Corrupt policemen were "turned" and kept on the job as investigators. Similar techniques were used in the Bronx investigation leading to the recent indictments referred to above.

There has also been a real effort to get away from a strictly complaint-oriented approach, and the Department has undertaken an extensive study of corruption hazards in an attempt to analyze situations which lead to corruption and acquaint operational personnel with them.

While these improved methods have vastly increased the efficiency and effectiveness of departmental anti-corruption efforts, the Department has yet to make one other change in its investigative apparatus which the Commission feels is essential if the apparatus is to be fully effective. As discussed in the Principal Recommendations, the Commission believes that the Department's Inspectional Services Bureau should be reorganized along the lines of the Inspections Office of the Internal Revenue Service. Under this system, officers would be recruited into Inspectional Services right out of the Academy and would spend their entire careers in anti-corruption work. This would serve to insulate the anti-corruption unit from the rest of the force and insure that no officer would be called upon to investigate a former associate or face the possibility of sometime serving with—or even under the command of—someone he had once investigated. Such a reform should not conflict with Commissioner Murphy's attempts to make field commanders responsible in the first instance for integrity within their commands since the Inspectional Services Bureau could select the cases it chose to investigate and provide a monitoring service for those dealt with by field commanders.

Chapter Nineteen

DEPARTMENTAL DISCIPLINARY ACTION IN CORRUPTION CASES

Investigation of misconduct is the first step in a sequence of possible actions against allegedly corrupt police officers. Within the Department the next step is the disciplinary process. The disciplinary options available to the Commission in corruption cases as well as others are limited. Moreover, even these options have not always been utilized fully or effectively. The formal disciplinary apparatus was and is overburdened and understaffed, and the range of penalties available to deal with officers convicted in Departmental Hearings is inadequate.

Today, the options available to the Commissioner are being used more fully than in the past, and the formal departmental machinery has been relieved of the burden of dealing with minor infractions. However, the range of penalties still remains inadequate.

Administrative Discipline

Short of taking formal disciplinary actions, there are six options available to police management for rewarding good police performance and penalizing bad, and these comprise the range of alternatives for informal, administrative discipline. First, the Police Commissioner has the authority to promote any captain to any of five higher ranks: Deputy Inspector, Inspector, Deputy Chief Inspector, Assistant Chief Inspector, and Chief Inspector. And he has the authority to demote any officers in these higher ranks back to captain. Second, the Police Commissioner has a very limited authority to reward lower-ranking officers with promotion in that, while selections for the ranks of sergeant, lieutenant, and captain must (by Civil Service procedures) be made from a list of eligibles, the Commissioner can select any one of the three men at the top of the eligibles list; however, he has no authority to demote officers in these ranks. Third, the Police Commissioner has the authority to appoint and remove detectives at his discretion. Fourth, the Police Commissioner can reassign to new duties any officer on active duty at will. Fifth, the Police Commissioner has the authority to terminate probationary patrolmen. Sixth, the Police Commissioner has the authority to return any probationary sergeant, lieutenant, or captain to his former rank.

These promotion, demotion, and reassignment options have not been adequately exercised in the past against corrupt officers and their superiors. The potential importance of such options to the members of the force was illustrated by a comment of one police commander:

> "Sure, there are 32,000 policemen in New York, but all the same the Department is really quite small. There are only 500-odd captains-and-up, and we all know, or can easily find out, each other's reputations and assignments for the last ten years and how those assignments were carried out. The way we find out what's going on in the Department is not by studying the general orders or the temporary operating procedures or the rest of all that paper, but by studying the promotion orders and the assignment orders."

Early in his tenure Commissioner Murphy clouded the general excellence of his promotions by elevating to high rank a few officers whose integrity was widely questioned throughout the Department. These promotions raised doubts in the minds of many officers about the sincerity of his intentions to root out corruption. On the other hand, recent personnel changes, including assigning men experienced in anti-corruption work to important command posts, should tend to re-establish the Commissioner's credibility in this regard. This is vital because whatever changes may come in the rules and in the organization charts, the men and women in the Department will make their final assessment of the Commissioner's plans for reform on the brutal basis of how many—and above all which—heads roll.

Discipline of Commanders by the Police Commissioner

Although in past administrations a commander was occasionally relieved of his command, or reduced in rank, or even dismissed from the Department, for personal derelictions of duty, it was previously unheard-of for such actions to be taken against him as a result of derelictions by the men under him. Joseph McGovern, a former Supervising Assistant Chief Inspector and Chief of Inspectional Services, testified before this Commission that he could not think of a single precinct commander who had been shifted for failure to maintain the integrity of his command. Indeed there is little evidence to suggest that such derelictions by subordinates ever seriously impeded a commander's rise to higher rank.

By comparison with previous administrations, a considerable number of high-ranking officers were demoted or transferred for such reasons during the first year and a half of Commissioner Murphy's tenure. As of March, 1972, five of fifteen assistant chief inspectors (ACI's), two of twenty-three deputy chief inspectors (DCI's), four of forty-three inspectors, five of 104 deputy inspectors, and nine out of 366 captains had been relieved of their commands. Of the sixteen officers ranking above captain who were relieved, seven have since retired. Four of the transfers of captains, it is worth noting, occurred as the result of unannounced spot inspections of the precincts they commanded. Such use of unannounced spot inspections is a major departure from past practice. Eight of the transfers of captains were for derelictions of the men under them.

However, the major test with respect to command personnel is yet to come. In March, of this year, Commissioner Murphy signified to his top commanders his intention of effecting each year a thirty percent turnover in each of the ranks above captain. This means that at the end of each year he intends five of the men who were ACI's at the beginning of the year, eight of those who were DCI's fourteen of those who were inspectors, and thirty-four of those who were deputy inspectors will either have been promoted or retired—or conceivably demoted. This policy would enable the promotion of thirty-four captains into the deputy inspector vacancies. More than half of all present top commanders will be gone within three years if Commissioner Murphy can fully implement this new policy. While this approach may have advantages with respect to eliminating past corruption problems, the wisdom of applying such a rapid turnover policy on a long-term basis is debatable.

To make the system of discretionary promotions more reasonable and combat the formerly pervasive influence system, Commissioner Murphy has created a promotion review board consisting of three deputy commissioners, the chief inspector, and the Department's next four highest-ranking officers to pass on all promotions above the rank of captain, and he has ordered that board to conduct a long face-to-face interview with each man being considered for promotion, in addition to studying his record and the evaluations of his superiors. Further, although the Commissioner has only selection authority in promotions to captain and below, the administration has attempted to impose some control on promotions by taking advantage of a previously unused civil service provision which specifies that each new sergeant serve a six-month internship—which is, in fact, a probationary period. During this time he may be demoted to patrolman. Of the first group of sergeants subject to this probationary period one has been demoted. This six-month probationary period has also been applied to the ranks of lieutenant and captain.

Removal/Appointment of Detectives

Detectives in all police departments generally occupy a position of privileged status. This may derive from the fact that their duties are considered by policemen to be the most honorific and the least onerous. Detectives are assigned to do what most policemen think all policemen should be doing, solving crimes and tracking down criminals. The fact of detective privilege is very real in New

York City. "Detective" is not a civil service grade in New York as it is in many cities, or a rank that is attained by departmental examination as in Chicago. It is an appointive post that carries with it not only prestige, but also a considerably higher rate of pay than that in the uniformed force. A third-grade detective earns more than a patrolman. A second-grade detective earns as much as a uniformed sergeant. A first-grade detective and a detective sergeant earn as much as a uniformed lieutenant. A senior detective lieutenant earns more than a newly promoted uniformed captain. Thus, removal from detective rank can mean the loss of several thousand dollars a year in salary. Nevertheless, the power to punish detectives by removing them from rank was seldom exercised by past police commissioners. In 1969, the last full pre-Murphy year, nine third-grade detectives, three second-grade detectives, and no first-grade detectives were reduced to patrolmen. In 1971, the first full Murphy year, the equivalent figures are twenty-eight, seven, and four. Moreover, detective appointments were seldom used in past administrations as a means of rewarding honest performance of police duties.

Although police commissioners have always had the power to appoint and remove detectives, they have seldom disapproved the appointment lists submitted by the Chief of Detectives. Moreover, it is in the appointment of detectives that influence peddling has always been most widely thought to play a significant part. As noted earlier in this report, Patrolman Phillips, working undercover for the Commission, initiated tape-recorded negotiations with a policeman serving as a chauffeur for a high-ranking officer to buy his way into the Detective Bureau. The usual price, he was told, was $500, but since Phillips had already been "flopped" from the Detective Bureau it would cost him $1,000. Because of the press of Phillips' other investigative activities the matter could not be pursued. There is no way of knowing whether this particular policeman's representations were true, but it is certainly a fact that detective positions were at the time widely considered to be for sale.

Criteria for appointment to the Detective Bureau in the immediate past apparently shifted frequently, but on the whole approximated these: four years in a plainclothes or narcotics assignments with a "satisfactory" record; or four years in the Tactical Patrol Force with an outstanding arrest record; or "in special cases,"—these are the Department's words—"men who had performed well in patrol precincts," which left room for anyone at all if his sponsor had enough influence.

The Department has now established a "career paths" program which sets out the assignments a patrolman must serve before he can be considered for detective status. The path that leads to detective rank requires that a patrolman, after spending a mandatory year in a "medium-activity" precinct and two years in either a "high-activity" precinct, the Tactical Patrol Force, or the citywide Anti-Crime Section, volunteer (with the approval of a screening board consisting of three deputy inspectors, one each from the Narcotics Division, the Public Morals Division, and the Patrol Services Bureau) to serve two years in plainclothes in either narcotics or public morals (gambling and vice) enforcement. If at the end of that service his superiors evaluate him favorably with respect to both efficiency and integrity, and another screening board again passes him, he will be eligible to become a detective when a suitable vacancy occurs.

This career path has existed only since December, 1971, and the earliest anyone treading it will reach the Detective Bureau is some time during 1973. There are reasons for not being optimistic that this program will drastically alter the face of the Detective Bureau. One is that the plainclothes units have been the Department's most corruption-prone because of the nature of their work, and no matter what managerial improvements are made, will continue to contain the greatest exposure to hazards and temptations. However, any step toward systematizing the selection of detectives in New York is a step in the right direction, particularly if its effect is to make detectives less dependent for their jobs on the private interests or quirks of other detectives or superior officers. Other steps that might be taken to systematize further the selection of detectives would be to require a promotion examination and to use a detective selection board including experienced investigators from other law enforcement agencies as is done in some other cities.

Extension of Administrative Discipline

Perhaps because of the seeming limitations on administrative actions, the concept of departmental discipline prevailing in the past was a rigid and legalistic one. Not even the most minor infractions —improper uniform, temporary absence from post, late for duty, and the like—could be handled without resort to a long and elaborate process of prosecution and adjudication. Commissioner Murphy has revised departmental disciplinary procedures so that precinct commanders can immediately and directly discipline the men under them with penalties of up to loss of five days vacation time for a number of violations of departmental rules. This strengthening of command discipline has led to huge increases in disciplinary actions in situations where commanders were previously loathe to invoke the Department's elaborate trial machinery. During the first quarter of 1971 approximately 198 cases of these minor infractions were processed by the elaborate trial machinery. For the same period in 1972, 2,461 such minor infractions were handled as command discipline cases at the precinct level.

With this important exception, the Murphy administration has been able to make few visible changes in the Department's disciplinary structure and procedures. On the whole, the structure and procedures are prescribed by the City's Administrative Code or the State's Civil Service Law and therefore can be changed only through the time-consuming and sometimes difficult process of legislative amendment. Consequently, the way the Department now handles major charges of misconduct against its members—including most charges of corruption—is the same way it has handled them for years.

The Police Justice Process

Once charges and specifications against a policeman are drawn by his commander, the Internal Affairs Division, or the Civilian Complaint Review Board, the charges go to the Department Advocate's office. He is, in effect, an in-house prosecutor reporting to the First Deputy Commissioner who has the additional responsibility of reporting on the total disciplinary climate of the Department. Once the Department Advocate and defense counsel have prepared a case for trial, much as the prosecution and the defense would in the outside world, it goes to trial by the Deputy Commissioner for Trials. Trials are decided on the basis of "the preponderance of the evidence" so that guilt does not have to be established beyond a reasonable doubt as in criminal trials. At the conclusion of the hearing the Trials Deputy makes an advisory determination of guilt or innocence and, in case of guilt suggests a penalty. His findings are forwarded to the Commissioner. It is the Commissioner's responsibility, under the Administrative Code, to make the Department's ultimate decision on the facts and on the punishment, if any.

In the past the police justice process has suffered from four principal deficiencies: overburdened trial machinery with insufficient resources; undue delays in bringing cases to trial; lack of punitive alternatives; and problems posed by judicial review.

Conduct of Departmental Hearings

The volume of cases reaching the Department Advocate and the Trials Deputy is seriously straining their capacity.

In the departmental system of discipline, the most overworked man—and the narrowest bottleneck—is the Trials Deputy. He has the responsibility of presiding over every departmental disciplinary hearing. The Administrative Code specifies that only a person of his rank, and with legal qualifications, is empowered to conduct such hearings.

Occasionally, when the pressure of cases becomes particularly intense, the two other deputy commissioners are drafted for a few days, and the Trials Deputy also uses a lower-ranking lawyer in the Department to pre-audit a certain number of cases. However, over the year he himself probably averages three or four trials per working day. Even granting that a majority of the cases are minor and that the evidence in many of them is conclusive, such a schedule makes it difficult for him to deal with serious, complicated cases either as promptly or as fully as they deserve.

The Department Advocate is only a little better off than the Trials Deputy. He has a staff of six uniformed and two civilian lawyers. These nine men processed 1937 cases during 1971. Of these, 292 were returned to the commands where they originated for command discipline procedure, and 1932 cases, many of which were pending from past years, were brought to trial. (Of those cases, the Department Advocate's figures show 186 were corruption cases in the categories of bribery, extortion, larceny, criminal receiving, gambling, and narcotics.) It is easy to see that if eight men have an annual caseload of 1900, whenever one man spends more than a day disposing of a case another man has to dispose of two or three cases a day—and that includes both preparation time and trial time.

Lack of adequate time for preparation in the not very recent past was so common that Detective Frank Serpico, the chief witness in the departmental trials of a number of Bronx plainclothesmen, was put on the stand without having been given any opportunity to refresh his recollection and asked to testify concerning four-year-old events. However, the advocate's caseload has been reduced by the new procedure which grants commanders authority to handle command discipline cases. Before this new procedure was instituted, the Department Advocate's caseload was approaching 200 a month. Now it is down to not much more than eighty. The consequent saving in trial time has had the effect of giving prosecutors extra time to prepare their cases when serious charges of corruption, excessive force, and abuse of authority are brought.

Delays: Since there were 909 cases pending at the beginning of calendar 1971 and 880 pending at the end of it, there was no great progress in clearing up the backlog. The Department Advocate estimates that the average time consumed between charges and disposition is six months or more. These delays pose a problem in terms of the thirty-day rule which governs departmental hearings.

Under this rule, an officer suspected of or charged with misconduct is permitted to put in his retirement papers and retire thirty days later, at which time he becomes immune to departmental disciplinary proceedings and eligible to receive his pension if he has served long enough to qualify for one. This results in a thirty-day race, with a suspected officer seeking to retire before the disciplinary proceedings against him can be completed. Although only a handful of policemen escaped discipline by this route, the ones who did escape often were the most serious offenders. For example, there were ten thirty-day cases in 1970. Trials were held in seven of them, resulting in five dismissals from the force and two acquittals. In the first of the remaining three, the defendant executed a complex technical maneuver that probably will never be repeated. In the second, the defendant was in a psychiatric hospital. However, in the third case, a bribe-receiving case against a lieutenant that may well have been that year's most important case, the lieutenant's lawyer was able to prolong the trial, which began twenty-five days before the deadline, past that deadline's expiration, enabling the lieutenant to retire with his full pension. In 1971 the record was better. There were eleven thirty-day rule cases, and all of them were tried. Six resulted in dismissal from the force and five in the next most severve penalty, thirty days' fine and a year's probation.

There are no statistics reflecting the number of situations where a police officer resigned before charges were brought but after he realized he was in danger of being charged. Under these circumstances, the Department might well never attempt to bring charges since it is virtually impossible to complete disciplinary proceedings within thirty days unless the investigation and preparation of the case has already been completed.

Penalties in Departmental Hearings

Perhaps the most troublesome issue in the disciplining of policemen found guilty in departmental hearings is the inappropriateness of the available penalties. The Administrative Code provides no gradations of penalty between outright dismissal from the force and a fine of up to and including thirty days' pay or vacation followed by a year's probation.* The Commission has recommended that the disciplinary alternatives available to the Police Commissioner be broadened to include greater periods than thirty days. However, even the available penalties were often utilized in the past to treat corrupt officers in a lenient manner.

Unfortunately, the Department does not maintain summary statistics on corruption case dispositions in terms of the charges brought. To obtain informaton on corrupton cases and the penalties invoked for corruption-related offenses, it is necessary to search the individual disciplinary record of each officer brought to trial.** In doing so, it is often difficult to determine from the record whether a case is corruption-related or not. (For example, an officer charged with making a false statement could either have lied during a grand jury investigation into his involvement in gambling operations or else in his memo book to cover up returning five minutes late from lunch.) Three separate counts were made of the number of corruption cases processed

---

* It should be noted that a fine of thirty days' pay or less of active-duty officers is usually not all taken out of the next paycheck, but is taken out one or two days at a time from each subsequent paycheck.

** The Department Advocate's office records only the dispositions that are handed down on the day of the trial, and most dispositions are reserved for later decision.

during 1971 and three different figures were reached. The Department Advocate's office counted 186 cases, Disciplinary Records Section counted 238, and the Commission staff counted 223.

Of the 223 corruption cases counted by the Commission for 1971, the complaint was dismissed before the hearing in thirty cases, the charges were filed* in six, and amnesty was granted in three. In another nine cases, the officer resigned without permission before the hearing was held; and in twenty cases the officer was dismissed from the Department before the trial, as is usual for officers on probationary status and those convicted in criminal trials. Of the remaining 155 cases, seventy-nine are pending. Of the seventy-six cases brought to disposition, eighteen resulted in an acquittal and fifty-eight in conviction. The following penalties were imposed on the fifty-eight convicted officers: Seventeen were dismissed from the force; five were placed on one year's probation, and four of these five also lost days of pay averaging twenty-two and one-half days per man; twenty-four officers were fined an average of 4.8 vacation days; eight were fined an average of thirteen and three-quarters days' pay; and four officers were reprimanded.

Judicial Review

The Police Commissioner's decisions on penalties in disciplinary hearings are subject to judicial review, and in fact have been reversed in several recent, well-publicized corruption cases. The reasons for reversal usually centered on the requirement for pension forfeiture upon dismissal for cause from the force. This was one of the considerations that motivated the Commission's recommendation, discussed in the Summary, for the separation of pension considerations from departmental disciplinary hearings. The Department should not be obliged to keep corrupt police officers in its ranks merely because some courts feel that loss of pension is too harsh a penalty for some offenses.

---

* "Filing" of a charge is a departmental disposition in which the filed charge is put aside due to lack of cooperation by the complainant or witnesses or because of lack of evidence or witnesses.

Chapter Twenty

CHANGES IN DEPARTMENTAL POLICIES AND PROCEDURES AFFECTING CORRUPTION CONTROL

During his tenure Commissioner Murphy has instituted numerous changes in policy and procedure aimed at improving the efficiency and effectiveness of the Department. To the extent they are successful, all such changes will have some impact in reducing corruption. However, the Commission has focused on those changes whose impact on corruption are expected to be most direct and significant: policies and procedures to provide accountability; policies and procedures to control corruption hazards; training of police officers; and officer evaluation procedures. These are discussed below in terms of past difficulties, corrective actions taken by this administration and the prospects for a reduction in police corruption.

Providing Accountability

On January 28, 1971, from 3:00 a.m. to 7:00 a.m., eight police officers in a Greenwich Village precinct were observed by Commission investigators removing packages from a meat packing company and transferring them to private cars. This incident was significant not so much because of the activities of the officers involved but because of the complete lack of concern with these activities demonstrated by their immediate superiors. The supervising sergeant of the officers drove by, apparently observed what was going on, and left; Commission investigators twice notified the precinct headquarters, but no action was taken; the supervising lieutenant (in charge of the precinct in the absence of the commanding precinct captain) could not even be found and later could not account for his time for a period of at least two hours. An investigation was finally initiated at 7:00 a.m. when Commission investigators notified division headquarters.

The patrolmen directly involved in the theft were suspended, and departmental and criminal charges were brought against them. Had nothing more been done, this incident would have been another example of what has been perhaps the Department's most fundamental managerial defect—the utter failure to hold supervisors and commanders accountable for the derelictions of their subordinates. This failure has been a major contributing factor not only to corruption but to the cynicism in the ranks that makes corruption possible.

In this case, Commissioner Murphy took action not only against the patrolmen who had been caught but also against those responsible for supervising them. He transferred the commanding captain of the precinct and eight sergeants and brought charges against the lieutenant in command at the time and against another lieutenant, three sergeants, and nine patrolmen. These actions were in line with the Commissoner's strongly stated policy to reverse the tradition of lack of accountability.

The pervasive failure in the Department to hold commanders and supervisors responsible for the actions of their subordinates has been a managerial failure, not an ideological one. Departmental rules have long emphasized command accountability. However, during the many years when the corruption that led to the creation of this Commission was growing, the Department never succeeded—despite the efforts of some police commissioners—in translating dogma into operating routine.

Making command accountability work is not an easy task. It takes considerable effort for a precinct commander to keep track of the multitude of things his widely dispersed subordinates are doing at any given time. And it takes considerable moral effort, given the fraternal atmosphere of a station house, for him to institute and enforce the unpopular measures necessary to control that multitude of men and activities. When a commander is not held to strict account for the performance of the men under him, he is likely to avoid as much of the tension and anxiety as possible that would attend his job if he were doing it well.

The Problem of Fixing Responsibility: Commissioner Murphy has taken a number of administrative and operational steps designed to force all officers to assume their full responsibilities. Many of these measures have been concerned with trying to ensure that the responsibility for a given activity at a given time in a given place could be clearly identified with the field officer on duty, the sergeant and lieutenant supervising him, and the captain and higher ranking officers in command.

This problem of assigning responsibility has not been easy for a number of reasons. First, a patrolman in the field does not work in the same assigned area during the same hours on every working day. Instead, all patrolmen follow a very complicated duty chart which requires that they rotate shifts every three to five days. They are not always assigned to the same walking post or patrol car sector because such factors as sick leave, vacations, and court appearances reduce the complement of men supposed to be in the field and often require leaving a post or sector vacant or having one man or car assigned to two posts or sectors. Second, because sergeants work a different duty chart from patrolmen and the patrolmen they supervise change from week to week, they have seldom been given responsibility for performance of specified groups of men. Moreover, sergeants have seldom been given long-term responsibility for the police work in specified geographical areas. Instead, their responsibilities have often varied from tour to tour depending on the exigencies of the moment. Third, lieutenants, who are the second-line supervisors, have in the past usually served in a staff capacity as desk and duty officers and have not been out in the field at all. (The exception was certain plainclothes units supervised by lieutenants instead of sergeants.) Fourth, while certain captains or deputy inspectors have been assigned command of a particular precinct in the past, there were also substitute or "fly" captains who had no permanent assignments but moved from job to job to fill in for commanders who for one reason or another were off their jobs temporarily.

All of this shifting around meant that it was virtually impossible to fix on any individual the responsibility for conditions that clearly suggested corruption was taking place. Moreover, the same shifting around also made it unrealistic to blame any one supervisor for the failures of the men under him since all the men worked for all the supervisors at one time or another.

Historically, lieutenants and sergeants have not supervised the men under them rigorously. Responsible supervision has simply not been insisted upon by commanders. Sergeants are only one rank— and in most instances, only a few years—removed from the duties and activities of the patrolmen they are supposed to supervise. Hence, they tend to identify with patrolmen rather than with the hierarchy above them.

Lack of fixed responsibility was not only confined to patrolmen but also extended to detectives. Although reporting to the Detective Bureau, detective squads used to work out of precinct houses and handled, more or less in rotation, whatever investigations happened to come up. Because most of the time no priorities existed, and the volume of work was extremely large, they could not be held responsible for failing to solve any particular crimes.

Improving Supervisory Accountability: Several approaches have been made in attempting to cure these many unsatisfactory conditions. At the heart of these efforts have been two closely related innovations in precinct structure and operations: Neighborhood Police Teams and the Lieutenant/Operations Officer Program.

A Neighborhood Police Team is a group of from 20 to 50 patrolmen and sergeants and a "commanding" sergeant that is permanently assigned to a given radio motor patrol sector or sectors. The commanding sergeant—of course under the direction and supervision of the precinct commander and the duty lieutenants—is in complete command of the team; he is, in fact, very much like a precinct commander in miniature. He is responsible for police work in his sector on a twenty-four-hour-a-day basis. He is expected to identify the sector's problems and needs, to deploy his men to meet them, and to supervise and evaluate their performance. He and his men will presumably become widely known in the sector and knowledgeable about it; they will become acquainted with its leading citizens and characters; they will become aware of its sociological and cultural patterns; and they will cease being more or less faceless embodiments of authority and become the individually identifiable helpers and protectors of the public that policemen ideally should be. At the present time, 141 of the City's 808 radio motor patrol sectors in forty precincts are covered by sixty-six Neighborhood Police Teams.

The Lieutenant/Operations Officer Program, which is in effect now in thirty-eight precincts, aims at the same goal of improving supervisory accountability as the Neighborhood Police Team Program. It gives each of the sergeants in a precinct twenty-four-hour-a-day responsibility for a given sector, under the supervision of a lieutenant who has been designated as the precinct Operations Officer and who, also on a twenty-four-hour-a-day basis, is responsible for the deployment of all the precinct's men and equipment. He is also responsible for reviewing the patrolmen's written reports of their daily activity.

Improving Command Accountability: A related reform has been the elimination of the fly captains and the assignment of specific responsibilities to all staff officers. Today every ranking officer is responsible for specific duties; many of the captains who in the past would have been "flying" (acting as substitutes) are the executive officers of busy precincts, where they are not only responsible for commanding in the absence of the commander, but more importantly, are responsible for handling the enormous amount of administrative detail that police work involves. Staff lieutenants and sergeants are no longer jacks-of-all-trades in the precincts, but are expected to perform the duties of Planning, Personnel, Training, Operations Officer and other staff assignments. Presumably the delegation of staff functions will enable a commander to spend more time commanding and less time on administrative ritual. Further, commanders have also been forced to focus on corruption.

All patrol borough commanders and the heads of all the specialized units—Traffic, Technical Services, Detectives and so forth—are now required to submit at regular intervals anti-corruption plans identifying the chief corruption hazards within their commands and detailing the measures that are being taken to reduce those hazards. The first set of plans arrived on the Commissioner's desk in July, 1971, and vividly illustrated a wide spectrum of sophistication and sensitivity about integrity. Some of the plans were detailed and precise and thoughtful. Some sought refuge in sociological and psychological verbiage about the "attitudinal" problems of corruption and the importance of "sensitizing" policemen. Some were useless. One borough commander whose command included a big part of the New York ghetto, with all its gambling and narcotics activity, identified "after-hours Puerto Rican social clubs" as the major corruption hazard in his command. Another reported that the principal corruption hazard in his command—which he no longer holds—was a small middle-class enclave where bar and restaurant owners were likely to try to bribe policemen so their customers could park illegally. Subsequent plans of rather higher quality have been produced and are being analyzed within the Department. In any case, requiring commanders to write and sign such plans is another step toward holding them to account for the conditions in their commands.

The program of requiring commanders to evaluate the corruption hazards within their areas of supervision could be expanded to include general evaluations in connection with specific incidents. Whenever an incident involving corruption comes to light in a command, such as the apprehension of a patrolman for a corrupt act, the commander should be obliged to report to his superiors and to the Internal Affairs

Division whether he thinks the incident is indicative of a broader condition. He should detail the reasons for his conclusion and outline planned corrective measures if needed.

Improving Detective Accountability: By the nature of their jobs, detectives are even more difficult to supervise than patrolmen. They roam about the City freely and sometimes are called upon to travel out of it. Their hours are often flexible—a flexibility that can and sometimes has been used to make substantial reductions in the working week. They deal extensively with informants, which allows many opportunities for the clandestine manipulation of information and evidence. They come across numerous incidents, from incompletely burglarized premises to narcotics pushers, in which it is easy to "score." In sum, a detective inclined to misbehave has always had plenty of chances to follow his inclinations. Under those conditions, the necessity to fix responsibility is paramount.

This has been approached by a major organizational change in the Detective Bureau called "detective specialization." As of January, 1971, detectives no longer work out of the precincts and are no longer generalists. They work only on a district basis (a detective district is coterminous with a patrol division and therefore includes anything from three to seven precincts) and are organized into specialized squads of homicide and assault, robbery, and burglary and larceny. Crimes that occur less frequently are assigned to one of these squads or are handled by small, specialized units. For example, the homicide-assault squads investigate rapes, and a special hotel unit operates in midtown Manhattan under the general aegis of the burglary-larceny squad there.

There are two principal objectives of this program. One is to improve the quality of criminal investigations and the other is, again, accountability. The Department hopes to make misconduct by detectives more difficult by pinpointing their responsibilities and curtailing their freewheeling activity.

238

Prospects for Long-Term Changes: It is still too early to determine if the many changes instituted to improve accountability will indeed force officers to act against corruption they know about. Continued monitoring will be necessary to determine if these programs are effective over the long term.

Controlling Corruption Hazards

In line with the concerted efforts to provide accountability, the Murphy administration has taken numerous steps aimed at the control of corruption hazards. These steps have been of two types. First, the opportunities for corrupt activity have been lessened by diminishing or redirecting the enforcement of certain laws which foster corruption. For example, Sabbath laws are no longer enforced, except upon a specific complaint, and the plainclothes units now concentrate not on street gambling but on putting gambling combines out of business. Complementary to these types of reforms have been measures to limit the exposure to corruption hazards, where such exposure must occur, to officers of higher rank who presumably have a greater stake in maintaining their reputations. For example, all important gambling and narcotics arrests are to be made by sergeants as are inspections of licensed premises.

While it is difficult to assess the impact of these changes on corruption, all indications are that there has been some reduction.

Improving, Training and Evaluation

The integrity of a police department depends in large measure upon adequate procedures to see that the new recruit is honest, that his training fortifies that tendency, and that his superiors accurately evaluate his performance once he begins the job.

Training and education are recognized approaches for changing the attitudes and motivations of police officers. Prior to the Murphy administration they were utilized as methods of combating corruption.

The part of the curriculum that dealt with the hazards of corruption and the proper responses to them was deficient—if not non-existent— prior to the present administration of the Department. At the Commission's public hearings, Edward Droge and Waverly Logan, both of whom had had their Academy careers interrupted by several months of emergency service in the street, testified with some emphasis how unrealistic, even comical, the Academy's skimpy material on corruption seemed to them after they had witnessed the real thing on the job.

Recruit Training: Corruption used to be one of several matters treated by the chaplain in the course of his six hours of Academy lectures. Copies of the Policemen's Code of Ethics were also distributed. During regular instructions on the Penal Law the bribery statutes were covered, but corruption was traditionally regarded as a matter of individual conscience and not in any large sense as an environmental or departmental problem. Moreover, the realities of the extent of corruption and the specific corruption hazards to be faced by new patrolmen were avoided on the ostensible theory that they should not be taught how to go wrong.

Corruption is no longer simply a subject of academic interest at the Police Academy. The new recruit is now instructed in every possible course as well as in special classes that the Department has a serious problem of corruption and what forms it takes. He is told that there have been corrupt policemen and very likely that many still remain on the force. His courses include tape recordings and other material evidence of corruption gathered by this Commission.

The new recruit program includes twenty hours of discussions and lectures that range through all known forms of police crime and corruption. These twenty hours are spread over the total days of recruit training. The old theory that discussing details of corruption might teach some recruits tricks they didn't know has been abandoned in favor of a more realistic approach. Extensive use is made of workshop and group discussion techniques. Role-playing is used to increase the impact and believability of the conditions to which the new recruit will soon be exposed.

A paragraph taken from part of the curriculum is illustrative of the new attitude at the Academy:

"As a practical matter, this is the point in your police career when you should decide what kind of police officer you are going to be. If your decision is, as we hope it is, to be an honest cop, then expect to live on the salary you earn and never start the slow corrosive slide into corruption. A slide that usually starts with a pack of cigarettes or a dollar and ends with disgrace and active criminality. If there is a cynic among you who feels that this hour has been a "snow job", to him we suggest that he become an honest crook. Leave the department and become an honest thief. Before you are caught you will make a great deal more money mugging old men or sticking up shopkeepers than you will as a chiseling cop. And, after you are caught you can expect fair treatment from the other convicts in prison. On the prison social ladder the crooked cop rates just below the child molester."

It must be kept in mind that the recruit's training period is a time when he should be evaluated as well as instructed. A recent New York City Rand Institute study found that the most reliable predictors of a policeman's ultimate performance are his performance in recruit training and during his probationary period as a patrolman. However, there is little evidence that in years gone by departmental superiors assigned new men on the basis of those indicators. In fact it had been a tradition not to dismiss a probationary patrolman except for the most flagrant kind of misconduct—which tradition vitiated the entire purpose of probation. There is some reason to believe that if the Department had gotten rid at the very outset of the men who scored worst at the Academy and conducted themselves worst as probationers, it would have nipped in the bud the careers of an appreciable number of corrupt policemen.

Academy Training of Superior Officers: Sergeants: The Academy's training for officers being promoted to the rank of sergeant does not spare their feelings, and it is no longer presumed that they are "clean" simply because they are being promoted. They are taught that they must make arrests for corrupt acts which other persons (including themselves) may have committed with impunity even a short time ago.

The pre-promotional training for patrolmen who are about to make sergeant has been extended from six weeks a year ago and as few as three weeks some years back to a present total of seven weeks. The training course is entitled "Basic Management Orientation" and is meant to develop management and leadership skills as well as imparting supervisory techniques. The course now also contains thirty-four-and-a-half hours of anti-corruption training. It includes field work, actual duty with the Inspections Division, training in all areas of anti-corruption activities and many hours of guidance sessions in small groups aimed at discussing and resolving on a mutual basis problems and problem situations that have and will confront these men as they progress in their careers.

Lieutenants and Captains: Pre-promotional courses for lieutenants and captains are entitled "Middle Management I" and "Middle Management II." They carry forward the theory that the Department needs effective management in order to do an effective job. The courses last two and three weeks, respectively, and each contains eight hours of anti-corruption activity.

Field Training: The most extensive anti-corruption training problem, however, is in the rank and file of the Department already on the job. The men on the beat, in the cars, and in the special squads have either participated in or been exposed to corruption for their entire careers. The Academy is trying to reach those men with a variety of field programs aimed at duplicating the "facts of life attitude" taken with recruits.

In keeping with the efforts at decentralization and command responsibility, the Academy supervises a program of workshops, lectures, and special classes at various command levels designed to penetrate to the places where anti-corruption strength is most sorely needed.

One of the Department's more encouraging innovations in anti-corruption training is a series of Ethical Awareness Workshops, run by a sergeant and a patrolman. In eight to ten three-hour sessions, using imaginative techniques like role-playing in a no-holds-barred atmosphere, the workshop leaders encourage the participants to explore what corruption really is and how it affects them, to confront their own attitudes toward corrupt acts, and to reach some conclusions about just what they feel is morally permissible and what is not. Surprisingly, almost all the officers who have been through the workshop have come to the conclusion that even accepting a free cup of coffee is compromising and even insulting.

While it remains to be seen how long these new attitudes prevail after the officers have left the workshop and returned to the pressures of the station house and the street, these workshops appear to be a most promising tool in the hardest phase of the anti-corruption fight, namely changing the attitudes of the rank and file.

Group leaders from every command in the Department are now being trained in these techniques, and will return to their commands to lead their own workshops, eventually reaching a substantial percentage of the Department.

In addition to special efforts being made at the Academy to professionalize the anti-corruption training of recruits in the Department, the Academy feels that in the long run future the Executive Development Program and the Management Techniques Program now being fully developed will be the strongest elements in the anti-corruption fight. From these programs will come the administrative and command staffs whose training and development hopefully will inculcate a professional attitude incompatible with dishonesty.

Evaluation: Training efforts and institutional reforms to combat corruption can have only a limited effect. The orders and instructions can go down through the ranks to the officer on the street, but whether they are obeyed depends on the mechanisms available for monitoring and evaluating performance and controlling compliance.

Performance evaluation poses special problems. Detective specialization has provided an improved means for measuring the effectiveness of individual detectives in executing their principal responsibility of solving serious crimes and apprehending their suspects. But the duties of the patrolman are far more diffuse, involving as they do a wide variety of activities ranging from the mediation of family conflicts and street fights to assisting the ill and injured, from directing traffic to patrolling an assigned area. Since most of the situations in which the patrolman intervenes are not criminal in the sense that they call for arrest and prosecution, crime and arrest statistics are consequently only partial measures of police effectiveness. For example, the use of arrest statistics as a measure of police effectiveness simply tempts the police to make large numbers of easy arrests. More complex measures of performance have to be instituted. Those used in the past involved assessments by superior officers of various personal traits thought to be crucial to good performance or indicative of poor performance along with a listing of the quantities of arrests in each crime category. These evaluations, however, were often made by supervisors who had few opportunities to observe the officer at work, because of the different duty charts of supervisors and patrolmen alluded to earlier.

Although the patrolman evaluation form still contains judgments about personal attributes, the evaluation procedures have been reformed. The form now places more emphasis on efficiency and integrity and less on number of arrests made. Working conditions on the streets are being altered, and evaluators are supposed to spend more time with the men they are expected to evaluate. Supervisors are also required to discuss their evaluations in detail with the evaluated officers. Evaluators, at all levels, have been told that they will be held accountable, if not for their infallibility, at least for the honesty of their judgments, and a board of high-ranking officers has been established to review all evaluations.

These changes in officer evaluation procedures have had an especially significant impact on the plainclothes units. The reform welcomed most heartily by policemen our staff talked with was the de-emphasis of "the Sheet" as it existed in both public morals and narcotics. In public morals, the Sheet was a wall chart, posted in the offices of every plainclothes unit. It displayed the number of arrests each member of the unit had made each month of the current year and each month of the previous year. A plainclothsman's performance was evaluated almost exclusively by the statistics on the Sheet. The arrest quotas were not absolute but relative. Each man was expected to make as many arrests each month as the same month of the prior year. New plainclothesmen were also expected to keep pace with their colleagues. As a result, supervision of plainclothesmen all too often consisted of the lieutenant—there were then no sergeants in public morals—studying the Sheet periodically and exhorting the men accordingly.

As a result of new procedures there is reason to believe that the quality of evaluations is improving and, even more to the point, the attention being given evaluations by those responsible for managing police careers is increasing. However, the effectiveness of evaluation as a personnel management tool depends ultimately not on orders or forms or systems but on honesty, perception, intelligence, and a host of other qualities that no Commissioner can decree or Chief of Personnel enforce. In short, subjective evaluations are only as good as the evaluators who write them.

Chapter Twenty-One

ANTI-POLICE-CORRUPTION EFFORTS BY THE DEPARTMENT OF INVESTIGATION

Under the City Charter, the Commissioner of Investigation ". . . is authorized and empowered to make any study or investigation which in his opinion may be in the best interests of the City, including but not limited to investigation of the affairs, functions, actions, methods, personnel or efficiency of any agency." However, the department's ability to investigate police corruption cases is, in practical terms, quite limited.

Judge Arnold Fraiman testified that while he was Commissioner of Investigation, the department had a staff of fifteen lawyers and sixteen investigators with which to perform all its investigations of all City agencies and that, in practice, it was impossible to cover all areas. Judge Fraiman stated that over the life of his department various commissioners had placed emphasis on different kinds of investigations and that, as far as he was aware, the Department of Investigation had never concerned itself with police corruption prior to his taking office. Judge Fraiman said that the feeling within the Department of Investigation was that it could not cope with the problem of police corruption and fulfill its other duties, especially in light of the fact that other units existed with the capability of dealing with police corruption.

In his testimony before the Commission in executive session, Judge Fraiman stated that when he assumed office in January, 1966, he made a "conscious decision" to combat police corruption "in some limited way." Fraiman stated, "I was more concerned about police corruption than other kinds of corruption because I felt and feel that this is the worst kind of corruption there is."

When asked later at the Commission's public hearings how many police officers had been brought up on charges as a result of the Department of Investigation's work during his three-year tenure, Judge Fraiman said that he could recall ten cases. When asked to specify, he listed seven relatively minor cases of individual misconduct by policemen, of which only four involved corruption. Three of the corruption cases were made against officers who received payoffs and the fourth involved an officer's possession of money apparently received from gamblers.

Commissioner Robert Ruskin, who assumed office in January, 1969, conducted seventy investigations into police corruption through 1971: seventeen in 1969; forty in 1970 (fifteen of which flowed from actions of the Rankin Committee); and thirteen in 1971. Of these, fifteen in 1970 resulted in the arrest and/or suspension of police officers, and one investigation uncovered an area of systematic widespread corruption (involving the sale of police arrest and conviction records to private agencies). As a result of this investigation in 1970, five police officers were arrested, and disciplinary action was taken by the Police Department against approximately one hundred others, including the suspension of one. Statistics are not kept on investigations the department initiated which lead to disciplinary action by the Police Department short of suspension or on those referred to the district attorneys.

As its record illustrates, the Department of Investigation never seriously concerned itself with police corruption. Several reasons have been put forth to explain this failure. The department has a limited staff to handle a large number of complaints involving all City agencies. Commissioner Ruskin is able to act on about 300 such complaints out of the 6,000 to 10,000 he receives yearly.

Only complaints containing specific allegations of serious misconduct, possibly criminal in nature, are retained for investigation. Judge Fraiman gave the example of an anonymous letter stating Sergeant X of the Police Department is being paid off by bookies at Joe's Bar on Tuesday nights. If such a complaint were received, it would be given a case number and then assigned to an attorney who would supervise the investigative work. The system does break down occasionally as evidenced by the fact that Serpico's charges, although far more serious in nature than complaints which became the subjects of investigations, were never given a case number or assigned to an attorney.

In addition to its limited manpower, the Department of Investigation faces two further difficulties one of which specifically undercuts its ability to investigate police. Its investigative staff is made up of police and a few civilians who work with the police unit under the supervision of a ranking police officer. According to Judge Fraiman this presented a problem contributing to his lack of success in many police cases since he recognized that policemen are not enthusiastic about this kind of investigation. The second problem is the absence of power to grant immunity. While the department does have the power to subpoena witnesses to testify under oath in private or public hearings, it cannot compel a recalcitrant witness to testify by giving him immunity. For years the department has tried to eliminate this problem. Bills seeking immunity power have been annually introduced into the legislature, only rarely even emerging from committee.

Since only very few cases can be handled by this relatively small department, the bulk of complaints are referred to other agencies for investigation. Complaints about the police are sent to the First Deputy Commissioner, often with a request for a written follow-up report. According to Judge Fraiman, the Police Department seldom reported positive results in these investigations. Yet his office did not evaluate the degree to which the police vigorously investigated the referrals, and no follow-up procedure was employed to make sure the charges were even investigated. Judge Fraiman expressed dissatisfaction with the Police Department's investigative techniques in police corruption cases. Nevertheless, he did not feel it was within his province to criticize such techniques.

Fear of interfering with the Police Department has been a definite restraint upon the Department of Investigation. Judge Fraiman characterized the Police Department as an autonomous and powerful agency which ". . . does pretty well what it wishes to do and is not answerable to the Department of Investigation. At least it was not when I was commissioner, and certainly was answerable even to a lesser degree when my predecessors were commissioners." This was clearly evidenced in the Police Department's failure to comply with Mayor Lindsay's May, 1969, directive instructing all City agencies immediately to notify the Department of Investigation of any allegation of misconduct or corruption involving a public employee. The Police Department did not comply until after the establishment of this Commission, when the Mayor issued an Executive Order in August, 1970, reaffirming this procedure.

In the Commission's view the best long-term solution to the problems of investigating police corruption is a properly organized Inspectional Services Bureau responsible to the Police Commissioner as described in our Summary and Recommendations. This will free the Department of Investigation from the burden of monitoring the day-to-day operations of the Police Department and leave the Department of Investigation free to make spot investigations, as necessary, or when requested by the Mayor.

Chapter Twenty-Two

THE CRIMINAL JUSTICE SYSTEM AND POLICE CORRUPTION

Information gathered in the course of this Commission's investigation makes it clear that police corruption does not exist in a vacuum and must be considered in the context of other elements in the criminal justice system. The Commission, which was appointed by the Mayor, only had power to command the cooperation of City agencies and, accordingly, did not conduct extensive investigations into the district attorneys' offices or the court system. However, it is obvious that both have an important role to play in the fight against police corruption. In addition, our investigation showed that the manner in which many policemen perform their duties is strongly affected by their opinions of how well the prosecutors and judges are performing theirs.

Police Corruption Cases

From information obtained from the district attorneys' offices and checked against court records, the Commission has tabulated all corruption cases brought against police officers over the past few years. (These figures do not include cases brought against police officers for crimes unrelated to corruption.)

The number of cases fluctuates widely from county to county, reflecting the diversity of the various counties in the number of policemen assigned to each and the corruption opportunities present.

The breakdown of criminal charges is as follows:

Police Corruption Cases 1968 to June 30, 1972

County/Year	Indictments*	Defendants	Dispositions			Sentences	
			Conv.	Dis./Acq.	Pend.	Total Jailed	1 Year or More
BRONX							
1965	No figures						
1966	1	1	1				
1967	2	3	3				
1968	1	1	1			1	
1969	13	14	9	4	1	3	2
1970	7	12	6	2	4	4	3
1971	8	11	6	2	3	2	2
1972	2	2			2		
TOTAL	34	44	26	8	10	10	7
TOTAL 1968-72	31	40	22	8	10	10	7

* Includes bills of information filed in criminal court.

County/Year	Indictments*	Defendants	Dispositions			Sentences	
			Conv.	Dis./Acq.	Pend.	Total Jailed	1 Year or More
NEW YORK							
1965-67	No figures						
1968	1	19	19			4	
1969	6	7	7			4	3
1970	11	14	8	3	3	5	2
1971*	22	26	8	1	17	2	1
1972**	5	8			8		
TOTAL	45	74	42	4	28	15	6

* 5 of the 22 indictments, involving 9 of 26 defendants, were referred by the Knapp Commission.

** 2 of the 5 indictments, involving 5 of 8 defendants, were referred by the Knapp Commission.

County/Year	Indictments	Defendants	Dispositions			Sentences	
			Conv.	Dis./Acq.	Pend.	Total Jailed	1 Year or More
QUEENS							
1965-66	No figures						
1967	2	3	3			1	1
1968	1	1		1			
1969	3	3	3			1	1
1970	1	1	1				
1971	2	4	2		2	2	2
1972	3	3	1		2		
TOTAL	12	15	10	1	4	4	4
TOTAL 1968-72	10	12	7	1	4	3	3
KINGS							
1965-67	No figures						
1968	3	7		7			
1969	4	8	2	6			
1970	19	25	11	13	1	2	2
1971	16	20	5	7	8	1	1
1972	7	31	1		30		
TOTAL	49	91	19	33	39	3	3
RICHMOND							
1965							
1966							
1967							
1968							
1969							
1970							
1971	1	1	1				1
1972							
TOTAL	1	1	1				1

In the four and a half years from the beginning of 1968 through the first six months of 1972, the five prosecutors initiated 136 Supreme Court and Criminal Court proceedings involving 218 police defendants in police corruption cases. There has been a noticeable increase in activity in recent years in most counties. In 1968 there were six cases involving twenty-nine defendants (nineteen of whom were named in one case); in 1969, twenty-six cases with thirty-two defendants; in 1970, thirty-eight cases with fifty-two defendants; in 1971, fifty-nine cases with sixty-two defendants; and, in the first six months of 1972, seventeen cases with forty-four defendants. Since then, arrests and indictments have been announced in a number of significant police corruption cases, indicating that the trend toward making such cases is continuing. Figures for the period before 1968 were available only for two counties: Queens, where there were two cases involving three defendants in 1967, and the Bronx, where there were three cases involving four defendants in 1966 and 1967.

Of the 218 defendants in this period, 158 were patrolmen, thirty-nine were detectives, nine were sergeants, eleven were lieutenants and one was an assistant chief inspector. Sixty-three defendants pleaded guilty, twenty-eight were convicted after trial, forty-six were acquitted or dismissed and eighty-one are awaiting trial.

Disposition of Police Corruption Cases

Of the ninety-one officers who have been convicted, eighty have so far been sentenced; forty-nine were either set free or given suspended sentences, and thirty-one received jail terms, fourteen for less than one year.

Bronx County District Attorney Burton Roberts testified before the Commission that light sentences were common in cases involving police officers, and went on to describe one:

"We worked hard and we convicted a man by the name of ———, a detective. He was found guilty after trial, guilty of bribe-receiving. We go into court. We ask for sentence. We ask for jail time. He winds up with a suspended sentence."

It is clear that the risks of severe punishment for corrupt behavior are slight. A dishonest policeman knows that, even if he is caught and convicted, he will probably receive a court reprimand or, at most, a fairly short jail sentence. Considering the vast sums to be made in some plainclothes squads or in narcotics enforcement, the gains from corruption seem far to outweigh the risks. Both William Phillips and Edward Droge said that they assessed the risk of meaningful punishment and determined that they had little to fear.

Dispositions in Non-Police-Corruption Cases

Criminal justice proceedings also have another more subtle effect on police corruption. According to Commissioner Murphy, of 94,000 suspects arrested for felonies in 1971, only 552 (slightly over one-half of one percent) stood trial. The other ninety-nine and one-half percent either had their cases dismissed or pleaded guilty, usually after having the charges against them reduced to misdemeanors or lesser felonies via plea-bargaining. "No doubt," said the Commissioner, "certain of the honest, dedicated policemen who made these 94,000 arrests last year came to the belief that conscientious police work is a waste of time, a waste of effort and a waste of devotion."

Most court cases are now settled via plea-bargaining, an arrangement made between the prosecutor and the defendant whereby the defendant agrees to plead guilty to a lesser crime than the one he was originally charged with, in return for a lighter sentence than he would have received if convicted of the original crime. This practice is inevitable in view of the unmanageable calendars with which the state criminal courts are faced. However, as more suspects are arrested and charged and the jails become more crowded and the court backlog increases, defendants tend to be allowed to plead to lesser and lesser charges and to receive lighter and lighter sentences. This process results in the frustration to which Commissioner Murphy referred.

Three studies of gambling and narcotics arrests illustrate the effects of plea-bargaining. These studies are of particular interest because gambling and narcotics are the most prominent areas of police corruption. A 1972 report of the Joint Legislative Committee on Crime of the State Legislature revealed that from 1967 to 1970, of 9956 felony arrests made for gambling in New York City only 921 (nine percent) resulted in indictments. Exactly sixty-one of those indicted were convicted of felonies. The disposition of the sixty-one convictions, punishable by imprisonment for four years, included twenty-nine fines, fourteen imprisonments for one year or less, thirteen probations, three conditional discharges, and the adjudication of two as defective delinquents. In short, 9956 felony arrests resulted in a total of sixty-one convictions and fourteen jail sentences—all of one year or less.

Another gambling study was done of high-level numbers bank arrests in Bedford-Stuyvesant. From 1961 through 1970, 356 arrests were made, of which 198 were dismissed. Sixty-three persons were acquitted and ninety-five were convicted. Of those convicted, seventy- seven were fined an average of $113, twelve received suspended sentences, five were sentenced to local jails for an average of seventeen days, and one was sentenced to prison for one year.

The Joint Legislative Committee's study of narcotics arrests revealed that only 43% of those arrested for possession of one pound or more of heroin or cocaine from January 1, 1969, through October 31, 1971, were convicted. Thirty-four percent of those convicted (fifteen percent of those arrested) received prison sentences of more than one year. Twenty-six percent were sentenced to local jails for one year or less. The remaining forty percent received non-prison sentences such as fines, conditional discharges, and probation. The disposition of these cases appears disproportionately lenient in view of the fact that possession of one pound or more of those drugs became punishable by life imprisonment on April 24, 1970.

Sentences like these are frustrating for the individual police officer who views the results of his arrests: a gambler given probation, or a drug dealer who offered a large bribe receiving a fine smaller than the amount of the bribe he offered. The officer who time and time again makes a good felony arrest, sees it reduced to a misdemeanor charge and then sees the offender receive a light or suspended sentence is likely to conclude that making good felony arrests is a waste of time. Under these circumstances, some officers see little wrong with accepting money to write up a weak arrest affidavit or to change testimony at trial, feeling that the offender is going to get off lightly anyway. These practices, in turn, contribute to high rates of dismissals and acquittals.

Reliance on Police Investigators

Although all but one of the five district attorneys' offices have civilian investigators, all of them rely chiefly upon the police for investigative work. The vast majority of cases they are called upon to prosecute are developed not by their own investigative personnel but by regular operational units in the Department. In police corruption cases, the district attorneys must rely on police officers working with the Department's Internal Affairs units.

This reliance upon police investigators necessarily affects the performance of the district attorneys since they must depend upon evidence gathered by men who are investigating their comrades. The natural reluctance of members of any group to look into accusations against other members of the group is accentuated by attitudes within the Department, discussed elsewhere in this report, which reflects an unwillingness to acknowledge the true nature and seriousness of the problem of corruption. Commissioner Murphy's administration has made significant headway in changing such attitudes, at least at command levels, but the Commission is convinced that the necessity of relying on police investigators is still a handicap to a prosecutor in police corruption cases.

The nature of this handicap is illustrated by the case of a lieutenant who commanded the detective squad in the office of Bronx District

Attorney Roberts. The lieutenant retired on August 30, 1971, after being found guilty in a departmental trial of "failure to take proper police action" after information was given to him regarding possible corruption of a detective in his command. A sergeant also assigned to the Bronx District Attorney's squad had reported to the lieutenant that a detective in the squad was engaging in serious criminal acts. The lieutenant took no action on the sergeant's report except to have the detective transferred to another squad. The detective was later arrested in an entirely separate case of extortion and conspiracy. It was only on the occasion of this later arrest that it came to light that the lieutenant had received a serious allegation against a detective under his command and deliberately suppressed it.

District Attorney Roberts, commenting to the press on the lieutenant's action in suppressing the report, said:

"[The lieutenant's] error, if any, was not an error motivated by venality. It was, if anything, an error motivated by compassion for a fellow policeman."

District attorneys working as closely as they do with police officers, also tend to be sympathetic to the police. Cases of outright and provable corruption are customarily pursued with appropriate vigor. However, a district attorney and his assistants, who work daily with police officers, often find it difficult to believe allegations of corruption among policemen who are brother officers of the investigators with whom they work.

The close relationship between prosecutors and police also affects public confidence in the district attorneys' willingness to prosecute policemen. Whether or not the district attorneys are in fact reluctant to conduct such prosecutions, large segments of the public believe that they are and this inhibits some people from reporting allegations of police corruption to them.

Case-by-Case Approach to Prosecution

Although district attorneys are empowered to conduct long-range investigations and initiate cases, Bronx District Attorney Burton Roberts testified in executive session that the current normal case load is so heavy that only limited time and manpower is actually available to conduct long-range investigations. This limitation of manpower forces the district attorneys to restrict their activities with respect to police corruption largely to the prosecution of cases that have originated elsewhere. Their approach remains necessarily case oriented, as they have not had the resources to identify patterns of corruption and take action for long-range control.

This does not mean that investigations have always been limited to short range cases. In the early 1960's the Police Department and New York County District Attorney Frank Hogan conducted an investigation which uncovered a massive citywide pad among plainclothesmen. Until the law regarding the admissibility in court of wiretap evidence was changed in 1968, it was not possible to bring these charges. In that year nineteen police officers were indicted. Many other charges arising from the investigation were by that time barred by the statute of limitations.

Investigative Techniques

Like the Police Department, the district attorneys have not until recently used certain investigative techniques which the Commission found most useful in uncovering corruption. Nor did they press the Department to adopt such methods as allowing a situation to develop, rather than making an immediate arrest, and using police officers caught in corrupt activities as undercover agents. The recent use of such methods in investigations in the Bronx and Brooklyn, referred to elsewhere in this report, proved highly successful. These cases have had significant impact on the Department. Indictments in Brooklyn and the Bronx resulting from the use of field associates and formerly corrupt plainclothesmen apparently have made police officers engaged in illegal activities wary of trusting supposedly corrupt comrades. Organized plainclothes pads in particular have become very risky.

Another approach not used until recently is that of looking critically into questionable police evidence such as illegal wiretaps, deliberately weak affidavits, and other practices like flaking and padding. In a recent precedent-shattering case in the Bronx, eight police officers were indicted for swearing to false affidavits in seven narcotics cases, even though this necessitated the dropping of the cases as a result.

Citywide Investigations

The fact that each district attorney's jurisdiction stops at the county line causes problems in pursuing police corruption cases. Although the fact that each prosecutor has jurisdiction in only one county also affects other investigations, it is particularly troublesome in investigations which involve a citywide Department with large numbers of men assigned to all five boroughs, many of whom are frequently being transferred from one to another—often in the middle of an investigation. The problems created by corruption investigations involving more than one county range from the difficulty of coordinating the efforts of several district attorneys' offices to the security problems inevitable when people in several different offices are privy to a secret investigation.

Federal Anti-Corruption Efforts

In recent years, due primarily to new legislative action by Congress, the Federal Government has significantly increased its efforts to help local authorities curb official corruption. These efforts have added to the forces available in combating police corruption.

Federal law enforcement agencies have certain inherent advantages in investigating police corruption because they rely for investigative work upon the Federal Bureau of Investigation and investigators assigned to the United States Attorneys' offices or the federal Organized Crime Strike Forces. Since these men are not members of the department they are investigating, they are not subject to the pressures, discussed elsewhere in this report, which necessarily affect the performance of policemen who are called upon to investigate other policemen.

The degree to which federal authorities can become involved in police corruption investigations rests upon the existence of federal statutes giving them jurisdiction. The increased federal effort in the area began with the passage in 1968 of the Omnibus Crime Control and Safe Streets Act which, among other things, made it a federal crime to operate a gambling establishment above a certain size. Corruption involving public officials in connection with any such gambling establishment was also brought within federal jurisdiction. This statute, giving federal jurisdiction over corruption in one area where it most commonly affects the police, laid the basis for a number of significant federal investigations. Other statutes allow federal authorities to become involved in anti-corruption work in connection with narcotics and various types of interstate transactions, particularly transactions involving organized crime.

Examples of the use to which these statutes have been put in recent years are the indictments of sixteen police officers in Detroit in 1971 following the investigation of a $15-million-a-year gambling operation and the work of the United States Attorney for the Southern District of New York who conducted a number of important investigations, including those which resulted in indictments based upon the undercover work of Patrolman William Phillips and Detective Robert Leuci.

Although increased federal efforts in prosecuting police corruption cases are most helpful, jurisdictional limitations prevent federal authorities from acting in many situations. No federal jurisdiction exists with respect to many of the corruption hazards found by this Commission and recognized by the Department. Therefore, federal effort, although valuable, cannot completely satisfy the need for the sort of supplementary assistance which the Commission feels is necessary in light of the conditions it found in the Department.

Chapter Twenty-Three

THE OUTLOOK FOR THE FUTURE

The Commission found that corruption within the Department was so pervasive that honest rookies joining the police force were subject to strong pressures to conform to patterns of behavior which tended to make cynics of them and ultimately led many of them into the most serious kinds of corruption. This situation was the result of an extremely tolerant attitude toward corruption which had existed in the Department for the better part of a century and had flourished despite the efforts—sometimes vigorous and sometimes not—of police commissioners and various law enforcement agencies.

Two important factors which perpetuated this attitude were: (1) a stubborn belief held by officials of the Department and of other law enforcement agencies that the existence and extent of police corruption should not be publicly acknowledged, because it might damage the image of the Department, thus reducing its effectiveness; and (2) a code of silence, honored by those in the Department who were honest as well as by those who were corrupt, which discouraged officers from reporting the corrupt activities of their fellows and which sometimes seemed to mark the reporting of corruption as an offense more heinous than the practice of corruption.

The effect of these attitudes was compounded by the fact that law enforcement agencies concerned with police corruption traditionally were commanded by persons who substantially agreed that it was contrary to the public interest to acknowledge the full extent of police corruption, and relied for their investigative efforts upon police officers who themselves were sympathetic to the code of silence.

We believe a beginning has been made towards a fundamental correction of these conditions. Our Commission, with the support of the Mayor and of Commissioner Murphy, has made full public disclosure of those patterns of corruption we found to exist. Commissioner Murphy and his administration, aided by the change in public opinion generated by our revelations, has instituted important and imaginative reforms. There has been official recognition that the appearance of honesty is no longer to be deemed more important than its actuality. The code of silence seems, for the time being at least, to have been weakened. Whereas two years ago it was thought inconceivable that rank and file police officers would testify publicly against the corrupt activities of their fellows, a number of officers have since followed the ground broken in this regard by Detective Leuci and by Patrolmen Phillips, Droge and Logan. Moreover, as already noted, Commissioner Murphy has been successful in instituting a program wherein officers volunteer on a regular basis to do undercover work in conjunction with the Departmental anti-corruption efforts.

The question is, will these new trends continue after this Commission has disbanded and public attention has ceased to be focused on police reform? It is the Commission's conclusion that there is a reasonable chance for an affirmative answer to that question if the momentum for reform can be continued until new attitudes can be institutionalized. It must become routine for the upper echelon of the Department to feel that integrity is more important than the appearance of integrity and for at least the honest members of the rank and file to consider that the exposure of corruption is both honorable and necessary to the proper functioning of a responsible police force. Once these attitudes become securely established, the Commission feels, the momentum toward integrity will have a chance to become self-generating and the Department's internal anti-corruption machinery, assisted by the district attorneys and other regular law enforcement agencies, should be adequate to cope with corruption. Until such time, we feel that some ongoing independent anti-corruption effort is essential.

It was to meet this need that the Commission made its first—and what turned out to be its most controversial—recommendation. The Commission envisaged a Special Deputy Attorney General who would have his own staff of investigators with no ties to the Police Department and who would supplement the efforts of the district attorneys and other law enforcement agencies. The Commission suggested that the job of this new official should be to continue this Commission's role of spotting patterns of corruption and providing impetus for reform as well as to prosecute corruption-related crimes. Because police corruption is only one—and not necessarily the most important —aspect of a much broader problem, the Commission recommended that this Special Deputy Attorney General have jurisdiction over all corruption in the criminal process. For the same reason, the Commission urged that the Special Deputy emphasize the prosecution of members of the public who offer bribes as well as those who receive them.

On September 19, 1972, Governor Rockefeller responded to our recommendation by taking two actions: He announced the appointment of Maurice Nadjari as a Special Deputy Attorney General to supersede the district attorneys in the five counties of New York City with respect to corruption in the criminal justice system; he established a special unit of the State Commission of Investigation, under the direction of Commission Chairman Paul Curran, to perform ongoing monitoring work in the same field.

These innovations represent an important addition to the anti-corruption forces in the City. The Special Deputy Attorney General's office will provide an independent prosecuting arm with the capabilities of being wholly independent of other law enforcement agencies and of devoting its full attention to the problems of corruption in the criminal justice system on a citywide basis. Equally important is the continuing focus which the new unit of the State Commission of Investigation can maintain on existing anti-corruption machinery through the ongoing examination of patterns of corruption and the means of combating them.

Any long-range hope of meaningful reform, however, depends upon the Department itself. If, as the Commission suggested, the Department's Inspectional Services Bureau is reorganized along the lines of the Inspections Office of the Department of Internal Revenue, with officers spending their entire careers in anti-corruption work, the Department's anti-corruption machinery will be strengthened and provided with a measure of continuity which will afford some hope of its surviving intact the tenure of commissioners less effective than Commissioner Murphy.

In addition, if the momentum already generated is to be maintained and the needed reforms implemented, Commissioner Murphy and whoever succeeds him must have the clear support of the public in taking the difficult measures necessary. New Yorkers must stop going along with demands for graft payments and must stop offering them. The business community, in particular, was most uncooperative with this Commission, apparently preferring to retain its ability to buy its way out of tangles with the law, while placing full blame for corruption squarely on the heads of the police. New Yorkers must realize that seemingly harmless small bribes made to policemen often lead to acceptance of larger and more serious bribes from gamblers and narcotics pushers. In addition, the prevalence of bribes from businessmen who are apparent leaders in the community, such as contractors and hotel executives, lends an aura of respectability to the practice, making it much easier for an officer to justify to himself the acceptance of payoffs from organized crime.

New York City policemen, whatever their other problems, are traditionally men of extraordinary courage. To protect our lives and property, they face armed men on darkened rooftops and a host of less dramatic dangers. New Yorkers must now find the courage to sacrifice narrow self-interest in helping these men to do their extremely difficult jobs with integrity. The goals of all of us should parallel those expressed by Captain Daniel McGowan during the Commission's public hearings:

"[I would like to] contribute in some small measure to rooting out the weaknesses in the system that permits fine young men with high ideals to come into the Department and within a few years be involved in corruptive practices. The tragedy of these men and their families [is] so demonstrably shown here with Patrolman Droge.

". . . I've spent over half of my life in the Police Department. I'm the son of a man who spent thirty-nine years in the Police Department. I want both of us to look back on that service with honor.

"And, last, I'm a resident and a citizen of this City. I have a vested interest that the quality of life in this City should become somewhat better, and that my wife and my children and my grandchild, together with all citizens, can point to the Police Department and truly say, 'It's the finest.'"

APPENDIX

EXHIBIT 1

THE CITY OF NEW YORK
LAW DEPARTMENT
Municipal Building
New York, N. Y. 10007

J. LEE RANKIN, *Corporation Counsel*

May 14, 1970

The Honorable John V. Lindsay
Mayor of the City of New York
City Hall
New York, N.Y. 10007

My dear Mr. Mayor:

As a result of allegations of corruption in the New York City Police Department you appointed this Committee and charged it with a three-fold responsibility: (1) to evaluate the procedures presently employed by the Police Department to investigate charges of corruption in order to ascertain whether these procedures provide the public with adequate assurance that charges of police corruption are dealt with vigorously, promptly and fairly; (2) to recommend improvements in these procedures; and (3) to investigate the charges of corruption and other allegations growing out of the announcement of the Committee's formation.

This assignment involves the integrity of the principal law enforcement agency of this City and is therefore of major importance to the community. In our brief period of existence the Committee has met four times and taken the following initial steps in what must now be regarded as an undertaking of far greater magnitude than that originally envisioned when this Committee was created:

1. At the Committee's request, Police Commissioner Howard Leary has furnished a report of the existing procedures employed by the Police Department for the investigation of charges of corruption.

2. The public has been requested to supply the Committee with any information it has concerning acts of police corruption. As of this date, 375 complaints have been received. The Commissioner of Investigation is evaluating and investigating these charges, in some instances in conjunction with the appropriate District Attorney.

3. The Committee has requested the five District Attorneys in New York City to provide summaries of prosecutions of police officers for acts of corruption over the past five years in order that we might ascertain the extent to which existing law enforcement agencies have delved into this problem.

4. Under present law a City employee is required to give 30 days notice before his retirement becomes effective. The Police Department has found that in many instances this time period does not permit a proper investigation and disposition of charges of corruption against members of the police force, particularly if criminal charges are also under investigation. Other City departments have encountered similar problems with regard to allegedly dishonest employees seeking to retire and obtain their pension benefits. The Committee recognizes that it would be unfair to require all City employees to be subjected to a longer period of notice. However, where charges have been filed against an employee, he should not be permitted to retire prior to 60 days from the date of these charges in order to permit the City, after fair hearing, either to dismiss or otherwise discipline the employee or to absolve him of the allegations. Consideration should also be given to changes in the law which would permit the divesting of pension rights in those instances where employees, after their retirement, have been convicted of crimes which relate to the performance of their City jobs. An employee should not be permitted to acquire pension rights under circumstances which, if they were known at the time, would have caused his dismissal from City service.

These steps represent only the beginning of the work which must be done in order for the people of this City to feel confident that its Police Department is free of corruption. A thorough evaluation of police procedures must go forward. Most importantly, however, a thorough investigation of specific charges of corruption must be undertaken backed by whatever resources of men and money is necessary in order to do the job. To facilitate this investigation members of the police force must be urged by the Mayor and by the Police Commissioner to advise the District Attorneys of any known acts of corruption. Commissioner Leary has stated unequivocally that no reprisals of any kind will be permitted against a member of his department who comes forward with such information. Any member of the department who feels that reprisals have been instituted against him should be assured that he can report this fact directly to the Mayor's office with full confidence that the Mayor himself will undertake to protect him against reprisals by the Department.

To state the magnitude of the task, however, is to indicate why this Committee would find it most difficult to perform it. An investigation only of the charges thus far received requires a full-time investigative body with a skilled full-time staff. The members of your Committee all have demanding responsibilities in connection with their respective offices. It is unfair to the public and to the positions they hold for the members of this Committee to attempt to perform the investigation which the job requires and which the public has a right to demand.

It has also been suggested that because of our several official positions there could be conflict between our responsibilities in our offices and as Committee members. While we do not accept the validity of this suggestion, we all agree that those undertaking so important a responsibility for the community should not only be free from any conflicts but also should be free from any appearance thereof. We, therefore, recommend to you that your Committee be disbanded and that it be replaced with an independent investigative body, appointed by you from the private sector, with full authority to carry forward this investigation. It must have the cooperation of the District Attorneys and all City agencies, most particularly the Department of Investigation and the Police Department, and should refer to the District Attorneys all cases which warrant criminal prosecution. Such an investigative agency should have an adequate staff and should be able to draw upon appropriate City agencies for assistance.

The Members of this Committee pledge their full cooperation to you and to the new investigative agency which we urge you to appoint.

Sincerely,

FRANK S. HOGAN

HOWARD R. LEARY

J. LEE RANKIN

BURTON B. ROBERTS

ROBERT K. RUSKIN

EXHIBIT 2

CITY OF NEW YORK
OFFICE OF THE MAYOR
New York, N.Y. 10007

Office of the Mayor
Executive Order No. 11
May 21, 1970

Appointing a Commission to Investigate Allegations of Police
Corruption and the City's Anti-Corruption Procedures

Section 1. Pursuant to the Authority vested in the Mayor, I hereby appoint a Commission to (1) investigate the extent of alleged police corruption in the City and any relationship of such alleged corruption to crime and law enforcement; (2) inquire into and evaluate the existing procedures for investigating specific allegations of corruption and present practices designed to prevent corruption and ascertain whether these procedures provide the public with adequate assurance that charges of police corruption are dealt with vigorously, promptly and fairly; (3) recommend improvements in these procedures, additional steps to provide stronger safeguards against corruption, and any improvements in methods of law enforcement which will tend to eliminate police corruption; (4) take evidence and hold whatever hearings, public and private, the Commission may deem appropriate to ascertain the necessary facts.

§2. The Commission shall consist of the following persons who are hereby appointed as members thereof:

Whitman Knapp, Chairman

Arnold Bauman

Joseph Monserrat

Franklin A. Thomas

Cyrus R. Vance

§3. The Commission is empowered to prescribe its own procedures and to employ such assistants as it deems necessary, within the amounts appropriated therefor.

§4. All departments and agencies of the City are directed to furnish the Commission with such facilities, services and cooperation as it may request from time to time.

§5. This order shall take effect immediately.

JOHN V. LINDSAY
Mayor

EXHIBIT 3

LOCAL LAWS
OF
THE CITY OF NEW YORK
FOR THE YEAR 1970

No. 13

Introduced by Mr. Cohen (by request of the Mayor)—

A LOCAL LAW

To amend the administrative code of the city of New York, in relation to the powers of the commission appointed by the mayor to investigate allegations of police corruption and the city's anti-corruption procedures.

Be it enacted by the Council as follows:

Section 1. Article one of title F of chapter fifty-one of the administrative code of the city of New York is hereby amended by adding thereto a new section to be section F51-9.0, to follow section F51-8.0, to read as follows:

§F51-9.0 Commission appointed by the mayor to investigate allegations of police corruption and the city's anti-corruption procedures; additional powers.—The commission established by the executive order of the mayor number eleven, dated May twenty-first nineteen hundred seventy, to investigate allegations of police corruption and the city's anti-corruption procedures, or any member of it designated in writing by the chairman, shall have the powers and duties set forth in such executive order and, in addition thereto, for the purpose of carrying out such powers and duties, such commission, or a subcommittee thereof, shall have power to administer oaths or affirmations, to hold hearings either public or private, require and enforce by subpoena the attendance and take testimony under oath of such persons as it deems necessary, and require and enforce by subpoena duces tecum the production of books, accounts, papers and other evidence relevant to the subject or subjects of its investigation or inquiry.

§2. This local law shall take effect immediately and shall cease to be of any force or effect on December thirty-first, nineteen hundred seventy.

THE CITY OF NEW YORK, OFFICE OF THE CITY CLERK, S.S.:

I hereby certify that the foregoing is a true copy of a local law of The City of New York, passed by the Council on May, 1970 and approved by the Mayor on June 25, 1970.

HERMAN KATZ, City Clerk, Clerk of the Council.

CERTIFICATION PURSUANT TO MUNICIPAL HOME RULE LAW SECTION 27

Pursuant to the provisions of Municipal Home Rule Law Section 27, I hereby certify that the enclosed local law (Local Law 13 of 1970, Council Int. No. 276) contains the correct text and:

Received the following vote at the meeting of the New York City Council on May 27, 1970: 29 for; 8 against.

Was approved by the Mayor on June 25, 1970.

Was returned to the City Clerk on June 26, 1970.

J. LEE RANKIN, *Corporation Counsel.*

EXHIBIT 4

July 1, 1971

Interim Report of Investigative Phase

The work of the Commission to Investigate Alleged Police Corruption, as stated in the report to LEAA of February 16, 1971, has been divided into two phases: investigation and analysis. The investigative aspect of the Commission's work was related to the subpoena power created by the City Council, which expired yesterday. Analysis of the investigative data and the formulation of recommendations will be continued throughout the summer. Detailed findings and recommendations will be presented at a later date. This is an interim report dealing in summary form with the investigative phase of the Commission's work.

It may be noted at the outset that the Commission's investigation has not aimed at ascertaining individual acts of corruption or establishing the guilt of individual police officers. Indeed, as District Attorney Frank Hogan has correctly observed, the Commission is not equipped to develop cases against individual police officers. In an interview with the New York Post, Mr. Hogan observed, among other things:

"They [the Commission] don't have the power to use the grand jury. They do not have the power of contempt nor do they have the power to prosecute."

The Commission has focused its efforts on identifying patterns of police corruption and on defining the problem areas in sufficient detail to lay the groundwork for the remedial recommendations.

A fundamental conclusion at which the Commission has arrived is that the problem of police corruption cannot—as is usually asserted—be met by seeking out the few "rotten apples" whose supposedly atypical conduct is claimed to sully the reputation of an otherwise innocent

Department. The Commission is persuaded that the underlying problem is that the climate of the Department is inhospitable to attempts to uncover acts of corruption, and protective of those who are corrupt. The consequence is that the rookie who comes into the Department is faced with the situation where it is easier for him to become corrupt than to remain honest. The Commission's ultimate recommendations will concern themselves with methods of reversing this pressure toward corruption.

In broad outline, the Commission's method of investigation has been: first, to postulate the patterns of corruption by interrogating a wide variety of sources, including aggrieved citizens, community organizations, trade associations, present and former police officers, and members of the underworld; and second, to verify the patterns thus postulated by ordinary investigative techniques, such as analysis of Police Department records, surveillance of police officers, examination of the financial books and records of persons believed to have made corrupt payments, and monitoring conversations with suspected police officers. As required by applicable law, the use of monitored conversations was confined to situations involving the cooperation of someone in a suspected officer's confidence who was willing to equip himself with a recording or transmitting device.

Among the areas of police activity that the Commission investigated were narcotics, gambling, prostitution, bars and restaurants, hotels, construction, tow trucks and bodegas (Spanish grocery stores). The reports concerning these investigations will be forthcoming when the evidence has been fully analyzed. However, certain preliminary observations seem now appropriate.

Narcotics: The Commission concurs with the statement by the State Commission of Investigation that police officers in the Narcotics Division engage in "various types and techniques of corruption ranging from extortion, bribery, contradictory court testimony designed to affect the release of a narcotics criminal, improper associations with persons engaged in drug traffic, and, finally * * * involvement by police officers in the actual sale of narcotics.''

Gambling: The Commission's investigation has substantiated allegations frequently made in the press with respect to the prevalence and extent of payoffs by gamblers to the police. Payments are made on a regular basis to plainclothesmen who are primarily responsible for gambling enforcement, and these payments are divided on the basis of shares—i.e., a full share or a fraction or multiple, depending upon the position of the police officer receiving payment. ''Show'' arrests of predetermined low-level employees of gambling establishments are periodically made.

Prostitution: The open way in which certain houses of prostitution are operated suggests that they are tolerated because of payments to the police. This has been corroborated by evidence developed by the Commission establishing the making of such payments.

Liquor: Payoffs are made by bars, restaurants and night clubs for a wide variety of reasons, ranging from the desire to avoid prosecution for outright violations of law to the mere assurance of cooperative attitudes by the local police.

Hotels: In addition to Christmas gratuities to practically all ranks in the Department, leading hotels were found to provide free food and accommodations to the local police in surprisingly substantial amounts.

Construction: The construction industry, in order to avoid compliance with a variety of regulations, was found generally to make regular payments which are usually earmarked for various police officers with jurisdiction in the area.

Tow Trucking: Despite wide publicity that had been given to scandals concerning collusion between police and tow truck operators, payments by such operators to police for favorable treatment at the scene of an accident are still prevalent.

Bodegas (small Spanish groceries): The Commission initially found a ritualized system of weekly police demands for payment from the bodegas which violated Sabbath laws. Police Commissioner Murphy subsequently ordered that Sabbath laws be enforced only on complaint, and the demands have apparently been greatly diminished.

Other areas which will be discussed in our final report include parking lots, garages, police property clerk's office, pistol permits, street vendors, gypsy confidence swindles, trucking companies. sale of police information, car rentals, and community taxis (gypsy cabs).

During the coming months, staff reports analyzing the evidence underlying the foregoing conclusions will be prepared, and the Commission will formulate its recommendations for dealing with the patterns of corruption which have been discussed.

EXHIBIT 5

Opening Statement by Whitman Knapp

First Public Hearings, October 18, 1971

I should like briefly to state the general purpose of these public hearings. As many of you know, the Commission was long undecided as to whether or not to hold public hearings. We were concerned lest the testimony at such hearings would—by its necessary relation to individual situations—detract from the basic findings of our inquiry.

The main thrust of our findings—and the point we wish to bring home to the public—is that the problem of police corruption cannot be solved merely by focusing on individual acts of wrongdoing. It arises out of an endemic condition which must be attacked on all fronts. The difficulty with any testimony is that it must necessarily relate to individual situations.

However, we believe that our counsel has succeeded in structuring these hearings in such a way as to focus on basic conditions and on the public's responsibility for giving support to steps taken to remedy such conditions.

It is of the utmost importance that the public be made aware of the critical problems facing the Department and its individual members. The police officer's job is perhaps more important than any other in our society. The average citizen's most frequent contact with government is through the police officer, and the manner in which the police officer performs his or her duties is what makes most people decide how government is functioning. Moreover, the police officer must at all times live with a realization of physical danger. This latter fact is obvious in the case of men and women assigned to high-crime areas. But no member of the force is immune from being called—at a moment's notice—into a situation where his or her life is at risk.

In addition to the physical danger of which a police officer must continually be aware, he or she is subjected to moral pressures the like of which we impose on no other person. Unlike almost all others subject to moral pressure, the police officer must frequently face these pressures alone and unobserved. He or she is constantly called upon to act in situations where the usual processes of audit and review cannot be used.

In such circumstances, it is as irresponsible for society to fail to provide the police officer with every possible support in resisting pressures toward corruption as it would be to let an officer respond to an armed robbery alarm without having provided training in self-defense.

What do we mean by support? The methods of accomplishing it may be—and indeed are—difficult. But the objectives are clear. A police officer who—totally alone and unobserved—is placed in a position where the mere acceptance of a proffered bribe may produce more wealth than an entire year's salary, or in the more usual position where the pressures are more subtle, is entitled to at least three elements of support to fall back upon:

(1) The officer in such situations should be entitled to feel confident that society is so organized that if a bribe be refused and the matter reported to superior officers, there is a reasonable chance that the corruptor will land in jail; on the other hand,

(2) such officer should feel that if he or she yields to temptation there is a reasonable chance that he or she—and any other officer similarly situated—will be apprehended, separated from the force and subjected to criminal prosecution; and, finally and perhaps most importantly,

(3) such officer should be confident that a refusal of the bribe and a report of the corruptor would produce commendation—and not hostility—from his superiors and fellows.

The need for focusing public attention on this problem of support has been dramatized by the nature of the opposition that has arisen to steps recently taken by the Police Commissioner to deal with the twin problems of corruption and discipline.

For example, some people have attacked the Commissioner's judgment on priorities. Instead of concerning himself with corruption and discipline, those people say, he should worry exclusively about "crime in the street." In our view such an approach would be futile and totally irresponsible. The Department's ability to take effective action in any direction depends on its discipline and integrity. Unless such discipline and integrity be maintained, it is ridiculous to expect the Department to be effective in dealing with "crime in the streets."

A word about what these hearings will *not* seek to accomplish. Being expositive in nature, those hearings will not deal with recommendations for reform or with attempts to fix responsibility for such conditions as have been found to exist. Those matters will be dealt with in our report, which is now in process of preparation and which will be published as soon as it is ready.

In brief, then, it is the purpose of these hearings to inform the public about—and to focus attention upon—the corruption-related problems faced by the Department and its individual officers.

EXHIBIT 6

Opening Statement by Whitman Knapp

Second Public Hearings, December 14, 1971

As a preliminary, I would like to give a word about the purpose of these hearings, which is different from the purpose of the previous ones.

The reason for having the first hearings in public, rather than behind closed doors, was to enable the public to share with us and understand the conditions our investigation had uncovered. As I then observed, we believed—and still believe—it to be of the utmost importance that public attention be focused on the conditions and causes of corruption, to the end that the public may give its constant support to official action taken to remedy such conditions and causes—and may, indeed, insist that such action be taken. The previous round of hearings, then, dealt with present conditions as to which action was—and is—imperative.

In line with our desire and purpose of producing action by focusing on present conditions, it had been our original intention to confine to private hearings our inquiries as to the past events, and to deal in our final report with the meaning of such events and their significance to the future.

However, it soon became apparent that there was intense public interest in one phase of past history—namely what official action or inaction had resulted from revelations made by Sergeant David Durk and Patrolman (now Detective) Frank Serpico concerning events in 1966 and 1967. Such interest appeared to be so intense that we became persuaded that to refrain from public hearings on the subject would not serve our purpose of focusing attention on the future, but would, on the contrary, simply divert such attention to the futile business of wondering about the past. It is to avoid such a result that these hearings have been scheduled.

It is obvious that these hearings, having a different purpose, will have a different format. The Commission itself has come to no conclusions as to any of the matters to be disclosed. Nor will it come to any conclusions in the course of these hearings. Any conclusions the Commission may make will appear in its final report.

In these hearings we shall simply endeavor to let each participant in the events under discussion lay before the public in an organized fashion his recollection and understanding of the events as they occurred.

EXHIBIT 7

Sources of Funds Received by the Commission

Grantor	Amount
City of New York	$325,000.00
U.S. Department of Justice— Law Enforcement Assistance Administration	215,037.00
State of New York— Office of Planning Services— Division of Criminal Justice	75,083.00
Edna McConnell Clark Foundation	50,000.00
Field Foundation	20,000.00
Fund for the City of New York	18,500.00
New World Foundation	10,000.00
The Rosenblat Charitable Trust	10,000.00
The New York Foundation	7,500.00
The J. M. Kaplan Fund Inc.	5,000.00
Joint Foundation Support, Inc. on behalf of the Joyce and John Gutfreund Foundation	2,500.00
Joint Foundation Support, Inc. on behalf of the Bernhardt Foundation	2,500.00
The Stern Fund	3,000.00
New York Community Trust	2,500.00
Howard Z. Leffel Fund in Community Funds, Inc.	2,500.00
Total	$749,120.00

EXHIBIT 8

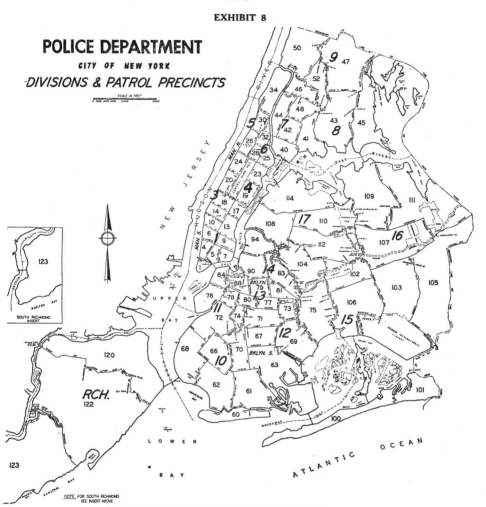

POLICE DEPARTMENT
CITY OF NEW YORK
DIVISIONS & PATROL PRECINCTS

Small numbers indicate precincts, which are gathered into divisions (indicated by large numbers). Divisions are in turn grouped into seven borough commands: Manhattan South includes Divisions 1 and 3; Manhattan North, 4, 5 and 6; Bronx, 7, 8 and 9; Brooklyn South, 10, 11 and 12; Brooklyn North, 13 and 14; Queens, 15, 16 and 17; and Richmond includes three precincts, but no divisions. This map shows boundaries which existed as of January, 1972.